INSURED FOR MURDER

INSURED FOR MURDER

Robin Yocum & Catherine Candisky

 Prometheus Books

59 John Glenn Drive
Buffalo, New York 14228-2197

Published 1993 by Prometheus Books

97 96 95 94 93   5 4 3 2 1

Library of Congress Cataloging-in-Publication Data

Yocum, Robin.
    Insured for murder / by Robin Yocum and Catherine Candisky.
        p.   cm.
    ISBN 0-87975-842-2
    1. Hawkins, John Barrett. 2. Hanson, Melvin Eugene. 3. Boggs, Richard
Pryde, 1933–   . 4. Murderers—California—Los Angeles—Biography.
5. Fugitives from justice—United States—Biography. 6. Murder—
California—Los Angeles—Case studies. I. Candisky, Catherine. II. Title.
HF5429.L7Y63   1993
364.1′523′0979693—dc20   93-30110
                                                                        CIP

Printed in the United States of America on acid-free paper.

Acknowledgments

We feel fortunate that, contrary to the way people often respond to reporters on television and in the movies, most people were anxious to talk about the Just Sweats case. For a variety of reasons, friendship and loyalty included, some were not always completely forthcoming. However, nearly all eventually provided us with the information we were seeking.

We are grateful to those who helped us piece together the stories for the *Dispatch* and the chapters of this book. Those who deserve special thanks are Erik DeSando, Melvin Weinstein, Austin Wildman, Albert MacKenzie, Edwin Laramee, Tom Tornabene, Marty Highfield, Dan Abraham, Vince Volpi, and Dale Rubin.

A great deal of credit goes to the management of the *Dispatch*— editor Robert Smith; his predecessor, Luke Feck; managing editor Gary Kiefer; and city editor Mark Ellis—for their support. Thanks goes to our co-workers who pitched in and covered for us, allowing us to dedicate time to our investigation. Equal credit goes to our agent, James D. Frost, for helping us through the early drafts of the manuscript.

Editors, whether they are at newspapers or a publishing house, are often viewed by writers as vicious people who seem to take great delight in mutilating copy: samurai editing, it is called. We were exceptionally lucky that our editor, Barbara Bergstrom, is a wonderful wordsmith and not the least bit vicious (although we believe she could be if properly provoked). Her help was instrumental to the publication of this book.

Editorial Note. This book was written from the perspective of *Columbus Dispatch* reporters Robin Yocum and Catherine Candisky. There are some instances in the book where brief monologues or dialogues occur in which the reporters obviously were not present. These passages were recreated by the authors from interviews, police reports, court records, and other documents. Also, the names of two tipsters in chapter 10 were changed to honor their request to remain anonymous.

Introduction

Most readers neither understand, nor care about, the behind-the-scenes efforts that result in a daily newspaper. As long as it arrives on their porch on time—and dry—they're happy. Readers may be enraged by a report on corruption in city hall or saddened by a feature on the death of a child, but they rarely think about the process by which those stories came to appear on the front page. This is typical. We don't consider the hours spent designing an engine when we get in our automobiles; rather, we simply expect them to go when we hit the accelerator. Similarly, readers open the pages of their town's daily newspaper searching for items of interest to them; but funny or sad, significant or inane, personal or distant, what they read remains just a story.

To a newspaper reporter, however, the story is everything. It is a newspaper's very reason for existing. The story. It is often engrossing, but never all-encompassing. Something always happened before it, and something will certainly always come afterward. Tidbits of information trickle in past deadline, too late for that edition. Those morsels will be saved for the next day and the next story. Rumors and wild tales abound, containing snippets, tiny shards, of truth that are tucked away, put on hold until the next slow news day. Nothing ever comes in neat little packages.

And as one story dies, another is born. Reporters sometimes even discard stories before they have run their course. An impatient lot, reporters are always searching for a better story. Their passion is also, and in no small way, an addiction. Stories, good stories, great stories, fuel reporters' ofttimes gargantuan egos.

Reporters feel a peculiar attraction to the seamier side of life. This inexplicable fascination with those who live their lives on the fringes of society produces fodder for the presses, the grist for the front-page by-lines. Stories of sin, sex, and slaughter captivate their readers.

If a reporter could devise the perfect story, it would have every evil element, every conceivable angle—murder, sex of every variety, deceit, theft, embezzlement, insurance fraud, beautiful blondes, a playboy businessman, bumbling cops, scams, a stun-gun-toting doctor, drugs, innocent victims, and an international manhunt.

Too perfect to be true—almost.

The story started with a classic newspaper cliché, a tip from a secret source. On August 25, 1988, two reporters from *The Columbus Dispatch* reported the facts of a simple lawsuit. An insurance company claimed it had paid $1 million to a Columbus businessman upon the death of his partner. Now, they had begun to doubt that the corpse was who everyone had claimed him to be.

Two reporters would unravel the mystery, an unbelievable story that contained all the elements. The Glendale, California, police scoffed at the reporters' questions. How dare they imply that the department's investigation had been anything short of thorough? There was nothing to investigate, police said, and therefore no story.

But there was a story, a bizarre tale that would play itself out on the pages of the *Dispatch* for the next year.

The story broke at a time when newspapers too often worried more about infographics, color reproduction, and bulletized nuggets of information than news stories. The late Ned Stout, a wonderfully skeptical and caustic reporter with the *Dispatch,* said the problem started when newspapers began referring to themselves as "products" instead of papers. Too many papers were forgetting their strengths—the ability to be insightful, probing, in-depth—and trying to be television news in print.

The Just Sweats case, with all its twisted plots, was a great story. Day after day the antics of John Hawkins, Melvin Hanson, and Dr. Richard Boggs spread across the pages of the *Dispatch*. The stories dominated the news and conversations around Columbus. Extracting the facts from friends, relatives, and co-workers was sometimes agonizingly slow. The *Dispatch* gave us every resource available; early on metro editor Gary Kiefer said, simply, "Stay after it."

More than five years have passed since the story broke, but we are still regularly asked: "Couldn't they have made a legitimate million with their business?"

Yes.

"So why did they throw it all away?"

We don't know.

Nothing ever comes in neat little packages.

1

She didn't have a regular beat, but pinch-hit wherever needed. One day she would be covering a drug trial in federal court, the next interviewing the mother of a teen-age homicide victim. This was fine with Catherine Candisky. She understood the pecking order, and dues had to be paid. After all, she was the youngest reporter—26—in *The Columbus Dispatch* newsroom, and the only woman assigned to the justice cluster, a close-knit group of five reporters who covered courts and cops.

Although the pace was sometimes overwhelming, Candisky liked the diversity. It was a decent assignment and certainly better than the suburban bureau—"the burbs"—where she had spent the previous two-and-a-half years. The NeighborNews bureaus served as farm teams for the *Dispatch,* training grounds for promising reporters awaiting openings downtown. Candisky had been the only reporter in the East Side Bureau, and she usually cranked out ten or more stories for each weekly publication, covering suburban city councils, zoning commissions, and school boards. She moved downtown in March 1988 after cluster chief Bernie Karsko hired her as swingman on the justice cluster.

On August 24, 1988, Karsko had pulled Mike Berens off the court beat to work full time on the capture of a rapist police had been after for several years. Candisky was assigned to make afternoon rounds at the courthouse. She shoved a notebook and a few pens into her briefcase, getting ready to head out for the Franklin County Courthouse.

Two desks over, Duane St. Clair was on the telephone, squeezing the receiver between his ear and shoulder as he scrawled on a scrap of note paper. St. Clair, a political writer, studied the tip for a moment before offering it up. "Karsko, who's doing courts?" St. Clair asked. "I just got a tip from a buddy of mine that might be worth checking out."

Karsko didn't look up from the story he was editing. "Give it to Candisky," he said, an unlit cigar bouncing from his mouth. "Berens is busy."

St. Clair rocked back in his chair and looked across the aisle.

Candisky had heard the exchange and was ready to add it to her list of things to check out. "Are you going to swing down by the clerk's office?" St. Clair asked, working over a piece of chewing gum.

Candisky nodded. "Yeah. What have you got?" she asked, not expecting too much. If she had learned anything in her first few months downtown, it was that reporters held on to good tips. Only the bad ones were tossed up for grabs.

"Take a look at the civil filings. A lawyer buddy of mine called and said there's an interesting lawsuit filed against a guy named . . ." St. Clair glanced down at his scrawled note. "John Hawkins."

"Who is he?" Candisky asked, taking the note from St. Clair's outstretched hand.

St. Clair shrugged. "He didn't say. He just laughed and said it was an interesting lawsuit and would probably make a good story."

"Is your buddy one of the lawyers on the case?"

"No. He just said he'd heard about it."

She nodded. "I'll check it out."

It was eighty-eight degrees, and as is typical for Columbus in August, miserably humid. Candisky elected to walk the six blocks to the Franklin County Hall of Justice, a modern structure that houses all the county courts, the sheriff's department, and the jail. Candisky had been a pre-law student at Ohio State and had easily developed several sources at the court, where stories were plentiful. She preferred the courts to the cop beat.

Candisky usually spent a couple of hours making rounds. It was after 3 P.M. when she finally made it to the clerk's office in Common Pleas Court to check the civil filings. She found the lawsuit St. Clair had told her about—case number 88CV-08-5750—listed on a clipboard at the front counter.

Farmers New World Life Insurance Company
Plaintiff

vs.

John B. Hawkins
Defendant

She scribbled down the case number and asked a clerk for a copy of the lawsuit. Candisky was in a hurry to get back to the newsroom and, without even looking at the suit, stuffed it into her burgundy briefcase and started back to the paper.

2

As the deadline for the first edition neared, the normal newsroom chatter ceased as reporters hurried to finish their stories. A handful of editors roamed the newsroom, reading paragraphs over hunched shoulders and searching for front-page candidates, the merits of which would be debated in the five o'clock budget meeting.

Candisky came off the elevator and walked down the narrow hall that emptied into the fifth-floor newsroom. She picked up her messages at the receptionist's desk and meandered through the newsroom to her desk in the back. She sat down and pulled the copy of the lawsuit from her briefcase.

It got to the point rather quickly.

The man who died April 16, 1988, in the Glendale, California, office of Dr. Richard P. Boggs was not Melvin E. Hanson. Farmers had paid $1 million to his beneficiary, John B. Hawkins. The insurance company wanted its money back.

The suit stated:

> Subsequent to Farmers' issuance of the check to Hawkins, the California Department of Justice ("DOJ") and Federal Bureau of Investigation ("FBI") performed scientific analyses [sic] to compare the corpse's fingerprints with known fingerprints of Hanson, and discovered that the corpse's fingerprints did not match those of Hanson.
>
> . . . Farmers' payment of One Million Dollars ($1,000,000) to Hawkins under Hanson's insurance policies was made under a mistake of fact as to Hanson's death.
>
> . . . Unless Hawkins is restrained from spending, transferring, encumbering or otherwise disposing of the insurance proceeds that were paid to him, and that rightfully belong to Farmers, Farmers will suffer irreparable harm for which there is no adequate remedy of law.

On November. 13, 1987, the suit noted, just five months before his reported death, Hanson had executed a new will and disinherited his family. Hawkins became sole beneficiary and executor of Hanson's estate.

If the dead man wasn't Hanson, Candisky wondered, who was he? She thumbed quickly through the lawsuit, but the corpse wasn't identified. As deadline approached, she knew she had a good story, even though the lawsuit posed more questions than it answered.

She had never heard of John B. Hawkins or Melvin E. Hanson. A check of the *Dispatch*'s computer library showed there was never an obituary on Hanson, but there had been one story with reference to the two men. The University of California at Los Angeles had sued the co-founders of Just Sweats, John B. Hawkins and Melvin E. Hanson, for trademark infringement. The company had apparently been selling sweat shirts bearing the university seal and the Bruin logo without paying royalties. Now the name Hawkins was a little more familiar to Candisky. She remembered seeing him in a Just Sweats television commercial. He was a handsome young man with curly brown hair, whose flexing biceps during the commercial had stuck in her mind.

With no other background on either the man or the company, Candisky made a blind call to the Just Sweats headquarters. "Good afternoon. Just Sweats," a woman said.

"Yes. Could I speak with John Hawkins, please?"

There was a moment of silence. "Just a minute."

A few minutes passed before another woman picked up the phone. "This is Melissa Mantz. Can I help you?"

"Maybe," Candisky said. "This is Cathy Candisky, I'm a reporter with the *Dispatch* and I'd like to speak with John Hawkins."

"He's not here."

"Any idea when he might be back?"

"He is no longer associated with Just Sweats. He doesn't own the company anymore."

"Do you know where I can find him?"

"No," Mantz said, abruptly ending the conversation.

Candisky thought Mantz had reacted somewhat harshly to a rather simple question. Scanning a Columbus phone book for Hawkins's home number, she found a John B. Hawkins on Ellerdale Drive in northeast Columbus. No answer. She called Dr. Boggs's office in California, but he was with a patient and couldn't come to the phone. Candisky left her name and number, but the doctor never returned the call. She called Melvin D. Weinstein, the Columbus attorney who had filed the suit on behalf of Farmers, but he wasn't in his office. It was past 5 P.M. Candisky knew she had to start writing if she wanted the story in the next day's paper. She made one last call to the Glendale police and was referred to Christopher Loop, the department's public relations officer. Loop acknowledged that the identity of the corpse was in question, but seemed unconcerned.

"So you're investigating the death?" Candisky asked.

"No," Loop stated. "You see, the coroner ruled the death was of natural causes, so there's no need for any further investigation."

"But do you know who the dead guy was? Was it Hanson?"

"No, the body has not been identified."

"Can you tell me anything about Dr. Boggs? Does he have any priors?"

"I can't tell you that. We're not allowed to discuss prior records, but I'll tell you he doesn't have one and he's considered a reputable doctor."

Thirty minutes later, Candisky was almost finished writing when she looked across the aisle at Karsko. He didn't appear busy, and Candisky asked him to add her story to the budget.

"Let me see that lawsuit," Karsko said, chewing on an unlit cigar. He quickly read the suit and frowned, handing it back to Candisky. He didn't appear too impressed.

About six o'clock Candisky had finished polishing the story. She took a computer printout of it to her editor. "Bernie, do you want to read this?"

Karsko shook his head. "Just put it in the basket."

Candisky put the story into the wire basket near the copy desk for the three or four copy editors who would check for errors in spelling, grammar, and style. Candisky was disappointed. No one seemed overly interested in the misidentified corpse. Without a pitch from her editor, the story would probably run on the obituary page.

3

Until downtown Columbus began revitalizing in the early 1980s and new buildings began dwarfing the old bricks, the sign was the most noticeable landmark in the downtown sky. Mounted on steel scaffolding atop the six-story building at 34 South Third Street, in blazing orange neon, was

Dispatch
Ohio's
Greatest
Home Newspaper
117 Years of Service

Some people considered the sign a garish eyesore. But most viewed it as a piece of Columbus's history, a landmark that had adorned the building top since 1925, looming above the state capitol building across the street. The *Dispatch* owners, the Wolfe family, had long prided themselves on being a family newspaper.

The paper was formed as part of a cooperative venture of ten printers, who first published the *Daily Dispatch* on the afternoon of July 1, 1871, for a newsstand price of three cents. The partners formed the Dispatch Printing Company and went without pay for ten weeks to get the fledging publication started.

Between that first issue and 1903, the *Dispatch* changed hands three times before it was purchased by Robert F. and Harry P. Wolfe. The Wolfe brothers had amassed a fortune as owners of the Wolfe Brothers Shoe Company, and two years earlier they had made their first venture into the publishing business with the purchase of the rival morning *Ohio State Journal*.

The paper has remained in the possession of the Wolfe family since then, conservative as the buff stone building that houses it.

The *Dispatch* was an afternoon giant with little competition for most of the 1900s. The *Ohio State Journal* and the afternoon *Citizen* were two dying papers by the time they merged to publish the first *Citizen-Journal* on November 9, 1959. The *Dispatch*, as part of joint operating agreement, published, delivered, and sold advertising for the morning paper, which also moved its offices into the *Dispatch* building.

Columbus became a one-newspaper town on January 1, 1986. After twenty-six years the newspapers' operating agreement expired and Scripps-Howard, which owned the *Citizen-Journal*, opted not to save the daily. It published its last paper on December 31, 1985. After nearly 115 years as an afternoon publication, the *Dispatch* published its first morning edition the next day. Soon afterward, the Dispatch Printing Company launched plans to build a $125 million printing plant on the far-west side of Columbus.

The new facility was only two years from operation in the fall of 1988, and that night Candisky and half a dozen of her colleagues talked of its completion at the Mohawk Bar in German Village, a favorite of *Dispatch* staffers. Candisky had endured a hectic afternoon, so she finished her beer and left the tavern just after eleven that night.

Her banana-yellow car bounced up brick-lined Mohawk Street and then over to Fourth. She whipped through the alley behind the *Dispatch* and left her car double-parked while she ran in to pick up an early edition at the security desk.

Her story had bumped the rape story, Dan Quayle, and an article on the commotion being caused by the movie *The Last Temptation of Christ* to down below the fold! Candisky was thrilled. No matter how long they've been in the business, reporters yearn to have the lead story on the front page. Even reporters who work for the same paper constantly try to one-up each other to avoid having their stories buried inside the local section.

The next morning, August 25, Melvin Weinstein picked up the *Dispatch* on his porch and stared in disbelief at the headline across the top of the front page.

Wrong corpse at the heart of insurance suit

He read the accompanying story.

An insurance company wants to get back $1 million it paid on life policies bought by the former owner of Just Sweats, charging it was duped into paying his partner on the death of the wrong man.

According to a suit filed Tuesday in Franklin County Common Pleas Court, a body identified as that of Melvin E. Hanson, 46, formerly of 1620 E. Broad St., Apt. 1001, is that of someone else. The suit also says Hanson's partner, John B. Hawkins, 25, of 3741 Ellerdale Dr., had no right to collect on Hanson's policies.

The body has been cremated.

Farmers New World Life Insurance Co. paid off on Hanson's policies July 7 and wants Hawkins to repay $1 million with interest.

The insurance company won a temporary restraining order yesterday from Judge Dale A. Crawford. The order prohibits Hawkins from spending the money.

Hawkins also was ordered to provide an accounting of the money and turn over the $1 million to the court until the suit is settled. He was not at the hearing and was not represented by an attorney.

A hearing to determine whether the order should be made permanent is scheduled for Sept. 6.

In 1985, Hawkins and Hanson founded Just Sweats, a Columbus-based clothing company with corporate offices at 4369 E. Broad St. The company runs 10 stores in Franklin County.

"Hawkins and Hanson no longer own the company," said Melissa Mantz, company vice president. She refused to say when or under what circumstances the men left the business.

According to the suit, the Washington-based insurance company issued a $500,000 life insurance policy to Hanson May 27, 1987. Hanson took out a second $500,000 policy on Oct. 7, 1987.

Both policies named Hawkins as beneficiary.

On Nov. 13, 1987, Hanson executed a will that named Hawkins beneficiary and executor of Hanson's estate. In the will, he disinherited family members.

Hanson reportedly died April 16, 1988.

That day, police in Glendale, Calif., were called to the office of Dr. Richard Boggs. Officers were shown a corpse that Boggs said was Hanson, according to court records.

Boggs told police that Hanson had come to his office and died of an apparent heart attack, court records say.

Police photographed and fingerprinted the corpse, and the body was taken to the Los Angeles County Coroner's office for an autopsy, court records say.

On April 17, the body was released to Hawkins, as executor of Hanson's estate, according to court records. The coroner signed a death certificate for Hanson, but a ruling on the cause of death was deferred pending tests.

The body was later cremated, court records say.

On April 29, Hawkins submitted a proof of death statement to the insurance company stating Hanson had died April 16 in Boggs's office.

The coroner later ruled the cause of death as "non-specific focal myocarditis," an inflammation of the heart.

On July 7, the insurance company paid off Hanson's life insurance policies, issuing a $1 million check to Hawkins. The check was cashed by Hawkins, court records say.

An investigation conducted by Glendale police, however, later revealed that the corpse was not that of Hanson, said Christopher Loop, department spokesman.

A friend of Hawkins and Hanson said yesterday, "Gene (Hanson) went out to L.A. and he never came back."

Boggs failed to return calls to The Dispatch. Hawkins could not be reached for comment.

"You've gotta be kidding," Weinstein said to himself. As attorney with the Columbus law firm Emens Herd Keggler & Ritter, Weinstein represented Farmers New World Life Insurance Company. He wasn't too keen about the publicity. The thought of his client's misfortune being scrutinized by the *Dispatch* made him queasy .

Weinstein threw the paper aside and started his daily run through the shaded streets of his suburban Bexley neighborhood. As he rounded the corner from Maryland to Stanberry, his Walkman blared the 7 A.M. WTVN radio news.

"Farmers Insurance Company suing the co-founder of Just Sweats for $1 million."

Weinstein doubled over as if in pain. Aloud, he said, "This is not good."

4

Candisky walked through the loading dock at 9:15 A.M. that Thursday, running fifteen minutes late, as usual. She took the back elevator to the fifth floor and grabbed a home final from a stack on a file cabinet in the photo department.

Over a cup of coffee at her desk, she re-read the story for any glaring deletions or additions the copy editors might have made. Like most reporters, Candisky had a general mistrust of copy editors, who considered themselves as the last line of defense between the reporters and their split infinitives, and the trusting reader. Since Candisky hadn't had any messages from work when she got home the night before, the copy desk either understood her story perfectly or had made wholesale changes, a frequent occurrence that made reporters grind their teeth. Another minor victory: the story seemed in order.

Across the aisle, Karsko was already working on Friday's budget. "Candy," he growled, not looking up from his computer. She was never quite sure if he knew her real name or just thought the hated nickname was easier to remember. Candisky put down her paper and walked over to Karsko's desk. "What do you have for tomorrow?" he asked.

She didn't know. Her story had broken so late the day before that she hadn't had time to think about a follow-up. At the *Dispatch,* you could win a Pulitzer Prize and be declared God of all Journalism on Monday, but without a story for Tuesday's paper you were in the doghouse. Thinking aloud, she responded. "Well, I've got some people I'd like to talk to, and I'm still trying to get an interview with Hawkins. Maybe . . ."

"Cathy," reporter Scott Powers interrupted from across the newsroom. "Telephone."

"Who is it?"

He shrugged and covered the receiver with his palm. "She wouldn't say. She said she wants to talk to you about Just Sweats."

Candisky wedged the phone between her shoulder and cheek while opening a notebook. "This is Cathy," she said.

"Are you the reporter who wrote this article about Just Sweats?"

"Yes."

"Why didn't you write about all the money those two embezzled?" the woman demanded, as if to imply Candisky was protecting Hawkins and Hanson.

Candisky scrawled "embezzlement" on the pad. "Embezzlement? I didn't know about any embezzlement. 'Those two,' you mean Hawkins and Hanson?"

"Yes, Hawkins and Hanson. They're crooks, both of them. This story doesn't tell half of what these guys were into."

The woman sounded like a jilted girlfriend, like someone with an ax to grind.

Candisky tried to wrestle back control of the conversation. "When did they embezzle money? Do you know?"

"Wait a minute."

The reporter heard the caller muffle the receiver and say, "She wants to know when they stole the money and how much they took." Then the informant continued.

"Hanson stole a bunch of money from the company last January or February, like $2 million, right before he left."

"Left? Left for where?"

"He went to California. He had some heart problem and he was dying, at least that's what he said. And Hawkins, he stole money from the company right before he left."

"That's interesting," Candisky said, taking down the information. "Who are you talking to?"

"My roommate. She works there."

Scott Powers slipped a note on her desk. "Caller waiting. Wants to talk about Just Sweats." Candisky signaled Powers to ask the caller to wait.

"Can you put your roommate on the phone?"

"She doesn't want to get involved."

"Tell her she doesn't have to give me her name."

"She's scared. These guys are crazy."

"I understand that, but I don't know who she is. I just want to ask her a few questions. I'll need her help to track down this embez- zlement."

Candisky strained to listen as the caller tried to persuade her roommate to come to the phone. "Sorry. She's too scared."

"Okay. I suppose you're not going to give me your name, either."

"No. No way. I can't get involved. But there's a lot more. If I find out anything else I'll call you back."

Candisky scratched out a few more notes—con artists, keep digging, only scratched the surface—then took the next call. "Are you going to write any more stories about John Hawkins?" a male voice asked.

"Planning to. You know him?"

"Sort of. I have some information about him if you're interested."

"Sure. I'm interested in anything you want to tell me."

"Did you know Hanson ripped off the company big time before he quit?"

"I'd heard something about it. Someone told me they stole $2 million, Hawkins and Hanson. You're saying it was just Hanson?" The man didn't answer for several seconds. "Are you still there?" Candisky asked.

"Yes," he said in a hushed tone. "It was just Hanson. It was right before he went to California."

"When did he go to California?"

"Earlier this year. He told us he was dying and moving to Los Angeles. Then he took the money and booked. Hawkins was on vacation. When he came back and found out Gene had ripped off the money, Hawkins went ballistic. Hanson about put him out of business. Call Just Sweats. Everyone at the office knows about it."

"You must work for Just Sweats, right?" Candisky asked. The phone went dead. "Evidently," she said to herself. As she started back over to talk to Karsko, Powers again held a telephone receiver in the air. "No big deal. I don't have any stories to write," Powers said with a grin.

She smiled and took the phone. "This is Cathy."

"Yeah, about the story in today's paper. Where did you get your information?"

Candisky rolled her eyes. This caller was looking for an argument.

"Mostly from the lawsuit."

"Man, I'm telling you, this is such total bullshit. How do you get off writing a story like this? Gene Hanson is dead. He had AIDS."

"AIDS? How do you know that?"

"That's what he told everyone at Just Sweats."

"I thought he was dying of a heart condition."

"He told people both stories. At first he said he had a bad heart, but everyone suspected he had AIDS. He looked terrible and told a couple of people he had AIDS."

"How did he get AIDS?"

"I'm pretty sure he was gay. He never flaunted it or anything, but I think he was. But trust me, Gene Hanson is dead. The guy was a zombie. When he left town in January he looked liked the living dead. I'm surprised he made it to California and lived as long as he did."

The calls, all anonymous, kept coming. Most conveyed an obvious bitterness or outright hatred toward Hawkins. It was nearly 11 A.M. before Candisky got a break. Her coffee, untouched, had long gone cold. She took a breath and slouched in her chair. "That's unbelievable," she said. "I thought that phone was growing out of my ear. I've never had so many calls about one story."

"Getting anything good?" Powers asked.

"I don't know. Maybe. I've talked to people all morning and not one of them would give me a name. Nothing is confirmed, but it looks like Hawkins and Hanson embezzled from their own company, and Hanson had AIDS or a bad heart, or both. One thing's for sure, these guys have some enemies."

Candisky found her notebook listing for Hawkins on Ellerdale Drive. After the phone had rung three or four times, Candisky figured no one was home and was about to hang up when a man answered, sounding as if he had just woke up. "Hi. This is Cathy Candisky at the *Dispatch*. Is this John Hawkins?"

The man's laugh was groggy. "No. John is not here. This is Erik DeSando; I'm John's roommate. Is there something I can help you with?"

"Maybe, but I really wanted to talk to John."

"That might be tough. I don't think John's going to be around for a while," DeSando chuckled.

Candisky missed the joke. She wondered why DeSando seemed amused by her questions.

"Well, I was trying to get a hold of him for a follow-up to today's story."

"Story? What story?"

"Haven't you seen today's paper?"

"No. Is there a story about John?"

"Yeah, on the front page."

"No kidding. What's it say?"

Candisky thought it odd that Hawkins's roommate didn't know about the lawsuit, but she didn't press him. He was probably just feeling her out to see what she knew, and Candisky didn't mind playing along. "It's about a lawsuit an insurance company filed. Evidently John received a million dollars last summer as beneficiary in Melvin Hanson's life insurance policy."

"That's right."

"Well, the insurance company claims Mr. Hanson isn't dead and they want the money back."

"Whoa! You're shittin' me. They're saying Gene isn't dead? You've got to be kidding me. Gene's dead. He died last April out in L.A."

"The insurance company claims it wasn't Hanson who died."

DeSando laughed. "If it wasn't Gene, then who was it?"

"No one seems to know. What do you think?"

"Christ, that's ridiculous. It was Gene. John went out and had the body cremated himself."

"Well, I'm just trying to piece all this together and it's pretty confusing. I'm hoping that John can straighten it out for me. The people out at Just Sweats told me he had left the company, but that's all they'll say. Do you know what he did with the insurance money?"

"The money sat in the bank for a little bit. Then one weekend he took it and left. I don't know where he is."

Candisky didn't believe him. Certainly DeSando knew the whereabouts of his roommate. No one just disappears.

"You really don't know where he is?"

"No. I really don't," he replied.

"When was the last time you saw him?"

"It was maybe two weeks after he got the money—on a Saturday, the middle of July sometime, I think."

"And he just left without saying where he was going?"

"Yeah."

"Isn't that a bit odd?"

"Not really, but you had to know John. He was like that. This is a slow time of year for the company and John was pretty far in debt. You knew that, didn't you?" he asked, as if to assure himself he hadn't revealed too much.

"I'd heard," Candisky bluffed.

"John was stressed out. Every day he had creditors on his back. It was just getting to be too much and he wanted to take some time off and enjoy the insurance money. He said he might take a cruise around the world. He might be back in a year, he might never come back."

Candisky sensed that hers wasn't the first call DeSando had fielded for his former roommate. She thought DeSando truly believed that Hanson was dead, but certainly he had some idea of Hawkins's whereabouts.

"So how can I get hold of John?" Candisky asked, making a final pitch for an interview.

"I swear I don't know where he is, but I might see him this weekend in Las Vegas."

"Vegas?"

DeSando explained that Friday he was leaving on a gambling junket and hoped to hook up with his old roommate in Las Vegas. Hawkins's mother—identified by DeSando as Jackie—worked in one of the casinos. She had told DeSando that Hawkins might come in for the weekend.

"So Hawkins might be there?" Candisky asked.

"Yeah, I hope. Listen, I can't talk right now. I've got to get to work. I'm already late."

Candisky kept DeSando on the phone long enough to set up an appointment for nine that night. She hoped that DeSando, in a face-to-face interview, would part with a few more details. He obviously knew more than he was telling.

5

Cathy Candisky came back from reviewing the lawsuit in the quiet of the newspaper's morgue and found a pink telephone-message slip on her desk. Farmers' attorney Melvin Weinstein had returned her call from the previous day. Candisky punched in the first three numbers for Weinstein but then hung up the phone. Better to call Shelly Navarre first, Candisky thought. She would be more likely to talk than an attorney.

Candisky had found Navarre's name on a letter attached to the lawsuit as an exhibit. Dated July 7, 1988, and addressed to Hawkins's attorney, Richard A. Curtin, the letter stated:

Dear Mr. Curtin,

We have concluded our routine evaluation of this claim. Enclosed you will find a check in the amount of $1,000,000.00 payable to John Hawkins, which represents the proceeds payable on the above policies.

We appreciate your patience and the cooperation shown by your client during our review of this claim. If you have any questions, please feel free to contact me at the Home Office address indicated above.

Sincerely,

Shelly Navarre
Life Claims Supervisor

Navarre had to know more than what was mentioned in the lawsuit. The sooner Candisky got hold of Navarre, the better. Company attorneys would certainly warn Navarre and her colleagues against commenting about pending litigation. Candisky flipped through the lawsuit until she found Navarre's letter to Hawkins, and on it the number for Farmers in Mercer Island, Washington.

"May I speak to Shelly Navarre?" Candisky asked, careful not to identify herself as a reporter until she knew who was on the other end.

Navarre might hesitate to reveal anything if her colleagues knew she was talking a reporter.

"This is she."

"Hello, Ms. Navarre. This is Cathy Candisky. I'm a reporter with the *Dispatch* in Columbus, Ohio, and I was calling about Melvin Hanson. His death was somehow faked and you folks have filed suit against his beneficiary, John Hawkins. Are you familiar with the case?"

Navarre laughed. "I know about it all right. I handled that claim. How did you get my name?"

"A letter you wrote to John Hawkins was included in the lawsuit," Candisky said.

"Oh. Are you going to write a story about it?"

"There was one in this morning and I'm working on a follow-up. That's why I'm calling. I was hoping you might give me a little guidance. This thing is awfully confusing. Do you have a few minutes?

"Sure."

"I'm not sure I know where to start. Any idea what happened to Hanson? Is he really dead?"

"The million-dollar question, so to speak. I wish I could tell you, but we don't know what happened to him. The only thing that's certain is he wasn't the man who died in Dr. Boggs's office."

"Who did?"

"We don't know. To my knowledge he's never been identified. We compared a picture of Hanson and his fingerprints to the corpse. It definitely wasn't the same guy."

Navarre's candor surprised Candisky. The reporter had fully expected the claims agent either to hang up on her or to regurgitate some prewritten company line. Navarre was a continent away from Columbus, Ohio, and that probably worked to Candisky's advantage. People who don't want their words to appear in the local paper will clam up to the hometown press, but will often be more talkative with out-of-town reporters. To a claims agent in Washington state, a reporter with *The Columbus Dispatch* probably seemed distant and harmless.

"Is this Dr. Boggs involved? What do you know about him?" Candisky pressed.

"He's involved all right," Navarre said definitively. "You should see the phony records he put together. Hanson applies for this life insurance and he's in perfect health, has been for years, according to the physical Boggs gave him. He hadn't gone to a doctor in years, then in March—boom, boom, boom, bad heart, bad heart, bad heart.

He goes to see Boggs three times the month before he supposedly died. You should see all the bills Boggs submitted. He even sent us a bill for treating Hanson the morning he 'died.' It was obviously a joke."

"So what about the guy in Boggs's office. How did he die? He certainly didn't drop dead for their convenience."

"Obviously not, but we really don't know how he died," she said. "I think he was murdered, plain and simple. And, if I had to bet, I'd say he was drugged, maybe by some kind of injection that induced a heart attack."

"Interesting theory. I suppose Boggs is in a position to know which drugs couldn't be traced."

"Exactly."

"So how did you guys figure out it wasn't Hanson?"

"It had all the signs of a fraud. The policies were new, all the visits to the doctor just before he died. I thought something wasn't quite right, so I asked the police in Glendale to compare photographs and fingerprints."

"You asked for the comparisons? Glendale police didn't initiate that?"

"No, I asked. When they got a copy of his driver's license and looked at the photo, half of the detectives thought it wasn't Hanson, and the other half were positive it wasn't him."

"Maybe I'm missing something here. If you guys were so sure that this was a fraud, why did you pay Hawkins?"

Navarre chuckled. "Good question," she said, as if to imply that the decision hadn't been hers. "There really was no reason to hold the check. At the time, the police said there was no question about identity and the coroner ruled death by natural causes. We had to pay it. By the time the police figured it out, we'd already mailed the check."

"I'd like to get hold of someone in Hanson's family. Did you ever talk to them?"

"No, but hold on and I'll check. I think they're from somewhere in Florida," she said. "Oh, here's something I forgot about. Hawkins tried to collect on a $15,000 corporate policy Hanson had; he wasn't even the beneficiary. He said he was executor of Hanson's will and therefore entitled to the money. We refused to pay that one."

"Who was the beneficiary?" Candisky asked.

"Some guy named Cecil Tanner from Atlanta."

"Did you pay him?"

"No. He's never filed a claim."

"Is Cecil Tanner related to Hanson?"

"Don't think so."

"Okay. Well, what about Hanson's family? Are any of their names listed in your records?"

"Yes. Let's see. Here it is, his father is a Cecil Hanson. He lives in Jacksonville."

"Terrific, Shelly. You've been a big help. Thanks. I'll keep you posted."

Candisky called information for Atlanta. There was no listing for a Cecil Tanner, but the operator found numbers for two individuals named "C. Tanner." Candisky got answers at both, but neither was *Cecil* Tanner.

She then called information for Jacksonville and located a Cecil Hanson. An older, raspy-voiced man answered the phone.

"Sir, I'm trying to locate Cecil Hanson."

"I'm Cecil Hanson."

"Are you Melvin E. Hanson's father?"

"Why?" the man asked, his voice turning defensive. "What's this about? Who is this?"

"My name is Cathy Candisky. I'm a newspaper reporter in Columbus, Ohio, and I'm trying to locate the father of Melvin Hanson."

"Why?"

"Well, that's a little hard to explain. Are you Mr. Hanson's father?"

There were a few moments of silence as the elder Hanson mulled over the question. "Yes. I'm his father. So what's this about? What do you want from me?"

"Has anybody talked to you about your son lately?"

"No. Hell no. I haven't talked to Melvin in fifteen years. Why? Has he gotten himself in some kind of trouble?"

"I'm not really sure what's going on," Candisky said, stumbling for a way to tell him that his son might be dead. "Melvin supposedly died last April. But now police don't believe it was your son who died. No one knows where he is and I'm trying to track him down."

"Dead? Hmm . . . Well, like I said, I haven't seen Melvin in some fifteen years." Candisky wondered if her words had sunk in. "Melvin was kind of a strange boy, the way he left his family and never communicated with us."

"I'm not sure where this story is going, but if I find out any more about your son, I'll give you a call. If you hear anything about Melvin, I'd appreciate a call."

"I don't expect I will, but if I do, yeah, I'll give you a call."

Candisky made another call to Just Sweats and this time asked for Ed Laramee. Earlier in the day, Ron Hatch, an advertising executive for the *Dispatch* who handled the Just Sweats account, had told Candisky that Laramee was now running the business. Hatch had met Laramee on several occasions, but couldn't offer much other information, except that Just Sweats was evidently having some serious financial problems. The *Dispatch* would accept the company's advertising on a cash-only basis, Hatch said.

Candisky got through to Laramee on her first try. "I'll tell you what I can, but there's a lot I don't know," he admitted slowly, in a barely audible tone.

Laramee said he had been hired as an accountant by Hawkins five months earlier. When Hawkins left town July 16, Laramee became president of a company in deep financial trouble. "We really had to scramble to keep our creditors happy," Laramee said. "Are you going to be in the office later?" Candisky said she would. "I'll probably be giving you a call in a little while. There's a lot going on right now and I've got to talk to our attorneys. I'll call you later."

6

The afternoon mirrored the morning. When Candisky got off the phone with one person, another was waiting. She hadn't even started writing by nearly four o'clock when Robert Smith, an assistant prosecutor for Franklin County, came on the line returning her call. Smith handled white-collar crime for the prosecutor's office, and Candisky had called to see if they were investigating the allegations of insurance fraud and embezzlement against Hawkins and Hanson. After grilling Candisky for details of what she had learned about the case, Smith acknowledged that the prosecutor was investigating a possible embezzlement. The possible insurance fraud had just come to Smith's attention, he said, assuring the reporter those allegations would also be looked into. But Smith had evaded many of Candisky's questions, making her suspect that his investigation had started during their telephone conversation. Police and prosecutors hate to be outmaneuvered by reporters and will often claim investigations are in progress just to save face. The status of Smith's case didn't concern Candisky. His comments would give credibility to the allegations she would make in her story.

Candisky now had enough details for a story, but the constant interruptions had given her no time to write.

Her struggle had not gone unnoticed by Mark Ellis, the general assignment cluster chief. The ten-year veteran reporter could see Candisky was overwhelmed. He waited near her desk until she was off the phone.

"Pretty busy?"

"Swamped."

"Want some help?"

"I'd love some."

Ellis had a staff of five general assignment reporters, but they were all busy. He walked across the newsroom to see if anyone on the special-projects desk was free. Reporters on the projects desk worked on long-term assignments, but usually were available in a pinch. Ellis returned

29

to Candisky a few minutes later. "Bob Ruth and Robin Yocum are both free. Who do you want?"

Candisky, already back on the telephone, dropped the receiver below her chin and thought for a minute. She had been downtown only for a few months, but she was well aware of the slash-and-tear reputation on which Bob Ruth prided himself. He had earned the nickname "Chainsaw" for his aggressive manner in chasing down a story. Candisky feared he would take over her story. She decided on the unknown but lesser evil. "How about Yocum?"

Yocum was hesitant. A former police reporter who was usually eager to help on a story—and this was obviously a good one—Yocum was also well aware of the reputation of the projects desk. Many fellow reporters considered the projects boys prima donnas, reporters who sometimes spent weeks and months on a story while the rest of the newsroom was cranking them out daily. Yocum didn't want to appear like a vulture, ready to swoop in and strip the meat off a good story. "I don't mind helping," Yocum said. "But only if she really needs it."

"She's buried," Ellis said. "Let's go."

At 32, Yocum had been at the *Dispatch* for eight years, the last three as the senior reporter on the projects desk. He had spent four years covering the police department under Karsko before newsroom reorganization established the projects desk. Yocum and Candisky spent a few minutes discussing the case and the next day's story.

Yocum had read Candisky's first story and was familiar with the lawsuit. "What's your follow?" Yocum asked.

"I'm not sure. I've got lots of tidbits that need to be pulled together. I talked to the claims agent for Farmers and she gave me lots of leads."

"Did she say why the insurance company paid Hawkins if they didn't know who the dead guy was?"

"She said they had no reason not to pay it. It wasn't until after they mailed it that they found out it wasn't Hanson."

"Okay, so we've got some comment from the insurance company. What about Hawkins or Hanson? Have you found them?"

"Hanson's dead, supposedly, and Hawkins is out of town, I guess. No one says for sure. I did talk to Hanson's father. He hasn't seen his son for fifteen years, but he did give me a few quotes."

"So, what can we hang a story on? What's your best hook?"

"The prosecutor's office says they're investigating an embezzlement from the company. Supposedly, Hanson ran off with $1.8 million earlier this year. But I don't have any solid details and I'm waiting to hear back from Laramee, the guy who's running the company now."

Yocum suggested he put together a chart showing the chronology of events from the time Just Sweats was formed in 1985 to the filing of the lawsuit. Candisky started writing a story on Hanson's alleged embezzlement.

As they were finishing up, about 5:15 P.M., Laramee finally called Candisky back, this time on conference call with Just Sweats' attorney Austin P. Wildman. Laramee said that within the hour Just Sweats had filed for protection from its creditors under Chapter 11 of the federal bankruptcy laws. The clerk's office was closed, making a copy of the filing unavailable, but Wildman offered to answer any questions. Candisky was unfamiliar with bankruptcy proceedings, so the filing caught her off guard. Only a few questions came to mind, and Wildman answered them all. The company owed $2.3 million and had assets valued at $1.4 million. The bankruptcy filing was designed to give the company time to reorganize without pressure from creditors.

Wildman also confirmed there had been embezzlement from the company, but remained vague when Candisky pressed him on the details. "I heard Hanson and Hawkins took $2 million. Is that right?" she asked.

After a pause, Wildman said, "The persons and amounts are inaccurate," he said.

"How much was it?"

"That's really all I can tell you."

"What about Hawkins? I've heard he took money from the company before he left town in July."

"Again, I really can't say anymore."

Candisky passed a note to Yocum. "J.S. filed for B-ruptcy."

Yocum went across the aisle to Ellis. "Just Sweats just filed for bankruptcy. Do you want a separate story or do you want it in with the embezzlement?"

"Better merge it. Put the bankruptcy angle up high. We're getting close to crunch time and we don't have that much space tomorrow."

Candisky got off the phone with Wildman and Laramee. Her interview had been the journalistic equivalent of a root canal. "What did he say?" Yocum asked.

"Not too damn much. They filed for Chapter 11 to keep the creditors at bay. He said they can keep their stores open, but they have to file a plan to repay their creditors."

"Did they have to file because Hawkins took the insurance money and booked?"

"He wouldn't say."

"How about the embezzlement? Was that part of the insurance scam?"

"I told him we had heard that Hawkins and Hanson had embezzled $2 million from the company in January. He said . . . ," she looked over her notes, " 'the persons and the amounts are inaccurate.' But he wouldn't tell me how much, and he wouldn't call it an embezzlement."

Yocum looked over the notes Candisky had typed onto the computer screen. "If he said it wasn't an embezzlement, what exactly did he call it?" he asked.

"A misunderstanding."

"A $2 million misunderstanding?"

She shrugged. "I'm just telling you what he told me."

"Ellis wants one story with the bankruptcy stuff up high."

As Candisky inserted the bankruptcy information into the story, Yocum called Wildman to see if he could pry any more details out of him. After listening to Candisky's fruitless interview, Yocum had expected Wildman either to spew forth lawyerly rhetoric, or simply to refuse to answer any questions. But without Laramee on the phone, Wildman apparently felt more at liberty to talk.

Wildman explained that Hawkins, the sole owner of Just Sweats, had simply abandoned the company. Hawkins left town in July, saying he was going to be gone for a couple of days on a buying trip, but he never returned. "We don't know where in the hell he went," Wildman said. "I don't know if the pressure got to him or what. He just took off and left us in a hell of a bind. We spent weeks just trying to get control of the company. When Hawkins left there wasn't anyone who could even sign a check. John finally sent a letter giving Melissa Mantz power of attorney and explained how he wanted the ownership of the company divided."

"And you never heard from him after he left?" Yocum asked.

"Oh yeah, he called a couple of times. Once he said he wanted to come back and resume control of the company because he had all these great ideas. I told him to forget it. 'If you come back, everyone's going to walk out. They won't work for you anymore, John, and neither will the bank.' That was the last we heard from him. As for the lawsuit, I'm as confused as you are. But I don't believe this 'Gene's not dead' crap. He'd been sick for months. He's dead."

"Did Hanson embezzle money from the company before he left?"

Wildman drew a deep breath when Yocum posed that sensitive

question. "I don't think it was an embezzlement. Gene was leaving and he took what he thought he was entitled to, which just about bankrupted the company. John talked to him, explained what the company was actually worth, and Gene gave most of the money back. That's all there was to it."

"Who owns Just Sweats now?"

"As of a couple of hours ago, Fifth Third Bank and the rest of the creditors."

Candisky's rewrite of the Just Sweats story featured the latest information on the Chapter 11 bankruptcy filing. The reporter also topped the story with a double by-line: Catherine Candisky and Robin Yocum. She told Ellis that since the work would be a team effort, all stories should carry both names. Ellis agreed.

7

Candisky picked up the plane tickets the secretary had tossed on her desk an hour earlier. Karsko now appeared excited about the story. He had arranged for a fight to Las Vegas in the morning, and a hotel room. "If DeSando is going out, maybe he can get you an interview with Hawkins," said Karsko. Candisky agreed, but felt uneasy at the thought of a blind trip to Las Vegas, in search of a man who had been hiding for six weeks. "What happens if I get out there and Hawkins isn't around?"

"Interview the mother," Karsko said. "She's been in touch with him. Maybe she'll help you out."

"This is wonderful," Candisky said to Yocum, softly enough so no one else could hear. "Now I have to tell DeSando I'm going out to Las Vegas with him."

"Do you think that will be a problem?"

"Well, he didn't exactly invite me, if that's what you mean."

Candisky and Yocum scrolled through the story on the computer screen. "You know what bothers me about this story?" Yocum asked. "No cops," he said, answering his own question. "What are the cops in Glendale doing? Shouldn't we have some comments from the cops investigating the death in the doctor's office?"

"There is no investigation."

"Why?"

"I talked to the flack for Glendale police, and he said they weren't investigating the case because the coroner ruled the man in Boggs's office died of natural causes."

"So he died of natural causes, but they still don't know who he is." Candisky nodded. "Don't they care?"

"I guess not," she said. "When I talked to the guy he acted like it was no big deal. No homicide, no investigation."

It didn't make sense to either reporter. At the very least, they thought,

Boggs had misidentified the corpse. Candisky grabbed her notes and she and Yocum headed for the basement lunchroom, away from the newsroom confusion. Yocum wanted to pick Candisky's brain about the case. The story fascinated him. He was eager to analyze the situation and to talk strategy with his new partner.

The two got off the elevator, walked past the display of autographed Ohio State University footballs and basketballs, and into The Den, a room of chipboard tables and vending machines. The room was empty except for the lady who kept the changer full and a guy from the print shop getting an ice cream bar.

"So, what do you think?" Yocum asked as he slipped a dollar bill into the change machine. "Did they just find some poor schmo dead in an alley, or did they kill someone?"

"I don't know," Candisky answered, spreading her notes on one of the circular tables. "If they killed someone, I bet it was some nameless face who wouldn't be missed."

"And what makes you think that?" Yocum asked, pouring change into the coffee machine. "Cream or sugar?"

"Just black. If it had been a person with a home and a family, they would be looking for him. I think it was probably someone who wouldn't be missed—a homeless person or a drifter."

"Good theory," Yocum said, setting two black coffees on the table and taking a seat across from Candisky. "Didn't a couple of these guys tell you Hanson had AIDS?" Candisky nodded. "If that's the case, maybe Hanson is dead."

"I'm not sure I follow."

"We know these insurance policies were bought within the past two years, and he must have had a physical to get them, and they always take a blood screening for AIDS. So, if he really did have AIDS, that means someone fudged on the blood work. When Hanson does die, the beneficiaries know they have to produce a clean body to collect on the insurance. Maybe he died and they just found a substitute body."

"Okay, so where'd the body came from?"

"They could have gotten it from a hospital or . . ."

"The morgue," Candisky said, completing the thought. "You're always hearing those wacko stories out of the L.A. County coroner's office. Boggs could have known somebody in the coroner's office who could switch the bodies. Who would know? Both bodies are cremated. No evidence."

"Seems like the perfect plan. So, you think he's dead?"

Candisky shrugged.

"If Hanson's dead, then the doctor had to be involved," Yocum said, sipping his coffee. "Do you think he was getting a cut of the cash?"

"I assume he did. Why else would he get involved? Besides, any way you cut it, Boggs has to be involved. If they switched corpses, he knew. If they killed someone, he knew. And, to boot, how do you misidentify someone who's been your patient for seven years?"

Yocum grinned. "I'd like to hear him explain that one. Have you talked to the good doctor?"

"No. He hasn't returned my calls."

"If he has a brain in his head he won't, either. So the doc's culpable. Who else? Hanson?"

"Depends if he's dead or alive. If he's alive he would have had to agree to stay hidden."

"Where's he hiding?" Yocum asked.

"Not a clue. Jesus, Robin. I've only been working on this since yesterday afternoon."

Yocum held up his palms in mock surrender. "Just asking. What about Hawkins?"

"It's a tough one to call. He's got a lot of enemies. I have an interview tonight with DeSando, Hawkins's old roommate. Maybe I'll find out a little more. DeSando says Hanson is dead and Hawkins isn't involved."

"If that's so, then what's the payoff for Boggs and Hanson?"

Candisky squinted. "That's right. They would have had to have Hawkins's cooperation to get their cut of the money. I'll bounce that one off DeSando."

"Any possibility he's involved?"

"I don't think so. Granted, anything's possible, but I think he was genuinely surprised when I called him this morning."

"Does DeSando know where Hawkins is?"

"He says he doesn't, but I don't buy it," Candisky said. "DeSando claims Hawkins left town right after he got the money. I think he knows where Hawkins is, or at least has a pretty good idea. He's probably just protecting his friend."

"How about the dead guy? Did the cops check missing persons reports?"

"I doubt it. I talked to their PR flack yesterday and he didn't know much about the case. Frankly, they didn't seem overly interested."

Candisky and Yocum gathered up their notes and documents and started back toward the elevator. "Have any of the people who called you given any clues to where Hawkins might be hiding out?" Yocum asked as they stepped off the elevator on the fifth floor.

"Not really. They tell me he's a big party boy, likes the ladies and likes surrounding himself with admirers. He shouldn't be too hard to find."

8

Yocum called home and told his wife Jill he was going to be late. Candisky headed out the door to grab some dinner and then to interview DeSando at his apartment. Her flight to Las Vegas left at ten the next morning. She and Yocum planned to meet in the newsroom at 8:30 A.M. to complete a list of leads that needed to be checked.

Yocum's main task for the evening was to try to get a copy of the autopsy report on the man who had died in Boggs's office. Candisky had called the Los Angeles County coroner's office earlier and spoken with a clerk in the records division. Coroner's office policy required that all requests for autopsy reports be submitted in writing with payment—a dollar a page—included. The bill for the complete autopsy report on the man they still called Melvin E. Hanson totaled $43. Candisky thought it a ridiculous figure, but supposed that the high cost was probably used to limit requests for copies.

Yocum got through to the records division at 4 P.M. Pacific Time. After arguing briefly with a clerk who insisted no exception could be made to the policy of pay-in-advance, request-in-writing, the reporter asked to speak to the media liaison, Bob Dambacher. Yocum first asked Dambacher about his reaction to Farmers' lawsuit. "I know the insurance company is claiming it isn't Mr. Hanson who died," Dambacher said. "But we're not so sure about that."

"Really? I thought the fingerprints didn't match."

"That's what Glendale the police say, but we're doing some checks of our own. We think it's him."

Yocum jotted down the comments, noting that Dambacher seemed defensive about the insurance company's allegations. The L.A. coroner's office had been criticized for years while under the direction of former coroner Thomas Noguchi, famed "Coroner of the Stars," who had directed investigations into the deaths of such Hollywood notables as Marilyn Monroe and John Belushi. Considering the number of deaths the coroner's office handled each year, it didn't seem impossible for a misidentified corpse to pass through the office without question.

"Look, Bob," Yocum started, leading into his request. "My partner on this story said she talked to somebody in your office earlier today who said it's your policy not to send out copies of autopsies until you've received the money."

"Right. I need a written request and a check. This one would be $43."

"Uh-huh. Bob, I realize you don't know me from Adam, but I'm in a real jam here. I really need that autopsy. Is there any way we could sidestep that request procedure? Let me tell you what I'm up against. The paper thinks this story is hot news and I've got a lot of heat coming down on me to produce that autopsy. The people from Just Sweats and now the coroner's office say the dead guy is Hanson, but my editors are screaming for a copy of the autopsy," Yocum said, resorting to a common reporter's ploy—blame the editor. "Anyway, if there's any way we could get around that I would really appreciate it. I need that overnighted to me so I can have it in the morning. I could give you our Federal Express number so it wouldn't cost you anything, and I'll have our business office send out a check first thing in the morning."

"All right," Dambacher said. "I guess I can do that. What's the Federal Express number?"

That was it. No begging. No pleading. It had been almost too easy, Yocum thought as he hung up the phone. He hadn't expected so much cooperation from one of the busiest morgues in the country.

When Yocum said he needed a check for $43, a disbelieving metro editor Gary Kiefer asked, "He's going to send it without the money? How did you pull that off?"

"It's a public record, and giving up a copy certainly wouldn't interfere with any investigation. The case is closed. Dambacher probably has to turn down the majority of requests he gets from reporters. But this one's easy. This isn't an OD'd celebrity or the work of the Nightstalker. This guy's been dead for four months and they think he died of natural causes. It's a chance for him to do a nice turn for some poor sap reporter out in Ohio."

"That still doesn't explain why he'd send it without getting the money first."

Yocum grinned. "Maybe I wooed him with my superior persuasive powers?"

Kiefer rolled his eyes skyward.

"Well, maybe he was awed by the journalistic clout of *The Columbus Dispatch?*"

"Try again."

"I guess there's always the chance that Bob Dambacher is just a nice guy."

9

Candisky had been waiting nearly an hour on the street outside DeSando's apartment, watching beads of rain roll down the windshield of her Nissan. It was nearly 10 P.M., and she was certain he wasn't going to show. In twelve hours she would be on a plane for Las Vegas with no clues on how to find Hawkins or his mother once she got there. Candisky slouched down in the car seat. She would wait DeSando out. He had to come home sometime.

A little after ten that night, a car pulled into the driveway and Candisky pulled in behind it. A tall, dark-haired man stepped out of the car. "Man, sorry I'm late," he said, slapping himself on the side of his head. "You must be Cathy, I'm Erik. Come on in."

DeSando's condominium was furnished in a somewhat sparse, but contemporary, style. A large, black-lacquered dining room table dominated the great room. A garish, three-foot statue of embracing nudes served as an oversized centerpiece. "John's mom got that for him. Pretty wild stuff, huh?" DeSando asked.

A good description, Candisky thought.

Across the room stood a matching black wall unit, its lighted shelves cluttered with knickknacks, mail, and photographs. A hot tub sat outside the sliding-glass doors on the patio. A mixed-breed cat brushed DeSando's leg and meowed for its dinner. "It's name is Hawk. John named it after himself," DeSando chuckled, flipping on the lights and snagging a box of cat food from the closet.

DeSando was polite and friendly and had a warm smile. Thick brown hair was feathered back off his forehead. He was an impeccably groomed, handsome six-footer, 24 years old, with chiseled features and pale blue eyes.

Candisky sat down at the table. "Do you work at Just Sweats?"

"No," DeSando said. "I was in some of their commercials, and helped out sometimes, but I didn't work there."

"Where do you work?"

"I have my own company," DeSando said as he poured the cat food into a dish. DeSando returned the box to the closet and fetched a Coke from the refrigerator. "You want something to drink? Coke? Beer?"

"No thanks," Candisky said. She took her notebook from her purse. "What kind of company?"

"Decks." DeSando fished his wallet from his hip pocket and gave Candisky a business card.

" 'Dreamdecks'?" Candisky asked.

" 'We turn your deck dreams into reality.' " DeSando grinned as he recited the company motto on the card.

"You're the president, huh?"

"President, salesman, carpenter, lackey. I do it all."

"Do you work out of here?"

DeSando nodded, turning around a dining room chair and sitting down with his legs straddling its back.

"Did you get a chance to read the article in today's paper?" Candisky asked.

DeSando laughed. "Yeah, after you told me about it I picked one up. Unbelievable. Like I told you this morning, Gene's dead. That's the wildest thing I've ever heard. And it makes John look really bad, like he ripped off the insurance company or something."

"It does. And it's going to keep looking that way until John gives his side of the story. Are you sure you don't know how I can get a hold of him, or at least get him a message? Maybe you can have him call me?"

"Honest to God, I don't know where he is," DeSando said, sipping from his soda. "If he calls I'll give him the message."

"Do you expect to hear from him before this weekend?"

"Not really. I haven't even talked to him about this weekend. His mom's the one who told me he might be in Vegas."

"Do you have any pictures of John?"

DeSando frowned. "Yeah. Somewhere." He walked over to the wall unit and picked a pile of mail and papers off a shelf. He sifted through it for several moments, then pulled a colored photograph from the stack. "Here's one from when we went to Hawaii," he said, passing Candisky the photo of him and Hawkins leaning against a balcony railing.

"When were you guys in Hawaii?"

"January, and just to give you an idea of the kind of guy John is, he took his mom, his sister, me, and two other guys to Hawaii and paid for almost everything. The plane tickets, the room. I'm telling you, John is one of the most generous guys I know. Before that he took another guy to Vail for his birthday. He was always spending money on his friends."

"Maybe so. But it's awfully strange that now he'd get all this money and no one, not even his roommate, knows how to get hold of him."

DeSando nodded, polishing off the last of his Coke. "Yeah, it probably looks a little funny, but John had been planning to leave for a long time. He wanted to sell Just Sweats and then buy a big boat in Hawaii and start a booze cruise."

"A what?"

"You know, a booze cruise—one of those boats that takes you out for a couple hours. They're big party boats. When we were in Hawaii, John went out on them twice so he could check them out firsthand. He was thinking about starting one with gambling. He thought that would be a big attraction. John was pretty serious about it. He was pricing boats."

Candisky held up the photograph. "Can I hold on to this? I'd like to have the photo department copy it and I'll get it back to you."

"Are you going to put it in the paper?"

"If that's okay."

DeSando grinned. "Yeah. Cool. That'd be okay."

Candisky slipped the photograph into her pocket. "Thanks. Who's she?" Candisky asked, pointing to a framed photograph of an attractive woman in the wall unit.

"John's old girlfriend, Missy. She's in some soap."

"An actress?"

"Yeah, and a model in New York."

"What's her last name?"

"Hughes."

"Missy Hughes. Do you know how I can reach her? Do you have a number?"

"No."

"So you're pretty convinced John wasn't involved in any kind of insurance scam?" Candisky pressed.

"No way. John even went out and had the body cremated."

"Did he actually see the body when he identified it?"

"I don't think so. But, so what? He talked to somebody at the coroner's office, then he went out and had the ashes spread at sea like Gene wanted."

"Was there a funeral or memorial service?"

"Nah," DeSando said.

"You said John was talking about leaving Just Sweats, but you didn't say why? Why would he abandon his company?"

"When he left Columbus he told me he was going on a buying trip. He said he was going to Atlanta because he had lined up a great deal on some sweats that he could resell for five times the purchase price, but it was a cash-only deal."

"Why cash only?"

"I don't know. I think he got a better price when he dealt in cash."

"So he had a lot of money on him when he left?"

"Yeah, but it's not like you're thinking," DeSando said, leaning back in his chair. "John always carried a lot of cash when he went on buying trips. He'd even take a portable safe with him."

"So why didn't he come back?"

"Oh, I don't know. I think the pressure of running a business and always having creditors breathing down his neck was just getting to him. Like I said, he'd been thinking about blowing town for a long time."

Candisky took advantage of a few minutes of silence and caught up with her notes. "How about the embezzlement earlier this year. I was told that Hanson embezzled $2 million from Just Sweats. Had you heard about that?"

"Well, sort of. I know what you're talking about, but it wasn't exactly an embezzlement."

"What was it?"

"Gene took the money from the company because he thought he was going to die in a week or something, and he didn't want the money going to his family."

"I knew Hanson made John his beneficiary just last November. Why? Did something happen between him and his family?"

"I don't think they were very close. But anyway, Gene left while we were in Hawaii. John comes back and finds the bank accounts empty. So he goes out to Los Angeles to look for him."

"Why L.A.?"

"I can't remember. Gene had friends there; he used to live there." He shrugged. "There was some connection. John thought that's where he'd go. And he was right. He found him out there and a few days later he comes home with a bag of money. I guess Gene had stashed it in a safe-deposit box."

"But why had Gene taken the money?"

"Supposedly he thought it was his. He was freaking out because he was dying. But, he gave it back."

"Did you know Just Sweats filed for bankruptcy this afternoon?"

"Really? I'm not surprised. They'd been in trouble for a while."

"What was the problem?"

"The bank got panicky when John left and called in a note."

"A note—like a loan?"

"Yeah, a note."

"For how much?"

"I'm not positive, but there were two loans worth right around $350,000. Call Fifth Third Bank and ask them." He chuckled. "They should know. It was their money."

"When John left, did he tell anybody or did he just disappear like Gene did?"

"No. He told us. Well, he told us he was going on that buying trip."

"Oh. Right," Candisky said, tapping her pen against her forehead. "It's been a long day. Okay. When did you find out he wasn't coming back?"

"John told me. He called one night and said he knew the insurance company was asking questions and he just didn't want to deal with it."

Candisky chewed on the end of her pen, staring at her notebook and silently contemplating. She had saved the most difficult questions for last. "How did these guys, John, Gene, and Dr. Boggs, how did they hook up?" Candisky began, choosing her words carefully.

"What do you mean? How do they know each other?"

"Right. It's my understanding that Gene is gay. Was he involved with John or Dr. Boggs?"

"John and Gene? Lovers?" DeSando laughed. "Hardly. John's about as straight as they come."

"What about Dr. Boggs?"

"Boggs, I think—and I don't know for sure so don't quote me—but I think he's gay. If he and Gene were involved it was a long time ago. John used to work at Studio 54 in New York, and that's where he said he met Gene. After John started Just Sweats, Gene needed a job so John cut him in. I'm not sure who knew Dr. Boggs first, but John and Gene both lived in Los Angeles and they were both his patients."

"So John actually started Just Sweats?"

"Yeah, in 1985, but Gene came in after a few months and they split everything."

"Did you know Gene very well?"

"Fairly well. I'd see him around, but I never socialized with him. Gene really stayed to himself a lot, very laid back. He smoked like a fiend and he was real flashy with fashion, you know; he wore Italian suits—silk. Gene was the stabilizing force of the two. He was like the father—he kept things on an even keel—and John was like a little kid. But John had the brains and was the creative talent for Just Sweats. John always had ideas, but he didn't know how to follow them through. That's where Gene came in."

"You called Gene the father. How so?"

"John was always running at ninety miles per hour. Gene never got riled. He was very easy-going."

DeSando told Candisky about an incident that occurred in 1987 when he was delivering merchandise from Columbus to the Just Sweats stores in Kentucky. On his way back, DeSando wrecked the company's leased truck. Fearful of Hawkins's reaction, DeSando asked Hanson what he should do. "Gene looked at me and said, 'Don't worry. That's what insurance is for.'"

Before leaving Columbus in early January 1988, Hanson invited DeSando to his penthouse at the Park Towers on the city's near east side. Hanson explained that he was very ill and had only a few months to live. He gave DeSando several expensive suits, a television, and a videocassette recorder, saying, "I won't be needing these anymore."

"So you think Gene is really dead?" Candisky asked.

"Oh yeah, no doubt," DeSando said, pausing for a moment. "If anything is screwy, it's that Gene maybe died of AIDS and not a heart attack. A lot of people thought he had AIDS."

After about an hour had passed, Candisky thought it was time to tell DeSando that he was going to have company in Las Vegas. She mulled over how to break the news without alienating him. De-Sando's cooperation was crucial if Candisky was to find Hawkins, or at least his mother. His mother's first name was Jackie, but she had divorced and had evidently changed her last name. Candisky figured the odds of finding a poker dealer named Jackie in all of Las Vegas at next to nil. After silently weighing her options, Candisky decided to use the reporter's standby—blame it on the editor.

"Uh, listen. I need to talk to Hawkins and his mother. This doesn't look too good, and John needs to tell his side of the story. So, my editors were thinking that it might be a good idea if I kind of tagged along to Las Vegas tomorrow," Candisky fibbed, conscious of the plane ticket already tucked inside her purse.

"Oh yeah? I agree, totally. John really needs to talk to you. He's got to clear his name," DeSando responded.

He bought it without a flinch, Candisky thought. She was lucky DeSando was so agreeable. "Do you think you can help set up an interview with John?"

"Well, I'm not positive that John is going to be there. He said he might show up. But I'm meeting his mother for sure on Saturday. She wants John's video camera and the tape of our Hawaii trip. I'm supposed to call her when I get there. I'll ask if she'll talk to you, but I can't promise anything."

10

Yocum hated the coffee in the newsroom. Decaffeinated. Why would anyone drink decaffeinated coffee? He once circulated a petition around the newsroom demanding the return of caffeine to the coffeepot. *Real* coffee reappeared for a couple of days, but Yocum's victory was short-lived. The managing editor, it seemed, preferred the decaffeinated kind, period.

Now Yocum bought his morning cup at the vending machine and checked his mail before making his way to his desk. Shortly before 9 A.M. he called the security desk for the third time that morning. A security guard growing short on patience again explained ever so clearly that Yocum's package from Los Angeles hadn't arrived. Federal Express never gets to the *Dispatch* before nine.

Candisky had left a few minutes earlier for Port Columbus International Airport, having talked a photo intern into giving her a ride. She had spent a half-hour re-creating for Yocum her interview with DeSando. Most of his comments could be worked into a weekend story. If Dambacher had sent the autopsy report as promised, it might give them a story for the next day. Yocum told her not to worry; he'd come up with something. Candisky had a layover in St. Louis and said she would call if she had time.

Yocum hoped the autopsy report might provide some leads. He also wanted to go to the clerk of court's office to review Farmers' case file for additional exhibits and addendums and to interview the insurance company's attorney, Melvin Weinstein. Yocum sent Karsko and Ellis electronic messages outlining his plans for the day.

Yocum had two messages waiting for him that morning. Reporters Grady Hambrick and Scott Powers had both picked up stray Just Sweats tips. Hambrick, a veteran reporter who usually worked the four-to-midnight shift and held down the fort after most of the editors were gone, had written:

I got a call last night from a woman who wouldn't identify herself. She works as a waitress at Max & Erma's on Rt. 161. She says a woman who works with her is John Hawkins's girlfriend. This girlfriend flew to L.A. to meet him early this week. The caller said they plan to buy a camper and go to Mexico. Hawkins supposedly told her to make sure her passport was up to date. The girlfriend's name is Amy Storm or Amy Buzzard.

A fellow reporter had provided them with their first clue to the whereabouts of John Hawkins. Yocum made a note: Call Max & Erma's and check on the Buzzardwoman.

The reporter then scrolled the computer screen down to Powers's message. Powers had recently been recruited to the *Dispatch* from a suburban news chain. His desk stood behind Candisky's and he frequently fielded her telephone calls. He would interview callers with Just Sweats tips and pass along detailed messages to both Candisky and Yocum. On Friday morning, Yocum's message from Powers concerned a call he had received the day before.

Robin:

I got a call from a woman who said she and her friend were with John Hawkins the night before he disappeared. She said he was telling them goodbye, because he was leaving the next day for Florida to visit his ailing father, and then he was going around the world.

I called her friend, who confirmed the story.

Neither of them want their names used and the information was taken with that understanding.

Here are the transcripts of what they said:

Heather:

I was out with John Hawkins the night of the 15th of July. We both were. He left town on the 16th. He told me he had sold the company that day and was on his way to Florida to see his father, who was dying. All I know is he said he sold the company and he was a millionaire and that he was going sailing around the world and would probably never come back. That's what he said. We met him at the Continental Athletic Club. He was very friendly. We talked with him about four hours one day. We all became really close. He used to live in the Continent. I met Erik DeSando as well. We met him at the pool. He never mentioned Hanson. I didn't even know he had a partner. I thought he was in it by himself. He was very friendly. He bragged a lot and he seemed to be very proud of his money and he made a point to tell us he was a millionaire. (She insisted he wasn't hustling them at all.) We felt very comfortable. I don't think he was a millionaire when he was talking to us. But I think he knew he was going to be.

Susan:

We were at a party with him and Erik and they came up in their limo. Yeah, they had a limo. Hawkins said he sold his company and tomorrow he is leaving for Florida to see his dad, then he is going to take a trip around the world. He said I would probably never see him again. He was a nice guy, kind of showy wih his money.

The tips kept rolling in, much to Yocum's delight. Let the cops sit around, he thought. Every telephone call put the *Dispatch* that much further ahead. Eventually, Yocum figured, the police would have to investigate the case. When they did, reporters Yocum and Candisky would be in the enviable position to barter background information for new leads.

Before leaving for Las Vegas, Candisky had entered her notes from the DeSando interview into a separate computer file and sent them to Yocum's personal queue. Yocum scanned the file, but found nothing earth-shattering in DeSando's information. However, the notes did provide answers to a few of the reporters' questions. Candisky and Yocum had heard from one caller that Hawkins had been dating a soap-opera star. DeSando said it was Missy Hughes. He couldn't remember which soap opera she had been in, but said she was also a model. Hawkins had met Hughes at Studio 54 while living in New York.

Yocum fired a computer message to reporter Dave Jones, a former television critic for the *Dispatch* who was now a general assignment reporter. "Have you ever heard of a soap opera actress named Missy Hughes? If so, which soap? She apparently was or is the girlfriend of John Hawkins."

Jones hadn't heard of her but promised to find out. After a few phone calls, Jones messaged Yocum that Hughes's real name was Ilanna Hughes and she had appeared briefly on NBC's "Another World." However, she was no longer acting, and Jones couldn't find an address or phone number.

The information on the story was accruing at an amazing rate.

Before it got out of control Yocum created a file in his computer to record all the notes, leads, messages, and unused quotes the reporters collected.

At 9:15 A.M. Yocum called security. "Not yet!" he was told. Yocum apologized, trying not to anger the security guard further. The security staff at the *Dispatch* was in charge of the company fleet. Aggravate a security guard and the next time you needed a press car, you were likely to end up with one of the clunky minivans—"*Dispatch* Winnebagos," the reporters called them.

Yocum opened up his *Dispatch* to the sports page, thinking he would wait patiently. As he scanned the pages for the baseball standings, city editor Mark Ellis came up with the next day's story budget. "Did you get your autopsy report?"

"Not yet. Fed Ex hasn't gotten here, and I can't be positive the guy sent it. He said he was going to, but you know how that goes sometimes. I really don't know what we'll have for tomorrow. Something, but I don't know what."

Ellis nodded. "Let me know."

Yocum grabbed a pen and notepad, intending to run down to the courthouse to recheck the lawsuit while he was waiting for the autopsy report to arrive. As the elevator door opened on the *Dispatch* lobby, the Federal Express delivery woman walked through the front door. The security guard sorted through the envelopes slowly, as if to even the score for all the bothersome telephone calls. Finally, the guard handed one to Yocum, who jumped back on the elevator for the return trip to the fifth-floor newsroom.

The package was a reporter's dream. Attached to the autopsy report was a three-page Glendale police report by Glendale Police Officer Timothy Spruill, with a two-page, typed summary of the death of Melvin E. Hanson by Glendale Sgt. Terry Jones; a three-page narrative from coroner's investigator Craig R. Harvey; the autopsy findings; and the toxicology report.

The packet Dambacher had sent had more information than the reporters could have tracked down in two weeks. Page after page revealed dozens of details on the reported death of Melvin E. Hanson, all courtesy of public records. A line from Harvey's narrative seemed to leap off the page: ". . . it was suspected the doctor may have sexually assaulted, either before or post-mortem, the decedent while he was at his office."

"Chee-suss," Yocum said, jumping out of his seat and practically sprinting across the newsroom to Ellis's desk. "You're absolutely not going to believe this," Yocum said.

"Something good?"

"Fabulous stuff. This'll make the hair on your neck stand up. Look at this. Sexually assaulting corpses. Look here—he attacked some other guy with a stun gun. Tell me this guy isn't the original mad doctor. I've got to go through this some more. It's loaded with great stuff."

The handful of reporters within earshot began crowding around, exhibiting the same morbid curiosity that made them peek at the bodies at homicides. Reporters are a hardy bunch. They cover shootings and ax murders and fires and car wrecks and nothing much bothers them. Yet, as Yocum read aloud the part of the report that stated police believed Boggs may have sexually assaulted a corpse, these same reporters quivered as if they had just woken up from a short nap behind the wheel at sixty miles per hour.

Yocum took the autopsy and a yellow highlighter and went back to his desk to begin piecing together a story for the next day's paper. The lead was never in question—Boggs sexually assaulted a corpse.

Harvey's report stated:

> Because of the past history of the physician, Glendale Police Department interceded when discrepancies became apparent in the doctor's story as to the sequence of events.
>
> . . . On 4-16-88, during the early morning hours, the decedent contacted his regular physician, Dr. Richard P. Boggs, (at home) and complained of chest pains which he described as, "an elephant on my chest." Boggs agreed to meet the decedent at his office later that morning for treatment. The decedent arrived and Boggs took his blood pressure (148/102; pulse 124) and then placed him on an EKG machine. The EKG was run and strip obtained (a copy of the strip is included with the medical file). The decedent then dressed and was left alone in the examination room, while the doctor attended to tasks down the hall. At this point, the doctor related hearing a thud-like sound and returned to find the decedent collapsed on the floor in a side/supine position. He placed the decedent in a supine position, elevated his feet, then began CPR. According to the doctor, he attempted to call 911, but received a busy signal. He continued on again for 40–45 minutes, then attempted a second call, which met with success. Paramedics arrived and pronounced death at 0715 hours, this date.
>
> Police arrived shortly afterward and while interviewing the doctor, found several discrepancies in his story as to what had occurred. The

doctor was taken to the Glendale Police Department for further questioning.

. . . The decedent's physician is alleged to be a homosexual, or to at least have those proclivities. The decedent is believed to be a homosexual also. According to [Glendale Police Detective James] Peterson, he has personal knowledge of the doctor's activities and related a recent incident where he investigated the use of a stun gun by the doctor against another man who claims to have been propositioned, then later rebuffed by Boggs. Because of the 40–45 minute time lapse the doctor claims occurred because of an inability to contact 911, it was suspected that the doctor may have sexually assaulted either before death or post-mortem, the decedent while he was at his office.

Ellis came over to Yocum's desk. "Does it say anything about what went on in Boggs's office the day that guy died?"

"Lots. It says Boggs claims Hanson called him about three-thirty in the morning complaining of chest pains. Boggs told him to go to the emergency room, but Hanson refused."

"Why?" Ellis asked.

"Apparently Hanson hated hospitals. So Boggs tells him to meet him at the office. He does some tests, an EKG, and decides Hanson isn't in immediate danger."

"Never sends him to the hospital?"

"No. Hanson supposedly tells Boggs he wants to rest, so the good doctor lets him sack out on an examination table. Boggs says he leaves the room, and about ten minutes later he hears a thud. He goes back in and finds Hanson on the floor, unconscious."

"So what's the bitch?"

"Well, what I've just told you is the only thing that makes any sense at all. Boggs tells the cops he starts CPR for a couple of minutes, then calls 911, but gets a busy signal."

"Nine-eleven busy? Think it's true?"

"No chance. It's early on a Saturday morning. So Boggs says he gives CPR for another forty-five minutes until he gets through on 911."

"What was he doing? Giving himself time to clean up?"

"Maybe he was gathering his nerve. Anyway, because of the time lapse, the cops think he banged the corpse."

Ellis winced. "Well, spare me the details there. Anything else?"

"There's something real interesting on the EKG. Boggs says he did an EKG on Hanson between 5:00 and 5:20 A.M. But according to the police report, the machine's electronic timing device says it was last used at two minutes after midnight. That's five hours before Boggs claimed he did the test, and three-and-a-half hours before Hanson even called."

"No indication anywhere of who the stiff is?"

"No," Yocum said, sitting back down at his computer terminal. "But whoever it was he felt no pain. The guy was bombed. The blood-alcohol was .29."

"Ouch. Good stuff. Anything else?"

"Not that I can tell. There was some blood in the stomach and mention of a fatty liver, but I don't know if that means anything. At some point, I'll take it over to Pat Fardel at the coroner's office and have him take a look at it for us."

"Sounds good. Write it." Ellis headed back to put the story on the next day's budget.

Yocum made a few notes to himself, including one to call Glendale police and find out if their 911 number was ever busy. When Yocum had the bulk of the story completed, he stored it in the computer. He then went down to the courthouse to take another look at the Farmers' lawsuit; he wanted to see if Candisky might have missed anything.

He asked to see the original file and found, tucked in the back of the manila folder, two exhibits that the secretary at the clerk of court's office had failed to include in the copy of the suit she had given Candisky. The exhibits contained two crucial pieces of information—photographs of the corpse and an enlarged photograph of Hanson's California driver's license. Yocum called the newsroom and asked for a photographer to come down and take shots of the two.

As he waited for the photographer, Yocum studied the photographs and played the judge's role in the case. It seemed obvious to him that the photographs weren't of the same person. One was obviously younger. One was bald, the other had a receding hairline. Yocum tried to analyze the photos, looking for any similar facial feature. If Hanson had plastic surgery, could he look like the dead man? No chance, Yocum thought. These photographs were not of the same man.

But Yocum had never met the real Hanson. All the stories that were surfacing about the man implied that Yocum couldn't even be sure the photograph on Hanson's driver's license was really of Hanson.

The corpse appeared much younger than 46 years old, Hanson's age at the time of his alleged death. But Yocum noticed that the physical description on Hanson's driver's license—blue eyes, brown hair, five-foot-ten, 155 pounds—was exactly the same as the corpse's. If someone had substituted another corpse for Hanson, it had certainly been a good choice.

When photographer Jeff Hinckley arrived, Yocum showed him the photographs. "Look at these. Is that the same guy in both pictures?"

Hinckley looked at the two and smiled, as if Yocum was kidding. "Are you serious?"

"Yes."

"No. Not even close."

Hinckley placed the exhibits on the floor and took shots of them. With the additional information from the driver's license, Yocum headed back to the newsroom to finish up his story. Now he only lacked identifications of the two photographs. Yocum wanted someone who knew Hanson to confirm he was the man pictured on the driver's license. Although the lawsuit claimed the photo was of Hanson, the story was getting bizarre. Yocum didn't want to risk the embarrassment of running the wrong photograph. He could ask the employees at the Just Sweats headquarters to identify Hanson, but they had been less than cooperative. Someone there might even find humor in causing the paper some grief. Later that day, however, the problem resolved itself.

That afternoon, Yocum received a call from a man who claimed to have worked at the Just Sweats headquarters. Yocum was growing suspicious of some of the callers, particularly after one woman had claimed to be Mrs. John B. Hawkins, screamed at Yocum, and ordered him not to write any more stories about her husband. However, this former employee knew some details about the company and seemed legitimate. Yocum asked for help identifying the photographs and the man agreed to meet with him at G. D. Ritzy's, a fast-food restaurant on East Broad Street.

Yocum clipped the information away from Hanson's driver's license, leaving just the photograph. When Yocum met the man and showed him the photograph of the corpse, the man laughed. "That's not Gene Hanson." Then Yocum produced the photo from the driver's license. The man tapped it twice with his index finger and said, confidently, "That's Hanson."

"You're sure?"

"Absolutely. I worked with the guy. That's him." The man went on to talk about working at Just Sweats and described Hawkins as "a total wacko and a real druggie."

"Druggie?" Yocum questioned. "All I've heard is that he's some kind of health nut who was always working out."

"Health nut!" He laughed. "Man, that guy used to go into the women's restroom out at the warehouse and lock himself inside for hours doing coke. He'd just disappear and you could bet that's where he was. We had this one little fat woman working out there and she used to beat like hell on the door trying to get him to come out so she could go to the bathroom. When he did come out his eyes looked like silver dollars. The boy liked his nose candy."

"You knew Hanson pretty well?" He nodded. "Was he gay?"

"I think so. I didn't know much about Gene's personal life. He really kept that to himself. But I think so."

"How about Hawkins?"

"I don't know. I don't think so, but you never know. You know, those two were a really strange pair. I could never figure out how they hooked up. Here's Hanson—older, quiet, probably queer, and Hawkins, who was this young turk. I didn't like him, okay, but he always had beautiful women around. Always. It was just a strange relationship."

11

At 10 P.M., the first edition of the *Dispatch* came back to the newsroom. The Just Sweats story spanned the top of the front page, accompanied by a photo of the corpse and another taken from Hanson's California driver's license.

"So how long are you going to milk this cow, Yocum?" asked Mike Curtin, the *Dispatch* public affairs editor who was strolling through the newsroom with a copy of the paper.

"I'll milk her 'til she's dry," Yocum said, looking over his paper. "And, maybe for a few weeks thereafter."

"I just saw a Channel 10 crew pull up out front and get a paper out of the box. Are they following this at all?"

Yocum shook his head. "Nah, they're all suckin' hind tit, just rewriting our stories. This isn't a good television story. Too confusing and no pictures."

"Well they better find a way to film it, because that's all anyone's talking about over at the statehouse. How'd you swing this?" Curtin asked, flicking the photo of the dead man on the front page."

Yocum shrugged. "Breaking new ground. First time a corpse ever made the front page."

Television news programs weren't climbing all over themselves to get to the story, and their absence certainly helped Yocum and Candisky. Since the *Dispatch* was the only one covering the story, its reporters were more apt to get the interviews they needed. People will generally talk to the first reporter to knock on the door, but the third and fourth reporters will likely find it slammed in their faces. With no one out there competing for interviews, doors stayed open for *Dispatch* reporters.

Yocum was trying to finish plugging some notes into his computer file so he could go home. So many tips were pouring in that he hadn't had time to check out all that he would have liked. The phone rang again.

"Newsroom. Rob Yocum."

"Yeah, are you the reporter working on the Just Sweats stories?"

"I'm one of them."

"Yeah, well are you guys interested in information on the story?"

Yocum pulled out his pen. "Sure. What have you got?"

"Are you interested in interviewing John Hawkins's girlfriend?"

"Excuse me?"

"John Hawkins's girlfriend. Would you be interested in talking to her?"

"Hell yes, but which one? I understand he had dozens."

The caller laughed. "He did, but this is the one who is out in California with him right now."

"Buzzard?" Yocum asked.

"Buzzard? What do you mean?"

"We heard her name was Amy Buzzard, or Amy Storm, something like that."

The man laughed again. "Blizzard. Her name's Amy Blizzard. She's a waitress at Max & Erma's."

"That's the one I heard about. Do you know her?"

"Yeah. I know her real well."

"Really, so you think there's a chance she might talk?"

"Yeah, I think so, if I ask her."

If I ask her, Yocum thought. The caller was trying to maneuver himself into a position of power and financial reward. "So, is there a chance you can line us up an interview?"

"I think so. I'll be talking to her when she gets back from California. Would you like me to ask her if she'll talk?"

"Absolutely," Yocum said, waiting for the catch. The caller was probably going to ask for money to set up the interview. But no request came. "I'm kind of curious," Yocum said. "What's your motivation?"

"Nothing. I don't care for Hawkins, particularly, but I just figured it might be a good interview for you guys."

Yocum had been in the business long enough to know that people rarely called to offer help simply out of the goodness of their hearts. Most were working an angle or grinding an ax. If the caller didn't want money, he had an ax to grind. Not that it mattered to Yocum. He knew it would be easier to get an interview with the girlfriend if one of her friends lined it up.

The caller didn't appear to be hiding anything and gave his name and telephone number without hesitation. Mike Martin. He worked for Continental Airlines at Port Columbus Airport.

"So when she comes back you're going to set up this interview for me?" Yocum asked.

"Yep. As soon as she gets back."

"Okay, partner." Yocum hung up the phone and said to himself as he started toward the door, "We'll see."

12

In the early afternoon of Friday, August 26, Candisky arrived at the California Club and Casino in downtown Las Vegas, the hotel where Karsko had booked her reservation. Although it was small by Las Vegas standards, the hotel's Hawaiian owners were known for their hospitality, Karsko assured her. They set her up in a slightly gaudy room with a less-than-spectacular view of an adjacent roof.

As soon as she got settled, Candisky called DeSando, who was staying on the strip at the Riviera Hotel, about two miles away. The telephone in his room rang six times before the hotel operator interrupted and offered to take a message.

DeSando had flown to Las Vegas several hours earlier on a plane chartered by the Columbus Fraternal Order of Police. DeSando, an avid gambler who read how-to-win books and made frequent trips to both Vegas and Atlantic City, had booked on the flight after a travel agent told him that it had a few vacant seats. He had promised to meet the reporter in Vegas. Candisky feared DeSando could easily be distracted in Vegas. What if he were winning at the craps table? She found it hard to imagine DeSando walking away from a hot streak to escort her around. Candisky prayed he would remember their arrangements. He was her only realistic means of finding Hawkins and his mother. She could track Jackie down through marriage licenses under her former name of Hawkins, but the county administration offices were closed for the weekend, making the task impossible.

Even though DeSando had agreed that it would be good for Hawkins to give his side of the story, Candisky worried that he might have only echoed her suggestion. Perhaps DeSando had already spoken with Hawkins and he had nixed the idea of an interview.

Candisky had a knack for pegging personalities, but she was having a hard time putting a peg on DeSando. Why was he being so cooperative? He seemed to like the attention, and he seemed to like being an expert on the subject of Just Sweats and John B. Hawkins even more. He had seemed sincere about convincing Hawkins to talk. Obviously, he had not even realized how much trouble his former roommate had gotten himself into.

The reporter began to wonder what she'd tell Karsko if DeSando didn't call. Contrary to his hard-nosed reputation, Karsko hadn't pressured Candisky; he'd simply told her to go to Las Vegas and "see what turns up." But those words gave her little comfort as she sat in her hotel room for the entire afternoon waiting for DeSando's call. She didn't want to come back empty handed from her first out-of-town trip for the *Dispatch*. Twice, the phone had rung and twice she had bolted off the bed to answer it, but twice it had been Yocum looking for good news.

At ten after six in the evening, the phone rang again. Candisky didn't get excited, figuring it was Yocum again. Instead she was greeted by a jaunty "Hey. How ya doing? It's Erik." Candisky took a breath and sat down on the side of the bed. DeSando said that he wasn't sure if John was in town, but his mother was coming by the hotel to visit the next day about noon. Jackie said she would be more than happy to talk to a reporter who had come all the way from Ohio to find out about her son. "So, what have you been doing? Are you having fun?" DeSando asked.

Fun? Candisky thought. It's been a blast—stuck in a room for three hours.

"Why don't you come and meet me and my friend here at the Riviera? We're going to the casino."

At the blackjack tables that night, DeSando, clad in a pair of running shorts and a T-shirt, with his money stashed in a black waist bag, shared some of the adventures he'd had courtesy of John Barrett Hawkins.

The two had met in June 1987 while playing basketball at the Continental Athletic Club on Columbus's north side. "I was just out of college and working at the club," DeSando explained, taking a hit on his seven of hearts and six of clubs. Queen of spades. Twenty-three. "Damn." DeSando tossed his hold card onto the table. "John used to come in and work out, and that's how I got to know him. We used to shoot hoops together. We just started hanging out together, barhopping and . . . you know . . ."

Candisky grinned. DeSando and Hawkins must share the same passion for women and fun. "So, you said you didn't work for Just

Sweats. What was the common bond for you two? Good times?"

DeSando took a king of hearts up and a nine in the hold. "I'll stay," he told the dealer. "That was part of it. John was a riot to party with. He spent money like crazy. But, to be honest with you, I think I was a little in awe of him. Here's a guy my age, no college—Christ, he never even finished high school—and he's running his own business and making a fortune. Here I was working at the club. John motivated me to get my own business started. So, we were spending all our spare time hanging around together, and we got to be real tight. John's roommate was moving out and he asked me if I'd be interested in sharing an apartment."

The dealer took a six of clubs. "House pays nineteen or better," she said. Erik showed his cards and pulled in his winnings.

"So you're telling me John liked to party and spend money?" Candisky asked. "I thought someone told me he was consumed with getting rich? Those don't sound like compatible traits to me."

"I know, but that's really the way he was." Erik took a ten of diamonds on the table and a seven of diamonds in the hold. "Wonderful. I'll stay. John talked about money all the time. He said he wanted to build himself a fortune, but he was real careless with it. He was constantly complaining about money problems at Just Sweats, but he'd turn right around and raid a cash register at one of the stores and leave an IOU. John used to brag about the money he was making, and I can't tell you how many times I heard him say he would be a millionaire by the time he was thirty. But money didn't stay in his pockets very long. He never thought twice about dropping a couple thousand to keep his buddies entertained." The dealer turned over two queens. "House pays twenty-one." DeSando tossed in his hold card.

DeSando had helped Hawkins with the business, driving a truck to pick up stock, and in return for his help Hawkins footed the bill when the two took vacations to Las Vegas, Chicago, the Bahamas, and Hawaii. While they had been living together, Hawkins and DeSando went out two or three nights a week. Hawkins frequently rented a limousine to chauffeur the two from club to club as they played "Let's see who can be the first to get a woman in the back of the limo." Hawkins was generous toward his friends, but he also delighted in saving a few dollars. One of his favorite penny-ante scams was ducking out of the airport parking lot without paying the full fee.

When Hawkins was out of town on business, he would leave his car in the short-term parking lot closest to the terminal. Airport personnel regularly checked the lot and would note any car that had not been moved for several days. However, Hawkins enlisted DeSando in a scheme to avoid paying a long-term fee.

DeSando would drive to the airport, park, and meet Hawkins when he returned from his trip. Then, DeSando would give his parking stub to Hawkins. Using DeSando's ticket, Hawkins could drive out paying for only an hour's stay. By claiming that he had lost his ticket, DeSando could get out of the lot by paying only the one-day rate. Net savings to Hawkins: about twenty dollars.

"It sounds like an awful lot of work to save a few dollars," Candisky said.

"It wasn't just saving money that was important to John. It was the thrill of getting away with something. He was always looking for little ways to jerk off the system."

"But why would you do it? What was in it for you?"

"Nothing, really," DeSando shrugged. "John's a hard guy to say no to."

DeSando conceded that Hawkins had his vices—marijuana, Quaaludes, steroids, mixed drinks.

"One of the people who called the office said he dealt 'ludes. Is that right?"

DeSando winced. "I don't know if you would call it dealing. He just got them for some of his buddies."

Candisky squinted one eye at DeSando.

His eyes widened. "Fuck no, not me. I never mess with that shit."

Candisky smiled.

"I swear," he said.

"Okay, Erik," she said, biting her lip to stem the urge to laugh. She wondered why DeSando felt it so important to claim his innocence on the matter. Image, she assumed. "How about all the women?" Candisky asked. "Are you counting that as one of his vices?"

"I should. I've never seen anyone like John. Seriously, he could not control himself. He loves women, all women. He's the horniest man I've ever known. There must be something wrong with his hormones. Sometimes he'd bring three women a day into the apartment. There were times—a lot of times—when he'd have some girl in bed and another would be knocking at the door, and I'd have to make up some story to get rid of her."

13

It was after 11 A.M. Saturday before Erik DeSando climbed out of bed and showered. Wearing blue jeans and a loose-fitting cotton shirt, DeSando was sitting on the edge of the bed, towel drying his hair, when the phone rang in his hotel room. A distant and weak voice said, "Erik, it's John."

"John, hey, wait a minute, I can barely hear you." DeSando turned down the volume of the television and ran back to the bed. "What's going on?"

"Not much. How 'bout with you?"

"Nothing with me. You're the one everybody's talking about. There's been a couple of stories in the paper about you."

"Yeah, I heard."

DeSando frowned. "How did you hear?"

"I don't know," Hawkins mumbled, avoiding the question. "Look, Erik, do you think this thing is going to blow over pretty soon?"

"I don't think so, John," DeSando answered, lying back on the bed. "The insurance company wants the money back. And the *Dispatch* is going crazy over the story. One of their reporters is in town right now. She wants to interview you."

"No fuckin' way. Tell her no."

"All right, John. Take it easy. But it might do you some good to get your side of the story in the paper. The *Dispatch* is kickin' the shit out of you. Everyone's coming down on you for skipping town. Can't you just give the insurance company its money back?"

"I wish I could, but that would be tough," Hawkins replied.

"Why is that?"

"Well, I don't have it."

"You've gotta be kidding me, John," DeSando said, bolting upright. "Jesus Christ, what are you thinking?"

"I know, I know."

64

"John, I've got to tell you, a lot of people think you're in way over your head, and they're starting to ask a lot of questions. Everyone's reading the stories. People think someone might have been murdered."

"Murdered! Look, I'm innocent. Don't believe anything you hear. If someone was killed, it wasn't me that did it. It was that dumb fucker Boggs, not me."

14

Candisky walked into DeSando's hotel room shortly after noon and caught him on the telephone. DeSando motioned for Candisky to sit down. "She'll be here. Don't worry," DeSando said. He pressed a finger to his open ear, turned his back to Candisky, and went back to his telephone conversation, whispering. Candisky wondered if DeSando might be talking to Hawkins and tried to listen in. She couldn't.

A minute later, someone knocked at the door and DeSando motioned for Candisky to answer it. She opened the door to a petite and pretty woman, with wavy blonde hair and a quick smile. "Hi. I'm Jackie Cirian, John Hawkins's mother," she said, extending her right hand. "You must be Cathy."

At 43, Jackie Cirian could easily pass herself off as ten years younger. She wore skintight faded denims and a light-colored blouse. A purse swung from her left shoulder and she carried an unopened can of Diet Pepsi. Personable and outgoing, Cirian reminded Candisky of a young Debbie Reynolds.

DeSando hung up the telephone and hugged Cirian.

"Have you talked to John?"

"That was him on the phone. He had been thinking about meeting me here, but he's not going to make it," DeSando replied, taking a seat in the chair nearest the window.

Cirian glanced at the two newspaper clippings DeSando had brought for her, then abruptly asked Candisky, "So, what would you like to know about my Johnny?" Her tone was light, yet very matter-of-fact. "I just can't believe you came all the way out here to talk to me." Jackie Cirian looked at Erik and smiled. "Can you believe that, Erik?"

DeSando squirmed in his seat, not sure how to answer the question. It was obvious to Candisky that Cirian didn't understand the seriousness of the allegations. "Jackie, are you familiar with . . . did Erik tell you about the lawsuit the insurance company filed against John?"

Cirian rolled her eyes. "Isn't that the most absurd thing you've ever heard?" punctuating her question by snapping open her can of soda. "I told Johnny he should sue the insurance company for slander. They've damaged his reputation."

"If he hasn't done anything, I guess I'd agree," Candisky said, choosing her words so she wouldn't alienate Cirian. "But where is he? Why did he leave town so suddenly?"

"Believe me, Cathy, there's nothing unusual about John leaving Columbus. He had outgrown that little town. After Gene left, Johnny lost interest in the company. When he was out here he told me, 'Mom, it's just not the same without Gene.' " Cirian picked up a pair of DeSando's shorts off the floor and folded them. "He was tired and burned out. He wanted to take a break. I guess I could have taught him a little better, but packing up and leaving is how John handles his problems. Johnny has this built-in ability—probably because I moved him around as a young boy—to pick up and go and not look back. It was just time for Johnny to move on and try something else. He needed new challenges."

The more Cirian spoke, the more obvious it became to Candisky that Hawkins had told his mother very little. Cirian spoke so sincerely that Candisky could not doubt that Cirian believed everything she said.

"Can you tell me what John told you about the case?" Candisky pressed. "Did he mention it to you?"

"Oh, of course," Cirian said, pausing to take a drink. "Johnny was just here three weeks ago, and I'll be honest with you, he was very upset. He told me that the insurance company didn't believe Gene was dead, and that Just Sweats was in trouble financially. I could tell the pressure was unbearable. One day, I suggested we go hiking in the mountains, just to get away. That was the most depressed I'd ever seen him. When he left, he told me he was checking himself into a clinic."

"A clinic? What for?"

Cirian hesitated for a moment. "Stress. He just needed some time to get his head together, that's all."

"Where at?"

Cirian shook her head. "Somewhere in California, I don't know. He didn't say."

"Didn't you ask?"

"No. I figured if Johnny wanted me to know, he would have told me."

This didn't ring true. What mother, especially one as concerned as Cirian appeared to be, wouldn't have asked where her son was going? Candisky looked over at DeSando, who was avoiding all eye contact. He had lowered his head and was kneading his hands in his lap. The reporter didn't believe Hawkins was in a stress center; she could tell that DeSando didn't believe it either. Candisky sensed that Cirian was just repeating what John had told her.

"One of the things I'm missing is background on John," Candisky said. "Could you fill me in?"

"Sure. Where would you like me to start?"

Candisky laughed. "How about at birth? If you don't mind."

"Mind?" Cirian tapped Candisky's knee. "Not at all." She crinkled up her nose. "I just love talking about him. Well, I got pregnant when I was just 17. My parents were very strict and they never taught me anything about birth control. So, I married John's father, John, Sr., in 1962. John was born on February 6, 1963. We were living in St. Louis at the time, but it didn't last. None of them did."

"None of them?"

Cirian's eyes suddenly grew more sullen, serious. "Four times. I've been divorced four times, but don't put that in the newspaper. Are you married?"

Candisky shook her head.

"Don't get married. They'll cheat on you every time," she said, nervously working the snap tab from the can. "I was working as a hairdresser and money was tight, but Johnny and I managed. I used to take John out to Busch Stadium to see the Cardinals. He loved baseball. He loved all sports, actually. I always encouraged him to play— basketball, hockey, football. And he was such a natural athlete. Wait until you meet him and you'll see what I mean. He's built like a god. All muscle."

"So, John grew up in St. Louis?"

"Not totally. That's a funny story. I came out here for a vacation and ended up meeting husband number three. That was in 1973, so John would have been about 10. I was in love, and there was more money to be made working in the casinos than cutting hair."

Cirian gave birth to a daughter, Kari, three years later, and soon divorced for the third time. Alone again, she tried to juggle the demands made by a job, a teen-age boy, and an infant daughter. Cirian said she did her best to keep John interested in school, but despite what she viewed as his sheer genius, Cirian conceded that her son had never shown much enthusiasm for the classroom. Even his earlier interest in sports waned. Hawkins's driving passion became making money. He delivered papers and peddled anything he could find. "By the time Johnny was 13, he was already tall and handsome, and he has those killer blue eyes. He'd just charm people into buying whatever it was he was selling."

"What year did he graduate from high school?"

Jackie shook her head. "He didn't. I tried to keep him in, but he just wasn't interested in book learning. He dropped out of school in the eleventh grade and moved in with his father in Florida. Johnny always said he learned more from the streets than he did in school."

"What did he do in Florida? Work?"

"No, he went to welding school. And, he worked as a welder for a while in Florida, and then he got a job on the pipeline."

"In Alaska?"

"No, some pipeline in California. But he didn't do that for very long."

"Why's that?"

"You have to understand, my son has a quick mind. He could never enjoy a labor job. He didn't want to be a welder—the life wasn't fast enough, it wasn't exciting for him."

"So, what did he do for work?"

"He was a prostitute."

Jackie Cirian rolled the words out of her mouth without hesitation. DeSando buried his face in his hands.

Candisky blinked. "I'm sorry. A . . . prostitute?"

"Um-hmm. A male prostitute. A gigolo. I'm not ashamed of it. For Johnny, that was just a steppingstone. It was his meal ticket. Johnny was blessed with a handsome face and a muscular body. Why not use it?"

Candisky looked to DeSando to gauge the truthfulness of the comment. He peeked over the tips of his fingers and gave a reluctant nod. "A prostitute?" Candisky asked one more time, figuring she had misunderstood something. "You mean he worked for an escort service or something?"

"No," Cirian repeated. "I mean a prostitute, a gigolo."

Candisky liked Cirian. Her honesty appealed to Candisky, and the reporter didn't want to take advantage of that candor. Candisky also felt sorry for Cirian. She'd had a tough life and her world seemed to revolve around a son who was now in way over his head.

"Jackie, I know you've never dealt with reporters much. I mean, we're on the record. I'm planning to use this information in my story. And frankly, I don't think you realize how that will look in print."

"Well, it's true, but I guess you better soften it in your story."

"Why don't we refer to him as a male escort? . . . So, he was working as an escort in Los Angeles. Correct?"

"Yes, but just for a while. Then he moved to New York."

"What prompted the move?"

"He hooked up with some middle-aged Arab woman in 1982. She was very wealthy," Cirian boasted. "Johnny was just 19 at the time. He traveled to New York City with her, and she introduced him to that guy—I can't remember his name, but he owned Studio 54."

DeSando finally took his face out of his hands and answered. "Steve Rubell."

"Right. Steve. He really liked Johnny and gave him a job as a bartender right on the spot. He worked in the VIP lounge, and he met all these famous people."

"That's where John met Missy," DeSando said.

Cirian nodded.

"Mantz?" Candisky asked.

"No, Missy Hughes. That was John's true love. She was a beautiful blonde, a model and actress, and she was on a soap opera . . ." Cirian looked to DeSando for help, but he only shrugged. "I think it was 'Another World,' the one with Mac and Rachel," Cirian continued. "Anyway, they dated for more than two years."

"Studio 54. Erik told me that was where John met Gene?" Candisky said.

"Yeah, maybe. I know it was somewhere in New York and not long after he moved there."

Despite their twenty-one-year-difference in age, Hawkins and Hanson became close friends and in 1984 started an Italian-shoe import business. "John went to Europe and bought all these shoes, and Gene used them to come up with designs. They paid to have copies made and started selling them," Cirian said.

"What happened to the shoe company?"

"They sold it to this big shoe company. I can't recall which one, but they made a lot of money from it."

"Is that when he started Just Sweats?"

"No, not right away. John left New York and went back to Los Angeles and just kind of goofed around. That's when he got the idea for Just Sweats. He'd saved all this money from bartending, plus the money they made from selling the shoe business, I assume," Cirian said. "Missy was involved, too. I think she was like a 10 percent partner."

Hawkins opened the first Just Sweats store in Hughes's hometown of Lexington, Kentucky. A few months later, an unemployed Hanson bought Hughes out and became vice-president of Just Sweats.

Cirian admitted that Hawkins and Hanson were the living odd couple: Hawkins the flamboyant playboy and Hanson a nervous, middle-aged homosexual. Cirian insisted, however, that Hawkins and Hanson were nothing more than good friends and business partners.

"Not lovers?" Candisky asked.

Cirian's eyes widened and her jaw tightened. Candisky had hit a nerve. "John's definitely not queer," Cirian snapped. "People suspected that he and Gene were lovers, but there's no way. My son loves women. He's had lots of girlfriends. He told me that he wanted to marry Missy, but he just wasn't quite ready to settle down and start a family."

Cirian said Hanson was asexual. "John told me Gene had real problems growing up. He hated his family—it had something to do with his stepfather—and he just couldn't have an intimate relationship with a woman."

DeSando interrupted to excuse himself, saying he had to go meet his friend. Candisky suggested that she and Cirian go downstairs for some lunch. Cirian glanced at her watch. It was about 1:30 P.M. and she didn't have to be at work until five. The two women went to the hotel cafeteria, where Cirian chose a large salad. "John told me I need to lose ten pounds," she said. Candisky, who had been eyeballing the turkey and mashed potatoes, looked at Cirian, pegging her as a size four. Candisky wondered how much weight Hawkins would tell her to lose. She, too, grabbed a salad.

"So, you want something to write about Johnny? I'll tell you one of my favorite stories about him. This tells you what a kind and thoughtful person he is. When John was in kindergarten I would drive him to school. We'd walk up to the school and I'd be holding his hand and I'd give him a kiss. One day I was picking him up and I heard some of the kids teasing him. They were calling him 'mommy's boy.' I asked him if he was okay, and he said yeah. So the next day I told him, 'I think you're old enough to walk to class alone and we can kiss good-bye in the car.' And John said, 'Okay, if that's what you want, mom.' He would have never brought it up. He wouldn't have wanted to hurt my feelings by asking me not to kiss him."

Jackie Cirian was more than a loving mother defending her child. She was a mother in love with her son. "I don't care what that insurance company says: Johnny didn't do anything wrong," Cirian said, squeezing a package of dressing on her salad. "John and I talked about it, and he told me there was nothing to worry about."

"Do you think he was just saying that to protect you?"

"Absolutely not. Johnny would never lie to me. He trusts me. I'm the only one John could ever confide in. His father was never around, so we've done everything together. When he asked me about marijuana, I rolled him his first joint."

"How old was he?"

"Thirteen."

"Thirteen! I can't even imagine my parents talking about pot, let alone offering me a joint."

"I'd rather he did it in front of me than out on the street somewhere. That's just the way Johnny and I have always been. He asked me questions about sex. Like, the different ways to have sex and which ways women like it best."

"What did you tell him?" Candisky asked, uncertain she wanted to hear the answer.

"I told him the only thing I could, which ways felt good to me," Cirian said between bites of tomato and lettuce.

Candisky swallowed hard, recalling the statue of entwined nudes Cirian had given to her son.

"When he walks into a room, he's so electric and so positive that when he leaves you know something's missing," Cirian said.

Hawkins had street smarts and a knack for getting what he wanted. He made his fortune in Just Sweats and Cirian couldn't have been more proud. She gushed over him. "I hope you get a chance to meet him someday. He'll melt your heart."

Hawkins had been concerned about the financial status of Just Sweats. When he received the $1 million in insurance money, he told Cirian that he put $600,000 back in the company. "He didn't tell me how much he took," she noted. "But I'm sure it was just enough to live comfortably on for a year or two until he started something else."

Cirian acted defensively when Candisky asked her about the embezzlement charges made against her son. "It was his money. It was his blood and guts. Why couldn't he do with it what he wanted? It was his." Cirian wiped some salad dressing from the corner of her mouth. "When Johnny left, he didn't realize how it would affect the company. Missy Mantz was calling every day to see if I'd heard from him. She said she was so upset that she had plucked out all her eyebrows. The bank was threatening to call in its notes. Johnny was going to go back and help get the company back on its feet. But when he called to say he was coming, Missy told him not to. She said that the banks would for sure call in their notes and some employees would walk out the door. They were that upset with him. Johnny was crushed. He told me, 'Mom, I was king of the mountain; now they all hate me.' "

Candisky returned to the hotel and wrote her story for Sunday's paper on a laptop computer. After three unsuccessful attempts to transmit the piece via modem, Candisky called Yocum and dictated the story to him.

It would run the morning of Sunday, August 28, under the headline:

Missing man is in stress center, mother says

After he had filed Candisky's story, Yocum brought her up to date with some new tips he had gotten.

In late July, Hawkins had tried to cash a check for $25,000 at a bank in Las Vegas. The information came from an employee at the secretary of state's office whom Yocum had called for copies of the incorporation papers on Just Sweats. The source said Hawkins presented a bank teller with a Just Sweats corporate check written out to, signed, and endorsed by himself. Suspicious, the Vegas bank teller called the secretary of state's office in Ohio to find out if the company was legitimate. The state employee told the teller that all he knew about Just Sweats came from a newspaper article that had appeared when the University of California at Los Angeles filed suit against them for copyright infringement. "That doesn't speak too well of his company, does it?" the teller had said. The bank refused to honor the check. Yocum wanted Candisky to ask Cirian about it.

"Also, see if she's heard of a woman named Amy Blizzard," Yocum said. "She's Hawkins's girlfriend in Columbus, a waitress at Max & Erma's on Route 161, and supposedly she's with him in Los Angeles." Finally, Yocum suggested Candisky leave telephone numbers with Cirian and, in the event Hawkins called her, instructions to call the reporters collect anytime. Candisky jotted down the questions and reminders. "She cut the interview a little short this afternoon because she had to go get ready for work," Candisky said. "I'm going to meet her again about midnight, toward the end of her shift at the casino."

*   *   *

The Frontier Hotel & Gambling Hall was on the strip, a good three miles from her hotel. Candisky took a cab. She found Cirian working a corner of the casino with fifteen poker tables. Candisky stood back for several minutes, watching as Cirian encouraged passersby to join in a game. She rounded up a group of older men and women—inexperienced players who looked as if they had come in on a bus charter —and herded them to a separate table. She ushered other, more experienced players to a table in the rear. Unlike the dealers, who wore a uniform of black pants, vests, and ties with white shirts, Cirian worked in a light-colored plaid suit.

Cirian smiled when she saw Candisky walk into the room. She grabbed Candisky's elbow and walked her around to meet her co-workers, introducing her as "a friend of my son's from Ohio." The billing gave Candisky a tightness in her throat. She knew Cirian would come to regret their association. When Jackie Cirian finally realized her son was in a lot of trouble, Candisky would be spelling it out across the pages of the *Dispatch*.

To kill the hour or so until Cirian's shift ended, Candisky sat down at the beginner's poker table next to a retired couple from Las Vegas. The woman had already lost her limit for the night and offered Candisky some tips. The reporter had lost thirty dollars by the time Cirian came back to say she was through for the night. They had planned to go out for dinner, but Cirian said she was tired and instead offered Candisky a ride back to the hotel. Candisky explained that she had a few more questions, but they could talk on the way.

"Does the name Amy Blizzard mean anything to you?"

Cirian nodded and smiled. "I know Amy. She was one of John's girlfriends."

"Was?"

"I think so. John said something about meeting Amy in Los Angeles, but I don't think it's anything serious. He just needed to be with someone before he goes into the clinic."

"Did you ever meet her?"

"Once, in St. Louis. John had asked me to arrange for Amy to meet with a plastic surgeon friend of mine."

"What for?"

"A breast enlargement."

Candisky stopped dead in the hallway. "I think you are the most forthright person I've ever interviewed."

Cirian shrugged. "She wanted to have the operation. All I did was put her in touch with the doctor."

Candisky pulled a notebook from her purse and jotted down a few quotes. "John supposedly tried to cash a $25,000 check from a Just Sweats account while he was out here a few weeks ago. Did he mention it to you?"

"No. I don't know anything about it," Cirian said. "But if he did, it was his money, wasn't it?" Carrying a glass of white wine in one hand and her pumps in the other as they walked through the parking lot, Cirian said she didn't expect to be working in the casino much longer because her son had promised to take care of her financially. "Johnny said this fall he was going to buy me a condo in Hawaii. And he has this Mercedes he's going to give me," she said, swinging her shoes at her side. Candisky and Cirian climbed into the rusting El Camino that rattled with the sound of a muffler beyond repair. "He said I could retire and that I'd never have to work again," Cirian said, finishing her drink and shoving the glass into the glove compartment. "I can't wait."

When they pulled up in front of the California Club, Candisky asked Cirian if she had a recent photograph of her son. From her wallet Cirian drew a snapshot of Hawkins and her daughter taken during his recent visit. "You can keep it, I have a copy," she said.

"Thanks. I'll have it copied and sent back to you," Candisky said as she tried to open the door. Only a shove with her shoulder would pry it open.

"I'm embarrassed to have you in this car. It's awful," she said. "Hopefully it won't be much longer before John buys me a new one. He promised."

15

"Sexual assault deepens Just Sweats mystery," Edwin Laramee read, pointing a lit cigarette at the banner headline on the front of the *Dispatch*. He picked the paper off his desk and dropped it in the trash, more a symbolic demonstration of his displeasure than tidiness. "A lot of people work real hard and you end up associated with that kind of headline and that kind of filth," Laramee grumbled, flicking his ashes in the general direction of an ashtray. "It shouldn't rub off on these people. That's wrong. These people are working sixteen-hour days trying to keep this company afloat."

Robin Yocum hoped to sidestep the issue. "Look, Ed, I'm sorry, but I don't write the headlines."

"It's unfair. I have two hundred good people working here and they deserve better than to be continually associated with Hawkins and Hanson, and whatever mess they may be involved in. Why do you have to call it the Just Sweats case, anyway? Those two aren't even involved with the company anymore."

"That's a good point," Yocum said. "I'll talk to my editors about the headlines. Maybe we can avoid that kind of reference in the future." Yocum knew that was a lie. Unfortunately, everyone still associated with Just Sweats was indelibly linked with the company's co-founders. The store was pivotal to the story and Yocum suspected there would be many more headlines that wouldn't meet with Laramee's approval.

Yocum had gotten up at seven o'clock and driven to the East Broad Street headquarters of Just Sweats. He was hoping that a face-to-face interview with Laramee and Missy Mantz might yield more information than he'd gotten on the telephone. The company headquarters occupied half of a one-story, cement-block building; a Just Sweats retail store, its windows painted with advertising, occupied the other half. The headquarters, consisting of a foyer, conference room, and three small offices, was modestly furnished with steel desks and chairs. The stark white of the walls gave the office a sanitized look that contrasted harshly with several ashtrays overflowing with cigarette butts.

Apparently satisfied that he had made his point, Laramee ushered Yocum into the conference room. Yocum moved a stack of sweat shirts and sat down on a folding chair. Laramee took an ashtray from a stack near the unplugged coffeepot and sat down across from the reporter. He was nothing like Yocum had envisioned. Yocum had thought Laramee would be one of Hawkins's proteges—young and handsome. Laramee was anything but. He was of slight build, fiftyish, with thinning gray hair and a moustache. His face reflected the hours he was logging at Just Sweats. Tired red eyes behind wire-rimmed glasses dominated a pale and drawn face. He blinked continuously and moved in short, jerky motions. Yocum speculated that Laramee's nervous mannerisms were likely borne from battles with bankers and other creditors, and not fear of a reporter.

Laramee ground the stub of a cigarette into the tin ashtray with his right hand as he reached into his breast pocket for another smoke with his left. "You know, if you want to write an article about this company, you ought to write about our people," Laramee said, lighting his cigarette. He dropped the still-lit match into the ashtray as wisps of smoke encircled his head. "They've been working overtime to keep the shelves filled and to order Christmas merchandise. That should have been done months ago, but it wasn't."

Yocum took the opportunity to get Laramee off his soapbox. "Maybe that's a good place to start. Why wasn't the Christmas merchandise ordered?" Yocum asked.

Laramee shrugged, drawing hard on the cigarette. "A lot of things didn't get done. Your guess is as good as mine. Apparently John had other things on his mind."

"Do you have enough time to get your stuff for Christmas?"

"Time, yeah. Money? Now that's another situation entirely," Laramee explained. "We've filed for bankruptcy, so no one is going to give us anything on credit. We can't buy anything unless we have cash on the barrel. Consequently, we may be short of sweat suits for the Christmas season, which—I don't know how much you know about the retail business—has to be your biggest sales period of the year. You need big Christmas sales to carry you during the slow times—January, February."

Yocum placed a yellow legal pad on the table in front of him and pulled a pen from his jacket pocket. "Ed, I know you haven't been thrilled with all the media attention. And like you said, the company is taking a beating because of its former owners. What I'd like to do is a profile of Just Sweats—the history of the company, how things got started, what it was like working for Hawkins and Hanson, Just Sweats' financial situation, and how you and Ms. Mantz are managing to keep it going."

"I can tell you what I know about the company's history, but you know I've only been here since March."

"Only since March?" Yocum asked. "I guess since you're the company president, I'd assumed you'd been here longer."

"No. I never even met Gene Hanson."

"Okay, let's start there. How did you come to be working for Just Sweats?"

"I just answered an ad in the paper that John had placed after Hanson left. He was advertising for a controller. I'd been with Revelation Shoe Corporation and was looking for work. I called and he told me to come on in. John interviewed me right over there," Laramee said, pointing with his thumb to the office next door. "Shortest interview I ever had. John sat there in blue jeans, his feet on the desk, told me about the company, and then hired me."

"So, was John interviewing for someone to take Hanson's place?"

"I assume so, but he didn't say that directly."

"Did John mention why Hanson had left, or where he was?"

"He didn't say much about Hanson. He said his former partner was dying of AIDS and that he would continue to draw a monthly paycheck until his death."

"We heard he told some people he had AIDS and others that he had some kind of heart . . ." Yocum interrupted himself as the door opened and a young woman walked in.

"Robin, this is Missy Mantz. She's our vice-president."

"Nice to meet you," Yocum said, standing as he extended his hand across the table. Mantz passively allowed Yocum to shake her hand. The vice-president was in her early to mid-20s. Her long, blonde hair was pulled back in a ponytail, and she wore a loose-fitting sweater over a pair of denims. Mantz took a seat next to Laramee and stared at her fingers, avoiding eye contact with Yocum. She appeared even less thrilled than Laramee to be talking to the *Dispatch* reporter.

"I told Robin about our displeasure over the headline in this morning's paper," Laramee said.

"It was disgusting. You don't realize how hard the people around here are working," Mantz hissed. "The whole thing has really hurt morale."

"Hopefully we'll be able to give Robin some information for a more positive story about Just Sweats. He's interested in the company's history and I told him I'd only been here since March and that you could help him there."

Mantz looked at Yocum with disdain.

"What do you want to know?" she asked. Yocum immediately knew that if he didn't ask the right questions he'd get nothing and like it. Something more than that day's headline was bothering Mantz.

"Well, for starters, how long have you been working here?" Yocum asked.

"Three years."

"All here at the headquarters?"

"No. I started at the campus store."

"Was that the first store?"

"First in Ohio," she said. "John had opened a store in Lexington a few months earlier."

"Do you remember the date?"

"The campus store opened in September 1985. The Kentucky store was a few months before that. Sometime in the summer."

"And there are how many stores now?"

"Twenty-two."

Even though Yocum already knew most of the information, he jotted down notes as if intensely interested. He frequently used this tactic in difficult interviews—easing into the questioning, allowing his target time to relax. If he could put her at ease, she was more likely to cooperate. He sensed Mantz would not be easy to interview: She was all business.

"You were hired as what, a store manager?"

She shook her head. "Clerk. I worked as a manager for a while, and eventually, about last fall, John brought me out here to handle merchandise and distribution."

"And now you're vice-president. That's happened since John left, right?"

Mantz glanced quickly at Laramee, apparently looking for his help.

"That's correct," Laramee answered.

"When did he leave? Do you remember the date?"

"Oh, yes," Laramee said, showing the hint of a smile for the first time. "July 16. A Saturday."

"Did you see him that day?"

"Just for a couple of minutes. He came by the office for a little while that morning. That was the last we saw of him."

Yocum leaned closer, hunkering over the table, resting on both elbows. "You saw him the morning he left?" Laramee nodded. "Right here at the office?" Another nod. "What happened. I mean, did you have any idea what he was going to do?"

"No. None. Paul Colgan, our accountant, and I were in trying to catch up on some work. Paul was just getting ready to leave, we were talking in the foyer, and John pulled up in his car." Laramee shook his head as he lit another cigarette. "I told Paul, 'You better get out of here. If you don't leave, John'll find something for you to do.' Sure enough, John walks in and the first thing he does is ask Paul to get him the balance in the company checking account."

"How much was that?"

"About $220,000."

"What happened then? Did he hang around?"

"No. He thanked Paul and left. He said he would be home if anyone needed him."

This, Yocum knew, was crucial information. Through Laramee and Mantz, Yocum knew he could begin to retrace Hawkins's last day in Columbus. He had to press this line of questioning. Not only was it important information for the reporters' investigation—more pieces of the puzzle—but it would also make great reading: "The desperate moves of a man on the run." Yocum turned to a clean sheet on his legal pad. "So, when John left that Saturday, that was the last you heard from him?"

"No. He called a few times, but I didn't talk to him. He talked to Missy."

Yocum continued to be cautious with Mantz. Erik DeSando had told Candisky that John and Missy had dated for several months. Perhaps, Yocum thought, it was not Just Sweats' problems Mantz feared seeing in the paper, but details of her personal relationship with Hawkins. "Can you tell me how many times you talked to him, Missy?"

She shrugged. "Couple of times."

"What did he say?" Yocum asked. "Did he tell you he wasn't coming back? Why was he calling?"

"No, he never said he wasn't coming back. He just wanted to see how things were going and to get his messages."

"That was all he wanted? Phone messages?"

"That, and a couple times he asked me to cancel appointments for him," she said.

"So, was he giving you some indication that he might come back?"

"I didn't even think about it at first, you know, that he wasn't coming back. He called me the Monday after he left and said he was on a buying trip in Atlanta, so . . ."

"And that wasn't unusual for John," Laramee interrupted.

"Right," Mantz agreed, seemingly relieved with Laramee's confirmation. "If John heard about a good deal on some merchandise, he'd just pick up and go."

"Okay, but back to the phone call. You said he asked you to cancel some appointments."

"He had a meeting with some officials at Fifth Third Bank on Monday and he asked me to call and reschedule it. He said his flight to Columbus had been canceled and he'd be in first thing Tuesday. Then he called Tuesday and said he'd missed his flight, but he'd catch a later one that afternoon." She shrugged and exhaled long and slowly. Her jaw tightened. "Obviously, he never came back."

Yocum frowned. "So he leaves, but he still owns the company. He didn't give it to you before he left, correct?" Mantz nodded. "So how did you two come to own Just Sweats?"

"Interesting story," Laramee said. "For weeks we were like a ship without a rudder. When John left he was the only one authorized to sign a check. We were in a helluva jam. We called all over the place looking for him."

In an attempt to locate Hawkins, Mantz said she had called all the numbers on a telephone bill she had found in Hawkins's desk. A woman in St. Louis said she had seen Hawkins on the afternoon of July 16. Hawkins had bragged of selling Just Sweats for $1 million and was taking a world trip to "see all the shores." Missy Hughes told Mantz she hadn't seen Hawkins. "I called a number John left in Florida that he said was his father's house. I called it and asked for John or his dad. Neither were living there. I called Erik DeSando a bunch of times, practically pleading with him to tell me where John was. But he always said he hadn't heard from him."

"Did you believe him?" Yocum asked.

She shrugged. "I don't know."

"So how did you get control of the company?"

"John eventually gave Missy power of attorney," Laramee said. "At least then we could start paying the bills."

"I realize my ignorance is probably refreshing, but what does all that mean? Power of attorney?" Yocum asked. "How did you get it?

Did you file something in court?"

"No, John had to give it to us," Laramee said.

"But . . ."

Laramee held up a palm. "It's just a signed and notarized document that John sent us. Basically it gave Missy control of the company."

"So you two got control of the company? I know things are probably screwed up because of the bankruptcy, but who owns Just Sweats now?"

"Missy and I each own 45 percent and there is a silent partner with 10 percent."

"Who's that?"

Laramee shook his head. "I can't tell you that. He's from out of state, he had nothing to do with this, and as you might imagine he's not too happy these day. He really doesn't want to be dragged into this."

There were other ways to learn the identity of the silent partner; Yocum made a mental note to check on that later. "What do you think prompted John to send you his power of attorney?"

"My personal opinion is that someone told him, maybe his roommate Erik DeSando, that all hell had broken loose and the company was going under," Laramee said. "I don't know, but whatever his reasons, one day near the end of July, Missy received a certified letter with his power of attorney. John enclosed a letter saying that he wasn't coming back."

"Do you have the letter?" Yocum asked.

"Well," Laramee started, "We do, but I don't know if . . ."

"No," Mantz said. She shook her head and looked at Laramee. "No. I don't see any reason for him to have it. No."

She left no room for negotiation, Yocum thought. He would have to find another source for the letter, too. "So, John gave you the power of attorney?" Yocum asked. Mantz nodded. "You two have been running the company for six weeks or so, since Hawkins left?"

Mantz shook her head. "Well, actually I've been handling it since the beginning of the year. John went on a long vacation in December and January and when he came back, he only came into the office about once a week. Trying to tie him down to make decisions was almost impossible."

"What was he doing?"

"I don't know. That was just the way John was," she said.

"Why would a guy work so hard to start his own business, build it up the way he did, then abandon it? Was the company doing that badly financially?"

"Not really," Laramee said. "Just Sweats grossed $8.5 million last year. They just lost their sense of direction."

"This can be a very lucrative business," Mantz interjected, apparently seeing an opportunity to speak about something with which she was extremely familiar. "In cities like Columbus and Lexington, big college towns, the demand is high for specialty clothing—school sweat shirts, stuff with sorority or fraternity letters. We had an artist right in the store to custom-design shirts. It was real popular."

Laramee looked at his watch; Yocum took it as a signal that the interview was nearly over. He got up and shoved his pen into his breast pocket. "I really appreciate your time," he said. "I know you're probably real busy now. Are the creditors still hounding you?"

"Every day," Laramee said, seemingly relieved that the interview was coming to a close.

"Oh, by the way," Yocum said, frowning, as if just remembering a question he had all along planned to save until the end. "We were told you had to file for bankruptcy because Fifth Third called in a couple of loans worth $350,000. Is that right?"

Laramee looked at Yocum as if he knew the question had been coming. "Yes, that's essentially true. When John left town, the bank felt he wasn't going to return. They're secured creditors, which means they're first in line for any money that's left. So, they called the notes due. There's no way we could pay them."

Yocum started to push on the door to leave, then turned back. "One more question. Did Hawkins and Hanson try to sell Just Sweats last year? We heard when Hanson left town with all that money last January, it was because he thought that was his share based on some kind of sale negotiations."

Mantz nodded the slightest of confirmations. Hawkins and Hanson were negotiating the sale of Just Sweats to a shoe corporation in December 1987. They decided against the sale, Mantz said, after learning that their contractual agreement would last two years after the sale.

"When the company got too large, they couldn't take the responsibility," Mantz said, offering her most candid comment. "I think they started with the idea that they would build it up, sell it, and sit out in the sun."

Yocum got back to the newsroom at 12:30 P.M. with enough time to finish the story and meet the early deadline for the Capital Edition. Katy Delaney, a summer intern from Ohio University, had spent the morning interviewing Just Sweats' suppliers. Jeff Scheiman, president of SOS Productions, a Columbus company that produced Just Sweats' television commercials, revealed that the company was about fifty days late on a $30,000 bill. "We were starting to wonder, but there was no big red flag going up. They seemed very solid," Scheiman said.

Max Joel, owner of LBJ Sales in Pittsburgh, a sweat-suit supplier, said Just Sweats owed him $120,000. Joel was surprised to hear the company was in bankruptcy because Just Sweats had always been prompt in paying its bills. "They were honorable and fulfilled every obligation to me. I haven't severed my business relationship with them."

Yocum smiled. "Sounds like Mr. Joel should have severed the relationship a long time ago."

"I know. Isn't that strange, calling them honorable?" Delaney asked.

"If someone owed you $120,000, and you thought you might not get paid, would you say nasty things about them?"

"I think I might," Delaney replied.

Yocum shook his head. "My bet is Mr. Joel is hoping if he says something nice they'll put him at the top of the 'to be paid' list."

Yocum and Candisky talked late that evening. Candisky planned to spend another day in Vegas with Cirian and DeSando, then to fly to Glendale early Monday to try to get an interview with Boggs. "Karsko really wants an interview with Boggs," Candisky said. "I'll be surprised if he talks."

"Me too, especially since he wouldn't even return your phone calls. But give it a shot. I know that's what Bernie's interested in, but I'd rather see you spend some time with the Glendale cops. See if you can find out why they aren't investigating the case."

"I can't help but think we're missing something," Candisky said. "If this looks so bizarre to us, why doesn't it look so bizarre to them?"

16

Erik DeSando stood up and began moving before the seatbelt light went off. He grabbed his duffel bag from the overhead compartment and worked his way up the aisle, inching around the slower passengers. He winked at a flight attendant as he passed, leading the coach travelers off the plane and into the terminal at Port Columbus. As he hoisted the bag over his shoulder, DeSando was blinded by the lights of three television cameras.

"Are you Erik DeSando?" one reporter asked.

DeSando laughed, putting up a hand to shield his eyes. "Yeah."

"Is it true that John Hawkins's mother said he was a prostitute?" another reporter asked.

"Jesus. Where did you hear that?"

"That's what the *Dispatch* reported."

"Um, well, yes. I guess that's true."

"Did you hear her say that?"

"Uh-huh. I was sitting there during the interview. She said it all right."

"Where's John Hawkins? Where's the money?"

DeSando started walking through the concourse. "I don't know. Really."

"So how much of the insurance money did you get?"

"None," DeSando blurted, stopping dead. "What are you talking about? Who told you I got some of the money?"

"You did—the message you left on your telephone answering machine."

"That! Oh, God," DeSando said, rolling his eyes. "That was just a joke. I wasn't serious."

The television reporters weren't so sure. They had eagerly waited to interview DeSando ever since they had heard the message he left on his answering machine before leaving for Las Vegas:

85

Hi, you have reached the home of John Hawkins and Erik DeSando. John and I aren't home. We've taken the insurance money and we are not coming back. Ha-ha. Please leave a message at the tone.

The television stations had already aired the message on their evening news programs while they awaited DeSando's return. The broadcast media greedily competed for footage in an otherwise pictureless story.

John DeSando watched his son stumble through the television interview. The English professor at Franklin University in Columbus decided it was time to tell his son the facts of life: his association with Hawkins wasn't doing him any good. "You could be in a lot of trouble, Erik," his father explained. "The FBI wants to talk to you about this. They think you got some of the money and you could go to jail. And, since you were friends with Hawkins and Hanson, most of Columbus now thinks you're gay."

DeSando pondered over his father's words. The seriousness finally struck him.

"Gay!" he said. "They think I'm gay?"

17

Yocum was in the newsroom by eight Monday morning, August 29, searching through the reams of paper heaped on his desk. Amid the clutter were all his notes on Just Sweats. Between those jottings and the electronic messages Candisky had sent, he hoped to find an angle for a story. Candisky wouldn't be available to help. Since she was on her way to Glendale in search of an interview with Boggs, the reporters both thought this would be akin to a snipe hunt, particularly since Boggs still hadn't returned any of their telephone calls. Still, when you knock on someone's door, there's always a chance. It's easier not to return a phone call than it is to turn away someone who is standing in front of you. Even if Boggs didn't talk, Candisky could still interview the Glendale police and ask why they weren't investigating the case.

"MESSAGE PENDING" flashed on Yocum's computer. Karsko had sent a one-word query: "Tomorrow?"

Yocum responded, "No clue. Still looking. Will let you know." The heat was on. Yocum sensed that Karsko smelled blood. He could be unrelenting on crime stories he liked, and this one seemed to be his current favorite.

The story was only five days old, but it was already the hottest topic in Columbus and it was starting to receive national attention. The Associated Press had begun shipping Candisky and Yocum's stories on their national wire. Locally, television and radio news were giving the story increasing airtime, though much of the electronic coverage was simply regurgitation of *Dispatch* stories. Perhaps the truest gauge of Hanson and Hawkins's notoriety was the number of parody songs that began popping up on local radio stations.

Yocum reviewed the autopsy material and found an attached investigative report that mentioned Boggs had attacked another man in his office with a stun gun. That police report would make a nice story. Candisky could dig it up in Glendale. Yocum decided to concentrate on the money angle, specifically, the whereabouts of the $1 million. Perhaps Melvin Weinstein, the attorney for Farmers, or Austin Wildman, the attorney for Just Sweats, could give Yocum some idea of what Hawkins did with the money. Weinstein was probably chasing the same information, so the reporter didn't expect him to be overly helpful. Yocum decided to focus on Wildman. The gregarious attorney for Just Sweats had by now probably drawn some conclusions about his former client and the location of the million dollars.

The reporter tried to reach both Weinstein and Wildman, but neither attorney, Yocum was told, was in his office. He continued to organize his notes, hoping the lawyers would quickly return the calls. A few minutes later, a guard called from the first-floor security desk. "There's a woman down here who wants to talk to you about Just Sweats."

Yocum winced. "Did she say what she wants?"

"Nope. Only that she wanted to talk to the reporters who were writing about Just Sweats."

"Okay, tell her I'll be down in a couple of minutes."

Yocum didn't want to leave his desk. He knew that as soon as he did, Weinstein and Wildman would call back, then promptly retreat into daylong meetings where they couldn't be disturbed. On the other hand, Yocum made it a policy never to turn down a chance to talk to a potential source. Some of his best tips on the police beat had come from screwballs who, in a moment of lucidity, muttered a fragment of truth that developed into a good story.

The woman in the lobby probably wanted copies of the Just Sweats stories to send to her psychic niece in Beaverdam, Ohio, who by reading them could pinpoint the whereabouts of Gene Hanson—be he alive or dead. To ensure that he wouldn't miss any calls, Yocum asked three reporters sitting in the general area of his desk to answer his phone and keep the caller on the line. "I'll just be a few minutes," he promised.

Downstairs, the security guard nodded toward an older couple sitting on a couch near the front of the lobby. The tall, lean woman had gray hair intruding on the black. Deep lines creased her face and neck. The heavyset man had thick, worker's hands. He was balding and holding what appeared to be a microphone in one hand. The woman stood and Yocum extended his hand. "Hi. I'm Robin Yocum."

She came right to the point. "I'm Katherine Lawley, Gene Hanson's mother. Can you tell me what's happened to my son?"

It took a few moments for the words to sink in. He still wasn't sure he had heard her right. "Who?"

"Katherine Lawley. I'm Gene Hanson's mother."

"I'm sorry, you kind of caught me off guard. I certainly wasn't expecting you. I thought . . . don't you live in Florida?"

"I do. Jacksonville," she said with a deep-southern accent. "I heard Gene was dead and no one will tell us anything. We drove all night to get here." She turned to the man standing next to her. "This is my husband, Doyle." As the man shook Yocum's hand, he held the microphone under his chin and spoke, pronouncing a guttural and tinny "Pleased to meet you." Doyle needed to press a microphone against his vocal cords to communicate; cancer had destroyed his larynx.

"I'll tell you what I can. Why don't we go upstairs where we can talk?" Yocum said, getting two visitors' passes from the security guard. Together they rode the elevator and entered the the smaller of the two fifth-floor conference rooms. Yocum then sprinted across the newsroom to Karsko's desk. "My Tuesday story just walked in the door. Hanson's mom and stepfather."

The Lawleys had appeared in the *Dispatch* newsroom as an indirect result of Candisky's research. The previous Thursday she had called Cecil Hanson in Jacksonville for information about his son, without realizing that Hanson's parents were divorced. When she and Cecil finished their talk, he called his daughter, Cecilia Kellum, and told her Gene had died. Cecilia, in turn, called her mother, Katherine Lawley. Desperate for the details surrounding her son's death, Lawley called her former husband, with whom she'd had little contact since the couple divorced nearly twenty years earlier. Although he knew his son might be dead, the senior Hanson refused to reveal any details of his conversation with Candisky. When Lawley asked for the reporter's name and number, her former husband again refused. "The reporter didn't give me permission to give it to you," Lawley quoted Cecil Hanson as saying. Frustrated and worried, she loaded Doyle and a suitcase into his Cadillac and started north, uncertain where they would find their answers. Fortunately for Yocum, they decided to stop at the newspaper first.

In the conference room, Yocum had mixed emotions over Lawley's visit. He was elated that he now had a story, but he felt sorry for Katherine Lawley. Her eyes were those of a woman who was tired and afraid. "Is my son dead?" she asked. The finality in her voice said she was prepared for the worst.

"I wish I could answer your question," he said. "But no one knows for sure. Gene supposedly died April 16 out in California," Yocum stated, handing her a copy of the story about the lawsuit. "But, they did some fingerprint checks and found out it wasn't him. The dead man was carrying a copy of Gene's birth certificate and a couple of credit cards, but it wasn't Gene."

"You're sure of that?"

"Yes."

Lawley looked confused. "Who was the dead man?"

"No one knows. There are two theories. One is that Gene and Hawkins and Dr. Boggs are all in on an insurance scam. The dead guy may have been killed and identified as Gene so they could collect the insurance money."

Lawley's mouth dropped open. "Oh my Lord," she gasped. "My Gene was involved in something like that?"

Yocum shrugged. "There is another theory. That is that Gene died and they substituted this body for his."

Again, Lawley looked confused. "If he died, why did they need another body?"

"Well, because if he died, he may have died of AIDS and they needed to get a clean body to collect the insurance money." This offered an opening to a question Yocum had hesitated to ask. "Mrs. Lawley, was Gene a homosexual?"

She seemed more taken back by the question of homosexuality than by the possibility of Gene's death. "Well, I don't know. I don't think so . . ."

For the first time that morning, Doyle Lawley made his presence known. He sat upright and jammed the microphone under his chin. "Dammit, Katherine, you can't lie to the boy," Doyle growled. "Yes, he's queer."

Reluctantly, she nodded. Katherine Lawley had paired AIDS and her son at least once before. In December 1987, Hanson revised his will, disinheriting his family. "When we received the will, the first thing I thought was that maybe he had AIDS. He might be out there now. He might be sick and need help." Katherine Lawley took a breath and seemed to fight back tears. "I just don't understand what makes a person that way. Do you?"

Yocum assured her he didn't know any more about that than he knew of the whereabouts of her son.

She shook her head. "Gene was a always a good boy, but sort of different," she said, in a slow, deliberate tone. "We were a close family, but Gene was always the outsider. He stayed away from the family. I spoke to my pastor about it and he thinks Gene stayed away to avoid confrontation about his lifestyle. I haven't seen Gene in twelve or thirteen years." Lawley pulled a tissue from her purse and dabbed the corners of her eyes.

"He talked to my daughter once and told her that he'd like to come home, but he couldn't. We never had any fights or anything."

"I'm glad I have the opportunity to talk to you, but I'm really sorry that Gene's father gave you a hard way to go."

"Oh, well, I sort of expect that out of him. And he's not Gene's father, it's his stepfather."

Yocum looked at Doyle and then back at Lawley. "Doyle here's my third husband. Cecil adopted Gene and his brother when they were little. Gene's named after his natural father, Melvin Eugene Snowden, but I haven't seen or heard from him in forty years."

"Mrs. Lawley, this is a confusing story to begin with. If you don't mind, I'd like to back up and take this from the beginning."

She nodded. "That's fine."

"Now, I have Gene's birthday as October 8, 1941. Is that accurate?"

"It is—in Ocala, Florida."

"And his father was Mr. Snowden?"

"Yes."

"But you divorced him."

"I did. He couldn't keep his eyes and hands off other women. We were married young and he wasn't ready to settle down; he wasn't ready to accept the responsibility. We stayed together for a couple of years, but he couldn't take it and I couldn't take it, either. I left. My parents were living in Leesburg and I moved back in with them. Donald was only eight months old."

"And Gene was . . ."

"Two. He's sixteen months older than Donald."

"So, did the boys ever see their father?"

"Oh no. He never paid me a dime of child support or anything. The last time I even saw Melvin was 1945 or '46."

"You're at home with your parents. Did you just stay home and raise the boys?"

"Oh, mercy, no. My mother watched the boys. I was working two jobs to help pay the rent. I was a telephone operator for Florida Telephone. At nights I worked at a drive-in restaurant making milkshakes and sundaes."

Yocum grinned. "You were a soda jerk?"

"Well, yes, I suppose," she said. "I did what I had to do to get by. My father was a Baptist minister and there just wasn't a lot of money."

Lawley smiled.

"Yes?" Yocum asked.

"Oh, I was just thinking about when Gene was little, about four years old, he used to imitate his grandfather. He would drag a cardboard box to the middle of the living room, then put an open Bible on it and deliver his own little sermon. It was darling. You couldn't understand much of what he was saying, but it was just precious. We all thought he was going to follow in his grandfather's footsteps and become a preacher."

"Did you stay with your parents until you met Cecil Hanson?"

"Yes, as a matter of fact, he had come to Leesburg to visit his cousins, two doors down. We got married in 1946 and moved to Jacksonville because he had a job there with Central Truck Lines."

The couple had two children of their own, and Cecil Hanson adopted Gene and Donald. "Cecil was never very comfortable with the boys," she said. "He provided for them and, I suppose, in his own way, he loved them. But he was very strict. Not mean, but very strict. I remember when Gene got in high school he really wanted to get an after-school job. He wasn't involved in athletics or anything like that at school, and his grades were always pretty good, and he wanted to work. But Cecil wouldn't hear of it. He said the boys could just come home and study after school. He let them cut grass during the summer, but he didn't think they needed to be out working during the school year. I remember that really upset Gene. He liked clothes and going to the movies, and he wanted the extra money. We always had enough money, but there was never anything left over for extras."

"So, Gene didn't get along with his stepdad?"

"Oh mercy, no. Neither he nor Donald liked Cecil. When they were in high school I always thought they liked him, but after we got divorced they told me they had hated him. Well, I didn't know. We were married twenty years and they never said a word to me about Cecil. They told me they didn't like the way he treated me. They thought he was mean to me."

"If we could back up a little, Mrs. Lawley. Can you tell me a little about what Gene was like in high school? You said he wasn't allowed to work and he didn't play sports, so how did he occupy his time?"

"Mostly with our church. He was a counselor for the Royal Ambassadors."

"Royal Ambassadors?"

"It's a youth group for boys. Gene took them on outings and camping trips. He really liked that. He did everything with the church. During youth week when he was 16, Gene was selected to deliver the Sunday sermon. Oh, and he did real well. We were so proud of him."

"So, Gene graduated from high school, when?"

"1960."

"And then what? Did he start working or go to school or what?"

"Oh, college. Gene was always very smart. He went to Florida State University, over in Tallahassee."

"What was his major?"

Lawley frowned for a moment, looked at Doyle, then back at Yocum. "Business, I think. But he never finished. He went for about two years, I expect, then he enlisted in the army. He had always been a good student, and his plan was to finish college later on the G.I. Bill. He told me, 'Mom, I might as well let the government pay for my education.' "

"Did he finish when he got out?"

"No. I wanted him to go back, but by the time he got out of the army he just wasn't interested in school anymore."

"And he was in the army how long?"

"Three years. He spent most of it stationed in West Germany. He even learned to speak some German over there. Like I said, Gene was real smart."

"So he didn't go back to school. What did he do when he got back?"

"Not much at first. He said he needed a little time to relax and unwind. He worked odd jobs for a while. Then, I guess it was about two years after he got out of the army, he moved up to Atlanta and got himself a job with Rich's."

"Rich's?"

"Oh, it's a big department store. He started out as a trainee in the shoe department. Then they made him an assistant buyer."

"I'm not very familiar with the retail business, but that sounds like a pretty good job for someone without much experience."

"Oh mercy, it was. It didn't pay a whole lot, but it got him started. Why, they eventually put him in charge of their women's shoe line. He picked out the shoes the store was going to sell."

"How long did he stay at Rich's?"

"About three years. Then he moved to a store in Richmond—Thalheimer's."

"Then where did he go?"

Katherine Lawley shrugged her shoulders. "I wish I could tell you, but I don't know anything about his life for the past thirteen years. The last time I saw Gene was in 1975. Donald and I drove up to Richmond for a visit, but I lost all contact with him after that."

"He just disappeared? No letters, no calls, nothing?"

Lawley took a breath, then slowly shook her head. "When my mother died in 1978, Gene sent flowers, but there was no card or letter. That was the last time I heard from him."

"What about his sister or brothers? You said he and Donald were close. Gene hasn't called him?"

"Donald died last year."

"Oh, I'm sorry. How did he die?"

"Well, the police say he committed suicide, but we've always wondered. They found him in his apartment. He'd been dead five days before they found him. He was shot in the head and the gun was laying right beside him. Donald just wasn't the type to kill himself."

"Had he been having problems?"

"I suppose. He was a disabled veteran. In the air force."

"Vietnam?"

She nodded. "It's hard to believe, but they said his fingerprints were the only ones on the gun. I'm certain Gene doesn't know that Donald is dead. I know it's going to bother Gene when he finds out. He and Donald were quite close."

Lawley showed Yocum several photographs of her son, and she went to the *Dispatch* photo studio to pose for another of her holding his high school graduation picture. The Lawleys intended to visit the Just Sweats attorneys, but expressed little hope of meeting with anyone. Katherine and Doyle planned to start back to Florida that afternoon. Yocum promised to stay in touch and to send them clips of future stories. "I just want to know what happened to him and where he is," Lawley said, pushing herself through the front door and into the bright midday sun.

18

While Yocum was interviewing Lawley, Candisky was en route to Glendale, California, after a day off in Las Vegas courtesy of Karsko. "Take a day and rest up, and then I want you to go to L.A. and interview Boggs," he told her.

Candisky had visited friends in Los Angeles a couple of times, so she knew enough to book a flight into Burbank. Arriving at the smaller Burbank Airport was a breeze compared to landing at the massive and congested LAX. By midwestern standards, the Los Angeles airport is a city in itself.

Candisky rented a car and headed south on the Golden Gate Freeway for the twenty-minute drive to neighboring Glendale. She checked into a room at the Glendale Holiday Inn.

Candisky made an appointment with Glendale Police for the following morning, Tuesday, August 30. She told Sgt. Dean Durand that she wanted to discuss some of the strange findings in Hanson's autopsy. To her surprise, Durand said he hadn't seen the autopsy and asked if she could bring a copy. Candisky checked her watch—it was about 4:20 P.M., forty minutes before the Los Angeles County coroner's office closed. Candisky called the office for directions and decided to take her chances on the unfamiliar L.A. freeways during rush hour. To her surprise, she had little trouble finding the coroner's Mission Road office, arriving there shortly before 5:00 P.M. The clerk in the reception area had already started packing up her purse, but Candisky approached her and requested a copy of case number 88-03963. "Sure," the clerk said, "I'll be right back." She disappeared through a doorway, emerging from the adjacent file room a few minutes later with a puzzled look. "Melvin Hanson?"

Candisky nodded.

"That's odd," the clerk observed. "The file is empty, but the card says it hasn't been checked out since June."

Candisky suggested that the autopsy report might be in Bob Dambacher's office. She explained that the public relations officer had sent a copy of the report to her partner on Friday. The clerk called the public relations office and asked a secretary to check around for the report. No one, however, could locate the autopsy proceedings.

Frustrated, Candisky left the coroner's office and drove to the Glendale bureau office of the *Los Angeles Daily News*. She had called there earlier and asked an editor for a desk and a telephone to use during her stay. In return, Candisky offered to trade information on the apparent insurance fraud and help the paper with the story. She was surprised to find the reporters there in awe of the *Dispatch*'s willingness to finance a trip to California. But they showed little interest in the stories that she and Yocum had uncovered about a doctor in their own backyard.

"We ran one of your stories off the wire, but frankly, they just don't think too much of it here," reporter Priscilla Lee told Candisky. "It's just an unidentified body and nobody's even been charged." However, Lee did suggest that she accompany Candisky to police headquarters the next morning; then the two reporters could stop by Boggs's office. If they had time, they could check the Glendale courthouse for any lawsuits or marriage or divorce records that might provide additional insights about the doctor.

When Candisky returned to her hotel, she called Boggs's office. It was after 6:00 P.M. Candisky was ready to leave a message on Boggs's answering machine when a woman answered the telephone. Candisky introduced herself and asked to speak to Boggs. "He's on vacation. He won't be back until September 20," said the woman, who identified herself as the doctor's receptionist.

"Shit," Candisky said as she slammed down the receiver. The sole purpose of her trip to Los Angeles had been to interview the doctor, but that seemed unlikely now. Even if he wasn't on vacation, as Candisky suspected, he wasn't going to talk. If the Glendale police didn't throw her a few bones the next morning, the trip would be wasted.

Early Tuesday, August 30, Candisky met Lee at the *Daily News* office where Karsko had faxed a copy of Hanson's autopsy. As they walked the couple of blocks to the police station, Lee talked about her paper's lack of interest in the story. "You guys can get away with saying that Boggs had sex with the corpse. You're clear back in Ohio. He's right here in town and he said he would sue us if we printed anything like that. He said he's going to sue the Glendale cops for putting that in the report, and you guys for putting it in the paper."

Lee, who covered the police department for the *Daily News,* led Candisky past the first-floor reception area to the second-floor office of Capt. Thomas M. Rutkoske. The reporters took seats facing his desk. Standing behind Captain Rutkoske was Sgt. Dean Durand, the department's public information officer.

"You're familiar with the case I'm working on . . ." Candisky began before Captain Rutkoske interrupted.

"Well, more or less, but why don't you fill me in."

Candisky detailed Farmers' lawsuit, but was careful not to give away too much of what she and Yocum had learned over the past five days. She hadn't been in Captain Rutkoske's office for more than two minutes before she realized they weren't investigating the case, nor were they particularly interested in talking to an out-of-town reporter.

Captain Rutkoske took on a condescending tone as he explained how one of the department's technicians, at the request of a Farmers' claims agent, had ordered a copy of Hanson's California driver's license. "The body in the doctor's office was not Hanson, based on fingerprints and photographs."

"So, who was it then? Do you know?"

Captain Rutkoske's brow furrowed as he stared at Candisky for several seconds. She knew the cops hadn't a clue, and Rutkoske knew she knew the answer. "No," he said, slowly shaking his head. "We don't know."

Candisky savored the comments for a minute, then scribbled them into her notepad. She relished even this small victory.

"So, you said you did this at the request of the insurance company. Were they pressuring you to move on the case?"

Rutkoske shrugged. "Just one of them."

"Excuse me?" Candisky asked.

"Just the one, Farmers. The other one we didn't hear from. You knew there were two policies, didn't you?"

Candisky nodded. "Sure," she said, feeling the redness of a blatant lie creep up around her neck. "I knew there were two, but I can't recall the name of the second one."

"Me neither," Rutkoske said, looking up at Durand, who shrugged. "It was for a half-million or so, but I don't remember who it was with."

Candisky jotted down the information. She'd call Yocum later and let him look for it.

"Captain, with all the odd circumstances surrounding this case, don't you think this could have been a homicide?"

"No," Captain Rutkoske said, slowing shaking his head. "We're not investigating a murder. There was no murder. The coroner says the cause of death was a heart attack."

Lee nodded in agreement with the captain and Candisky suddenly realized she was without an ally. She wondered for a moment if she was truly missing something, but figured she had little to lose and pursued her line of questioning.

"Yeah, but don't you think it's odd that this guy had this insurance policy and his beneficiary has disappeared? Don't you think homicide is a possibility?"

Captain Rutkoske glanced out of the corner of his eye at Sergeant Durand. "Look, the coroner's report is cast in concrete," Rutkoske said. "Now the body is gone and there's no way you can go back. There's no way to prove a homicide."

Captain Rutkoske admitted that his officers were wary of the situation at the time of the death. "Our detective got suspicious of the hour and Boggs's claim that 911 was busy. The coroner's office took fingerprints, although they're not required to by law. Normally the prints go to the department of justice to check. In this particular case, the coroner didn't send them because they felt they had a good ID from a reputable doctor."

Captain Rutkoske said police requested a copy of the driver's license from the California Department of Motor Vehicles and determined the photos didn't match. Police then got the thumb print from the driver's record and found it didn't match, either.

"When we determine who the other person is, we'll have to determine if he had a heart condition or if he drank a lot, but we can't do a single thing until we identify the body." Captain Rutkoske said Glendale police had no leads on the identity of the dead man.

Nor, Candisky thought, were they making any effort to identify him. The cops were talking out of both sides of their mouths. They admitted they had suspicions; yet they insisted there was nothing to investigate, even though they knew the body had been misidentified. And the reporter with the *News* was causing Candisky to grind her teeth. Candisky needed help and she was getting none from her colleague, who was swallowing the spoon-fed bullshit from the Glendale police. Candisky tried another frontal assault.

"Yes, but don't you think there's still the possibility he was murdered?" she persisted.

"The report said the man died of a heart attack and the body has been spread over the ocean. This report has to stand," Captain Rutkoske said.

"Have you talked to the doctor about this?"

"Boggs was questioned that day," Sergeant Durand replied.

"Have you talked to him since?"

"No."

Candisky took a moment to jot down some notes. "What are the chances that Boggs really got a busy signal when he called for help that morning?" she continued.

"Anything is possible," Sergeant Durand said. "But it's highly, highly unlikely that 911 was busy at that hour."

When asked if Boggs had a criminal history, Durand said, "California law prohibits us from releasing criminal records." He might have been reading it off the wall behind Candisky's head.

"How was the body identified?"

"Well, Dr. Boggs had been treating him for seven years."

"You mean he was treating the real Hanson, not the corpse?"

Candisky hit a nerve. The officers nodded, appearing weary of the questioning. Rutkoske had been forced to admit that police knew Boggs had intentionally misidentified the corpse. Candisky knew it was time for a final question. For the fourth time that morning she asked why they were so convinced the dead man hadn't been murdered.

"There is no way to prove a murder. The coroner ruled he died of natural causes. You just can't refute that report. We aren't investigating a homicide; there was no homicide," Captain Rutkoske said.

At first, the law officer had appeared curious to learn why the *Dispatch* had sent a reporter to California to investigate a death that his department had considered a closed case. Now, he was annoyed at Candisky's repeated suggestions that his department was overlooking the obvious. She continued. "You have a man here who supposedly died, but didn't; you still don't know who the dead guy is; and his partner collected a million dollars in life insurance, and now he's gone," she said. "Doesn't that strike you as a little odd?"

Captain Rutkoske was no longer amused.

He stood up with a deliberateness that revealed his agitation, walked around to the front of his desk, and sat on its edge. He was a big man—solid—and wore an angry expression. Candisky, who was just over five feet tall, knew Rutkoske was trying to intimidate her with his size. "Let me explain it to you this way, honey. We aren't investigating a homicide because the coroner ruled the man died of natural causes. The coroner's report is cast in concrete and the body has been cremated. At best we have an unidentified body. Do you have any idea how many people are reported missing here each year? This may be a big deal in Columbus, Ohio, but we're in L.A."

19

On August 30, at 2:00 P.M. Columbus time, Yocum received Candisky's first call of the day. She was calling from the *Daily News* office; she was not happy. "I have nothing," she told Yocum. "What's going on back there?" she asked.

"Not much. You're the one out where the action is. What's going on?"

"Robin, it's pathetic. Bernie's going to be furious. Nothing's going right."

"Did you try and talk to Boggs?"

"Yes, but his secretary or receptionist—somebody in the office—said he was on vacation for a month."

"Did you talk to the cops?"

"Yes . . . they were dicks."

"What happened?"

"They treated me like I was ignorant. You know, like they were humoring the rube from Ohio. All they would say was they weren't investigating because they didn't have a homicide. I kept asking questions about the death, but they just kept getting more disgusted, like I was too stupid to understand." She lowered her voice, whispering so the *Daily News* reporters couldn't hear her. "Even the reporter from the *Daily News* who went with me was looking at me like I was stupid. All they kept saying was, no homicide, no investigation."

"But they have a body who isn't who the doctor . . ."

"I know, I know. But that doesn't seem to matter to them. They said the coroner's report is cast in concrete and they haven't looked into the case in months."

"Months? You mean they're still not investigating?"

"No. Nothing. They couldn't care less. They think it's ridiculous that the paper would spend all this money to send me out here. I was hoping to get a story saying they had reopened their investigation, but there's no way I can write that."

"I don't understand how they can ignore their own suspicions?" Yocum said, his voice starting to climb. "What about 911 being busy? Do they have an answer for that? The corpse was cold when they arrived at the doctor's office! That was in their own report."

"I know, but they say, 'No big deal.' They said they're not going to investigate. Period."

"They refuse, huh?"

"Completely."

"Cathy, that's wonderful," Yocum said. "It's perfect."

Candisky looked at the phone receiver and winced. "What?"

Candisky was so concerned with keeping the editors happy that she was missing the big picture. Yocum could tell they were well ahead of the police in investigating the case. "We're on to something really good, Cathy. At best, there's been a homicide. At the least they've substituted a corpse as part of an insurance scam. Eventually, someone is going to start investigating this. We've got a jump on them all; we've just got to keep after it. The Glendale police are going to have to investigate sooner or later. 'Cast in concrete.' Right. They'll eat their words, believe me."

Candisky felt somewhat relieved upon hearing Yocum's opinion, although it did nothing to solve the more immediate problem. She still didn't have a story for the next day. "I did get a tip on something while I was over at the police station. Rutkoske said Hawkins was trying to collect on another life insurance policy worth a half a million."

"That's great. From Farmers?"

"It isn't with Farmers; that's all I know. Rutkoske mentioned it and I acted like I knew what he was talking about. Maybe you can track that down. I'm going to go to Boggs's office. Maybe I should tell Bernie what I'm doing."

"No. Just go do what you've got to do. I'll talk to Karsko."

Candisky's editor, Karsko, had been pressuring Yocum for a story to put on the next day's budget. Yocum had been trying to track down the whereabouts of the $1 million Hawkins had received, but wasn't having a lot of luck. "I just got off the phone with Candisky," Yocum told Karsko. "Evidently, Hanson had another life insurance policy."

Karsko's brows arched. "Good, we need that for tomorrow," he said, already typing it into the budget.

When, Yocum wondered, was he ever going to learn never to mention a story to an editor unless you have it in the bag? "Bern, I don't have any idea who held the policy. I don't know if I can find it today."

"We've got nothing on the budget. We need it."

*   *   *

At nearly 3:00 P.M., Yocum started making a flurry of phone calls. Austin Wildman, Hawkins's attorney, was out. Melvin Weinstein, the attorney for Farmers, had, to Yocum's surprise, flown to Glendale to take depositions in the case. His secretary said she didn't know about any other insurance policy. Yocum called a source at the Columbus police department and Bob Smith at the prosecutor's office, neither of whom were aware of the second policy. Ed Laramee at Just Sweats said he had heard of a second policy, but didn't know who it was with. Yocum called Candisky back at the *Daily News* office. "Any luck?" she asked.

"I'm striking out all over the place. If you hear anything, call me back. Karsko's hot for this and I've got to come up with something." Yocum started going through the notes and documents they had accumulated, searching for a clue tucked away somewhere. Nothing.

It was 4:00 P.M. and he sent notes to Karsko and Ellis. "No luck on the insurance policy. I don't think we can write a story unless we have the name of the company and a confirmation nailed down."

Yocum glanced over the Farmers' lawsuit again, but found nothing. Then, on a document marked "Exhibit C," the beneficiary-claimant statement for the Farmers policy, Yocum spotted a notation under "Remarks—Special Instructions."

Golden Rule Insurance Co. for $450,000.00

Yocum grabbed the business index and found the company headquarters in Lawrenceville, Indiana. How could he get confirmation of the suit without a blind call to the company? Insurance companies and banks were notoriously uncooperative, particularly when the information in question might make them look bad. Yocum called Sol Sokol, a local insurance agent who for years had written a column on insurance for the *Dispatch*. Like Austin Wildman, Sokol was a news junkie who had always seemed more interested in the newspaper than in the insurance game.

"Sol, any chance you've heard of Golden Rule Insurance?" Yocum asked.

"Sure. As a matter of fact, I have a very good friend who works there. Why?"

"Hanson, the guy who may or may not be dead in the Just Sweats case, he had policy with Golden Rule for $450,000. I'm trying to track it down. Do you think your friend would help me?"

"I don't know, but I'd be glad to give him a call and see. Are you going to be in the office?"

"I won't move."

"Give me ten minutes."

It took fifteen, but Sokol called to say that his friend, a company vice-president based in Indianapolis, had agreed to talk, but wanted to remain anonymous. "He says the company is real touchy about this," Sokol said. "Evidently they came real close to paying the claim. He said he'll talk, but only if you agree not to identify him in the story."

Yocum didn't like unnamed sources, but he couldn't afford to dicker this close to deadline. He called the man, who was very familiar with Hanson's policies. "Oh yes," the man said. "I'm familiar with Mr. Hanson, all right. He and his buddy tried to pull a quick one on us."

"So you never paid him, correct?"

"That's right. We refused to pay Mr. Hawkins's claim. We knew it was a hoax."

"How many policies did he have with Golden Rule? Just the one?"

"Right, he had one policy with us, which he received in," the man paused while he checked his records, "September of '86. Four hundred fifty thousand dollars. He applied for three others, all within twenty months or so of his untimely demise." The insurance executive chuckled at his own humor. "According to our records, Hanson applied for the $450,000 policy, it was approved, and then he applied for the other three. He probably thought we'd be a soft touch, but we don't pass out insurance policies like candy. I can't believe the other company paid off on the policy. We've known for a long time that it was fraudulent. He's not collecting from us. We're not paying."

20

In the *Daily News* office, Candisky and Lee were checking a city directory and telephone book for Boggs's home address. Candisky doubted his receptionist's claim that he was on vacation and called his office again. This time a young man answered the telephone.

Candisky identified herself and asked to speak to the doctor.

"We're giving out no information," the man said. "The office is closed."

"Who is seeing Dr. Boggs's patients while he's gone?"

"There are no patients and the doctor's not here. I'm just here to answer the phone."

And hang it up, Candisky thought as she heard the click of the receiver followed by the dial tone.

Lee had found an address for Boggs at 301 North Belmont Street in the California Woods condominiums. The three-story wood-and-stucco apartment building was only a few blocks from Lee's office. The secured, U-shaped building had mailboxes and buzzers for each unit placed outside a black iron gate.

No one answered when the reporters buzzed unit number 205 or any of the units on Boggs's floor. While Candisky jotted down the names of some of the tenants, a small man in his sixties appeared from behind some shrubs in the courtyard.

"Who are you looking for?" he barked.

"Dr. Boggs. Does he live here?" Candisky answered.

"He moved a few months ago."

"Do you know where?"

"I don't have to answer any of your questions," he snapped, before turning and marching back into the building.

Candisky and Lee looked at each other, stunned, for a minute and then started laughing. After grabbing a sandwich from an open-air vendor, the reporters decided to try Boggs's office. Candisky still didn't believe the doctor was away and hoped that by showing up unannounced, she might catch him.

A directory in the lobby indicated forty doctors had offices in the three-story building. Riley's Pharmacy occupied much of the first floor. Candisky tried the door at Boggs's office on the second floor but it was locked.

"Who's there?" a woman asked from inside the office.

"Is Dr. Boggs in?" Lee asked.

"Are you a patient?"

"No. I'm a reporter."

"Well, we're closed."

"Why are you closed?"

A male voice interrupted. "We're closed because we don't have any patients and the doctor is not here."

Lee and Candisky found the handful of other workers in the building equally uncooperative. An employee of Riley's Pharmacy said Boggs had been renting office space in the building for two or three years, but he refused to answer any other questions.

Candisky and Lee returned to the *Daily News* office late in the afternoon. Candisky decided to check back with the Glendale police. She wanted to ask about allegations included in the autopsy report that Boggs had attacked a man with a stun gun. If such a report existed, she wanted to see it. Candisky left a message for Captain Rutkoske to call her at the *Daily News* office. He returned the call and launched into a tirade, apparently thinking he was talking to Lee.

"I don't know about that reporter from Ohio; she seems a little dense," Captain Rutkoske said. "She kept asking the same questions. She just didn't get it. There was no homicide."

Priscilla Lee walked to another corner of the *Daily News* newsroom to speak to an editor about a story. As soon as she was out of earshot, Candisky grabbed the phone and punched in the number of the Los Angeles County Coroner. Although Lee had been helpful, she was still the competition. Candisky didn't want her conversations overheard by anyone on the *Daily News*.

Candisky called Bob Dambacher more out of curiosity than necessity. She and Yocum had their copy of the autopsy, but she couldn't help wondering why the original was suddenly missing from its file at the coroner's office. She asked Dambacher if he had been able to locate the autopsy on the suspect body. He had.

"I was in the office on Monday, but the woman I talked to said it was missing," Candisky said.

Dambacher explained that it had actually never been lost. After talking to Yocum the previous Thursday, Dambacher had passed the autopsy on to investigators with the fraud division of the California Department of Insurance.

"Why did you send it over there?" she asked.

"I wanted them to take a look at it," Dambacher said. "We . . . I really don't want to get into specifics, but the coroner now believes that the man who died in Dr. Boggs's office may not be Melvin Eugene Hanson."

Candisky scrawled a few notes on a piece of scrap paper from the desk. "I guess I'm a little confused. I thought you told my partner, Robin Yocum, that the case was closed. He told me that you weren't putting any stock in the insurance company's claim."

"Well, when I talked to Mr. Yocum, we really didn't . . . we weren't sure. We weren't prepared to comment."

"So what does this mean?" Candisky asked, lowering her voice and glancing over at Lee, who was still busy with her editor. "Are you reopening the investigation?"

Dambacher paused for several moments. Candisky sensed it was the prelude to a painful admission. "Yes. We're reopening the investigation officially today. Due to the fact that Dr. Boggs apparently lied about the identification of this gentleman, we have sufficient reason to reexamine the case."

Candisky could barely contain herself. "You know, Bob, we've been writing about this for a week and . . ."

"I'm well aware of your stories," Dambacher said, his voice an even monotone.

"Is that what prompted you to change your mind?"

"Oh, not really, it was a combination of things. Not one in particular."

"Okay," Candisky said, writing in the margins of her paper. "But when I talked to the lady in your office, she said the autopsy hadn't been out of its file since June something, the middle of June. But, just so I have this straight, since you spoke with Robin last Thursday, you've removed the file, sent it to the investigators at the California Department of Insurance, and reopened the investigation. Correct?"

After another moment of uneasy silence, Dambacher admitted, "Yes. That's correct."

Candisky was elated. Dambacher had stopped just short of acknowledging that the stories prompted the coroner to reopen the case. But that was fine with Candisky—the evidence seemed pretty overwhelming in her favor. "I'm real anxious to see what you folks find out. What's the next step?" Candisky continued. "When might we expect to hear something?"

"We'll have our forensic pathologists review the autopsy. It won't be today or tomorrow, it's going to take a while. We'll give it a pretty thorough going over to see if there's anything we might have missed the first time around."

"Such as?"

"I can't get into specifics," Dambacher said. "Suffice it to say that we'll be looking for a more specific cause of death."

Lee walked back toward Candisky. She sat down and started making calls on another phone, trying to line up interviews for her feature story.

"If you no longer believe it's Hanson, then do you have an ID on the corpse?" Candisky asked.

"No, but that's one of the things the investigators will be trying to establish," Dambacher said.

"Shouldn't that have been done months ago?" Candisky countered.

"At the time we had no reason to question anything because the man was identified by his own private physician," Dambacher said, reciting a line already quite familiar to Candisky. "At this point it is going to be quite difficult to identify the body. We have fingerprints and a photograph, but if this fellow doesn't have a criminal record . . ." Dambacher's voice trailed off. "I don't know how we're going to do it. There is always the hope that somebody will come up with a missing person report."

21

Mel Weinstein slid a copy of an addendum to Farmers' lawsuit across his desk to Yocum. "This is it, huh?" Yocum asked, licking the tips of his fingers as he flipped through the pages.

Weinstein nodded. "That's it, as far as we know," he said. "I'm sorry I couldn't give it to you yesterday, but I didn't think it would be proper to give it to you before Farmers got a copy of it."

Yocum chuckled to himself. "Proper." Weinstein's photo was probably next to the word in the dictionary, Yocum thought. He had talked to Weinstein several times over the past few days, each time attempting to wheedle more information from the lawyer. Not much worked. Although at times Weinstein seemed anxious to talk, he choked back anything that wasn't public record. Weinstein was keenly aware of his obligation to his client and was, in turn, very protective of them.

The reporter knew that, like himself and Candisky, Weinstein had been trying to track down the whereabouts of the million dollars Hawkins had received from Farmers. While Yocum was calling all over town trying to piece together the financial trail, Weinstein was obtaining the figures with a few well-placed subpoenas.

"So this was filed . . . ?" Yocum asked.

Weinstein shook his head. "It hasn't been filed yet. We may not even file it. It's not critical to the suit, but we wanted to track down the money for Farmers."

Yocum nodded. "Good. Then there's no problem running with it tomorrow?"

"Go ahead."

Yocum continued to scan the document. "So, he deposited the entire $1 million in his personal bank account to begin with?"

Weinstein nodded.

"And now there's less than $125,000 left?"

"Correct. That's what's left in his personal account. I don't think he's spent it all, of course, but with this guy, who knows. The only thing we're sure of is that it's not in his account now."

"Do you know where it went from his personal account?"

"To some point," Weinstein said. "Some of it was cash withdrawals. Some was transferred into a Just Sweats account."

The addendum stated that Hawkins had deposited Farmers' million-dollar check into his account at the Broad Street branch of Fifth Third Bank on July 8. Over the next two weeks, some $875,000 was removed from the account. "Looks like the boy was a little panicky when he left town," Yocum noted, looking at several large withdrawals in mid-July.

On July 15, Hawkins transferred $150,000 from his personal account at Fifth Third to another personal account at BancOne, and he immediately converted the sum to cash. He transferred another $150,000 to his account at Blunt, Ellis & Loewi and withdrew $28,000 cash. From the $500,000 he had transferred to the Just Sweats account, he withdrew another $154,000.

On July 16, he withdrew an additional $84,000 from the Just Sweats account. "The sixteenth?" Yocum asked. "Wasn't that the day he . . ."

"Left town? Yes. About the same time he found out we were questioning the identity of the corpse."

"How did he get $84,000 in cash on a Saturday?"

"Excellent question," Weinstein said. "Why don't you pose it to Fifth Third? Better yet, go try and make a large cash withdrawal from the bank and see how far you get."

"Assuming I had $84,000," Yocum replied. "But you seem to be implying that Hawkins had some help."

Weinstein grinned. "All we know is that Hawkins goes to a few Fifth Third branches on a Saturday and they give him everything he wants. You make your own inferences, but it doesn't make sense to me."

Weinstein's secretary, Marty Highfield, poked her head in the door. "It's that call you've been waiting on from California."

"I'll take it," he said, turning back to Yocum. "I think it's all pretty self-explanatory. If you have any questions, give me a call."

"Great. But, one more bug I'd like to put in your ear. If you do decide to file this or anything else with the court, do me a little favor and file it as close to five in the afternoon as possible."

Weinstein frowned as he grabbed a clean legal pad from his desk drawer. "Why? What difference does it make?"

"The closer to five o'clock you file it, the tougher it will be for the TV news to get their hands on it. I won't have to hear about it on the evening news before it gets in the paper."

The phone rang and Weinstein waved good-bye. "We'll see." He wouldn't commit one way or the other.

It wouldn't be proper.

22

The reporters had first learned that Dr. Boggs had attacked a man with a stun gun when Yocum caught a passing mention of the incident within the packet sent to him by the Los Angeles County coroner. Candisky followed up on the information by asking Glendale police for a copy of the incident report.

Sgt. Dean Durand tracked down and handed Candisky the one-page report—a standard police summary of an assault.

On April 1, 1988, two weeks before Hanson's reported death, Dr. Richard P. Boggs attacked a 44-year-old Hollywood computer programmer, Barry C. Pomeroy, with a stun gun during an after-hours visit to the physician's office.

"Can you just burn me a copy of this?" Candisky asked.

Durand folded his arms across his chest and shook his head. "No. You can take any information you like, but you can't have a copy of it."

"This is public record, isn't it?"

"It is, and it's been made available to you. But we don't make copies."

"Not even if I pay for it? It's easier to be accurate if we have a copy."

Durand shook his head. "Sorry."

"Okay, but I'm going to copy this word for word. It might take a while."

"Go right ahead. I've got the time."

Candisky began the painstaking process of duplicating the report in her notebook. "Were there ever any charges filed in this case?"

"No," Durand said. "The report was filed by the alleged victim and then forwarded to the prosecutor's office. They made the decision not to press charges."

"Why not?"

"Well, you should address that question to them, but from what I understand, it boiled down to one person's word against another's. There was no physical evidence and the attack wasn't reported for a week. It might just be a lovers' spat."

Candisky continued to copy the information. When she read Pomeroy's physical description, she set down her pen and picked up the report from the table. She read it again, then a third time. "Have you read this report? 'Barry C. Pomeroy—5' 11", 144 pounds, brown hair and brownish green eyes'—that's the same physical description as Hanson, the same as the corpse."

Durand nodded in weak agreement. "We talked to you yesterday about Mr. Hanson's death. I see no reason to delve into that again."

"Fair enough," Candisky said, hoping to avoid another fruitless confrontation.

She finished copying the information, then walked to a pay phone on the street to call Yocum. "Good stuff, here," Candisky said, reading Yocum the description of Pomeroy.

"And two weeks before Hanson supposedly died?"

"Right."

"Looks like they were out trolling for a would-be Hanson."

Early that evening, from Lee's desk at the *Daily News,* Candisky called Barry Pomeroy at his home. She had talked to him briefly that afternoon, calling him at Peterson Publishing, the Los Angeles firm where he worked. "Can I call you later?" Pomeroy had whispered. "I don't know how you got my name and number, but I really don't want to talk about this at work."

"I got your number from the police report you filed. I'm looking into Dr. Boggs and his involvement in an insurance scam and a possible murder. I've got your home number. I'll call you there later."

Pomeroy was still upset when Candisky reached him at home. "I just don't understand what you want with me," Pomeroy said. "I don't know anything about this insurance thing you're talking about. I hardly knew Dr. Boggs, and I've never heard of this other guy, Hanson."

"I know. There's no doubt in my mind that you weren't involved. In fact, I think you were almost the man they found dead in Boggs's office."

"What?" Pomeroy shrieked. "How? Oh, my God. I don't understand. You're scaring me, Cathy. What do you mean? Are you saying they were trying to kill me?"

"I think so. Look, Barry, I'm not trying to scare you, but I think it's really important that we talk. Have the police ever contacted you about this?"

"No. Never. Not since I filed that report."

"I didn't think so. So, you probably didn't know that Hanson, the dead guy, and you have the same physical characteristics?"

"Oh, this is very disturbing. How do I know you are who you say you are? How do I know you're really a reporter?"

"Well, if you don't want to take me at my word I'll hang up and you call the *Los Angeles Daily News* and ask for their Glendale office. Ask for Cathy Candisky, the reporter from Columbus. I'm working out of here."

Less than five minutes later, Pomeroy was on the phone. "I would still like to meet in person. I'd like to see some identification."

"Fine. I can meet you right now. Can you give me directions to your place? Or, if you want to meet someplace else . . . ?"

"Oh, I can't tonight," Pomeroy said. "I have a previous commitment. How about tomorrow after work?"

"That's no good for me. I've got a four o'clock flight back to Ohio. How about tomorrow morning?"

"Sorry. I just can't. I just can't meet with you until sometime after five."

"Okay, let me see if I can stay over another night. But, if you've got a few minutes, could we just go over a few things?" Candisky was afraid to let Pomeroy get away without extracting some information. She feared he would renege on his offer if he had time to think about it. "Could you just tell me a little bit about how you met Boggs?"

Pomeroy was shooting pool at The Spike, a gay bar on Santa Monica Boulevard in West Hollywood, when he noticed a nattily attired man watching him from across the room. A few minutes later the man walked over and introduced himself. "He said his name was Dr. Peter Richards and that he was a doctor from Glendale. He seemed quite nice. We started talking about pool and he asked if I'd like to join him for a late dinner."

They left The Spike about 2:00 A.M. They got into Richards's black Cadillac and drove a mile down Santa Monica Boulevard to Theodore's, an all-night restaurant. Pomeroy had the "scrambled burger"; Richards, a cup of coffee.

"He was a wonderful conversationalist," Pomeroy said. "He had a wide range of interests. He seemed consumed with talking about architecture. I guess we had been there about an hour, and he practically insisted that I take a ride through downtown Glendale to look at some of the new high-rises."

"So, did you go?"

"Oh, yes. We drove around for a while and we stopped by his office. He said he had to call a patient."

"Kind of late to be calling a patient, wasn't it?"

"Yes, but I guess I wasn't thinking about that at the time."

Pomeroy said he busied himself in the lobby while Richards went into his office to make the call. Richards returned a few minutes later and showed Pomeroy some literature on an import-export venture he was considering. "He said it would involve importing gourmet wine, cheese, and gifts," Pomeroy recalled.

"So, then you left?"

"Well, first he gave me a tour of his office. And, you know, I didn't see his name on any of the certificates that were hanging on the wall. They all were for this Dr. Boggs."

"Didn't you ask him about it?"

"Yes, and he said, 'Oh, that's my partner.' "

It was almost 4:00 A.M. when Richards dropped Pomeroy off at his apartment. The doctor suggested dinner the following week and Pomeroy agreed, giving Richards his telephone number.

The doctor called a few days later and set up a date for the following Friday, April 1. They met at 8:00 P.M. at Denny's Restaurant on Sunset Boulevard, a block from Pomeroy's apartment on Harold Way. Pomeroy arrived first and sipped a cup of coffee while he waited for Richards, who was about twenty minutes late. The men talked while Pomeroy finished his coffee and then left in Richards's car for a seafood restaurant in Glendale. "Once we got to Glendale he said he needed to make another quick stop by the office to call a patient."

"Weren't you a little suspicious?"

"Not really. Everything seemed normal at the time."

They arrived at Richards's office about 9:30 P.M. Pomeroy wandered through the examination rooms while Richards made his call.

"I was just wandering around, looking at things, and he came out of his office and I asked him about this heart-monitoring machine, oh, what's it called?"

"An EKG?" Candisky offered.

"Oh, that's it. And he hooked me up for a test."

"I've never had one of those," Candisky said. "How do they do it?"

"They hook these little suction-cup things to your chest and legs. The machine reads your heart rate and the results get printed out on paper. It took about ten minutes."

"So, how'd you do?"

"Okay, I guess. He said my heart was in good shape."

"Is this when he attacked you with the stun gun?"

There was a brief pause. "I'm really not comfortable talking about this on the phone," Pomeroy said. "I still want to see identification to make sure you're really a reporter."

"We'll do that tomorrow night," Candisky said. Candisky doubted that Karsko would approve an extended stay. She needed to keep Pomeroy talking, but she sensed that was going to be difficult. "You're really lucky, you know that?"

"I'm beginning to realize that. I just thought he was stressed out or something. But this explains why he went so berserk, why he just kept lunging at me."

"So, how did you get away?"

"I just overpowered him," Pomeroy said.

"Really?" Candisky said, trying to drag Pomeroy slowly back into the interview. "Can you explain how it started. I mean, did he just pull out a stun gun and charge after you?"

"See, I really don't want to . . ."

"I'm sorry," Candisky said. "I'm just amazed because this all fits so well. Boggs is really a creep, isn't he?"

"Well, from what you've told me, it seems to me he's a murderer."

"Can't you tell me a little bit? Don't go into a lot of detail if you're uncomfortable, but just tell me how it all started. I mean, I've never even seen a stun gun. What do they look like?"

"It's a little box, about the size of a pack of cigarettes, and it has these two steel prongs sticking out of one end. That's where the electric current comes out. It crackles and makes this electric blue arc."

"Ouch," Candisky said. "That sounds painful."

"It was. He cut my neck. I nearly passed out, but then I took a deep breath and started fighting back. I got a burst of energy from somewhere, knocked his right hand against the table, and the stun gun fell to the floor."

"God, you are so lucky," Candisky repeated, still hoping to win Pomeroy over. She knew she would only get the story piecemeal. "You said he lunged at you. Did you see it coming?"

"No. Not at all. I was putting on my shirt and he held up his arm like he was going to give me a hug. I went to hug him back, and he started jabbing me in the back with that thing."

"So when you knocked it away, what did he do? What did he say?"

"He didn't do anything, thank God. He was all out of breath."

"So, did he say what the hell he was doing?"

"No, not really. He said, 'I'm sorry. I don't know what happened. I have these spells sometimes. I'm going to get help.' Then he tried to look at the cut on my neck and offered to stitch it, but I said 'no thanks'—like I'd let him near me after that."

"Good move on your part. I assume you never made it to dinner."

"No. Hardly. I couldn't have eaten anything after that. I just wanted to go home."

"How did you get home?"

"He drove me."

"Weren't you a little afraid to get in the car with him?"

"At first I was hesitant, but he seemed to have calmed down."

"Were there any problems on the way home?"

"No, none. He drove by his house to get more sedatives."

"More sedatives?"

Candisky could hear Pomeroy exhale on the other end of the line. He was tiring of the interview and had, Candisky thought, already told the reporter more than he had intended. "Well, he, uh, he had given me a couple of sedatives at the office, and he said he wanted to give me a couple more to take home, but he was out at the office and he wanted to swing by his apartment to get me some."

"Barry, you've got to be kidding me? You took pills from this guy after he tried to kill you with a stun gun," Candisky said, beginning to question Pomeroy's mental abilities. Why, she wondered, would he get into a car with Boggs, go to his apartment, and pop a few pills from him? "Weren't you worried about what he might be giving you?"

"I guess I wasn't thinking about it at the time. Listen. I gotta go. You give me a call tomorrow and we can pick a place to meet."

"Okay, thanks. Oh, one more real quick question. I'm just curious. Did you ever hear from him again?"

"He called me a few days later to see if I was all right, but I told him not to call me again. Really, that's all I want to say. Goodnight."

Bernie Karsko pulled the cigar from his teeth and winced, leaning back in his chair. "What do you think she'll get out of it?" Karsko asked.

Yocum knew the look. He could make his best pitch, but the effort would be futile. Once Karsko had made up his mind, little could be done to change it. "I think this is the best thing she's dug up. This guy was probably supposed to be the first dead Hanson. It'll make a great interview and it'll only take one more day. I think we're wasting a hell of an opportunity if we make her come back."

Karsko exhaled. "I just don't think we're going to get much." He put the unlit cigar on the edge of his desk. "I can't see keeping her out there any more. This story's about run its course, anyway."

"I don't think so, Bern."

Karsko swirled his chair back to the story he was editing on the computer screen.

"Fine," Yocum muttered, heading back across the newsroom.

"Why don't you miss the plane?" Yocum suggested. "You tell him, 'Bernie, the traffic to the airport was hell and I just couldn't make it.' Catch a red-eye."

"My ticket's nonrefundable. I miss the flight, I eat the ticket. What's one more night?"

"I don't know, but there's no arguing with him. Anyway can you get Pomeroy sooner? Meet him for breakfast or something?"

"I've tried and tried. He refuses to see me until after work. The only thing I can think of is to give this to the *Daily News,* see if Priscilla will do the interview and share it with us."

"Do it. Make her agree that we run our stories on the same day. That should be okay, since we're not exactly fighting for the same readers."

Lee was happy to oblige, even though the *Daily News* had little interest in the story since no charges had been filed. Nevertheless, Lee met with Pomeroy and called Candisky in the *Dispatch* newsroom the next morning.

"He wanted to see every piece of ID I have," Lee said. "The guy is really paranoid. He thinks Boggs is going to come after him."

"Did he tell you why he waited a week to go to the police?"

"Yeah. I asked him about that and he said . . ." Candisky could hear Lee flipping through her notebook. "Here. He said he wasn't going to tell the police, but a friend convinced him to. They went back to the medical building to check the directory and found out there was no Dr. Peter Richards, so they figured Dr. Richards was really Dr. Richard Boggs. He said that convinced him that he had been set up."

"It took him that long?"

"That's what he said."

"Did the cops ever tell him why no charges were ever filed against Boggs?"

"He said Detective Peterson called about a week later and really gave him a hard way to go. Pomeroy said Peterson acted as if he was protecting Boggs. Here's a direct quote. This is what Pomeroy said Peterson told him, 'Do you realize what allegations you're making against Dr. Boggs? I've known the family for twenty years, and he's a well-respected physician.'"

"Sounds like the good doctor has some friends on the force," Candisky said.

"His brother was on the force with Peterson, you know."

"Do you think that had anything to do with it?"

"I don't know. Might have."

"Peterson mentioned the attack in Hanson's autopsy. He wrote it off as a homosexual spat. Have you had a chance to ask Peterson about it?"

"No. Peterson hasn't talked to reporters for years and I don't think he's about to start now."

23

Yocum pushed open the door to the State & Fourth Grill, allowing Candisky to go in ahead. At 8:00 P.M. the reporters were wrapping up yet another twelve-hour day, a stint that was becoming more the norm than the exception. Yocum was tired, but Candisky was exhausted. Her five-hour flight from Los Angeles had landed at Port Columbus at one that morning and she was at work by eight. She had put in a long day on Ohio time while her internal clock was still operating on California time.

Yocum directed her to a vacant booth in the back of the bar. "Two Buds," he told the bartender, dropping three bills on the bar.

Yocum looked up and down the bar. Two men from the *Dispatch* composing room were at the far end drinking their lunch. He didn't recognize anyone else in the bar, which was a half-block from the paper and a popular hangout for the *Dispatch*'s blue-collar workers—pressmen and the composing staff. Older reporters who frequented the grill referred to it not as the State & Fourth, but as the Fourth Estate.

Candisky slouched in the booth, her back to the bar. She struggled to keep her eyes open. "This will probably put me to sleep," she said, taking a sip of beer.

They sat in silence for several minutes. Tiny beads of rain were starting to streak the windows of the State & Fourth. An old Glenn Miller song played on the jukebox. Yocum finished his beer and fetched another.

About 8:15 P.M. a face familiar to Yocum walked into the back room. Yocum made eye contact and the man in a damp beige overcoat approached the booth. His slight grin—maybe a smirk—disappeared when he got close enough to see Candisky. "I thought this was going to be just me and you," he said to Yocum.

"She's all right," Yocum said in a tone a little louder than a whisper. "This is Cathy Candisky. We've been working on the stories together. Cathy's been out in California working on this and I figured it was a good time for you to meet her." Yocum introduced his partner to the man. He nodded, barely, and sat down next to Candisky.

"This is nothing personal," he said to Candisky, then turned to Yocum. "But it was supposed to be me and you. That was the deal. I'm not real comfortable giving this to you, anyway."

Yocum was normally very protective of his sources, but he thought it was important for Candisky to meet this one. "You can trust her," Yocum said. "You're not going to get burned."

"No one can know I was the one who gave it to you."

"Understood," Yocum replied.

The man turned to Candisky, who tried to be reassuring. "Rob explained the ground rules before we came over. I won't say anything."

The source nodded. "Okay." He looked back at Yocum. "How'd you guys find out about this, anyway?" he asked. "There are only a few people who even know it exists."

"Laramee and Mantz told me a little bit about it last week, but they wouldn't give me a copy. Laramee might have, but Mantz nixed it. I wouldn't ask you for it, but I don't know where else to go, and we really need it."

"A lot of people are going to be upset when this gets in the paper. Do you think they'll try to figure out where you got it?" he asked.

"No doubt," Yocum said.

"What if someone asks me if I gave it to you?"

"Lie," Yocum said. "Don't ever admit to it. Guaranteed, neither of us will ever say anything."

"What if the lawyers or the cops want to know?"

"Tough. They don't control us. We don't give up our sources."

The man took a breath and reached inside his trench coat. He pulled out a blank white envelope with a corporate logo in the corner. "I'll keep the envelope," he said, pulling out several photocopied pages. "Here you go," he said, handing them to Yocum. "Do you think someone is sending Hawkins your stories?"

Yocum looked at Candisky, who shrugged. "Probably," she said. "He's probably got an old girlfriend sending him clips. Why?"

"No reason," the source said. "I was just trying to imagine what he's going to do when he sees this outpouring of emotion in the paper. He's not going to be happy."

"Breaks my heart," Yocum said, unfolding the pages that contained the letter John Hawkins had sent to Missy Mantz after he left Columbus. He held it so he and Candisky could read it together.

Dear Melissa:

This is undoubtedly the toughest letter I've ever had to write. There is no other way I can do what I am doing except through a letter. The pressures of running the business have totally driven me almost crazy. I know you think I'm a wimp for running from the responsibilities like this, but my happiness is more important to me than the power and prestige Just Sweats gave me.

I'm going to ask a very important thing of you. I need you to take care of everything for me until I return. You are the only friend I have who is responsible enough to handle what I am going to ask. The enclosed power of attorney will give you the ability to do everything I want. First take the power of attorney to Jim Connors [Columbus lawyer and Hawkins's friend] and retain him as your personal attorney. Give him a retainer of no less than $5,000 as he will need it. Use Jim as your advocate at all times. He is a good man and you can trust him. I wouldn't advise any other counsel.

I have $150,000 in a money market account at Blunt, Ellis & Loewi. The details are specified in the power of attorney. My contact lady is Jody Scheiman. I want Jody to invest those funds in tax-free bonds and transfer ownership to a joint account of mine and my mom's. There is $450,000 owed to me by another insurance company. Dick Curtin [Just Sweats attorney] will give you the details. When the check comes in have the money invested in the same way. I also have an account at Fifth Third Bank which has approximately $109,000 in cash. You may use those funds as collateral for Just Sweats to borrow against for one and a half years. After that time, I want my mother to have the money. As with Just Sweats, it's yours to do with as you please. With what you are about to go through it's the least I can give you. It's your decision, but I would like you to give an equal share of ownership to yourself, Paul [Colgan, Just Sweats accountant], Dianne, Erik DeSando, as I feel he deserves an opportunity in life, and Dave Kessler from Fifth Third. Dave is a free agent right now and without his expertise in finance you won't survive, with you controlling the voting power. The stock certificates and bill of sale from Gene are in my safety deposit box at Fifth Third Bexley branch. The Kentucky corporation papers are in the office of E. Lawson King in Lexington, Kentucky. If you don't wish to be the owner of Just Sweats, it can be sold very easily as Dan White has expressed a strong desire for a quick sale. In order to sell the business, you must first finish the audit currently being conducted.

Missy, I'm very sorry I'm dumping all of this on you. You have no idea how bad I feel. I'll make it up to you some day and that's a promise. I miss you guys already, but the only way I can get my sanity back is to walk way from all the pressures for a while. I'll call you, but it's going to be at least six months. I have a friend in London, England, and I plan to stay there for a while. You can't let anyone see this letter as they will try to take the power of attorney away from you saying I wasn't sane at the time of writing it. You will be asked repeatedly where am I and why did I leave. The best response will be that I wanted to take some time off and enjoy the insurance money. Good luck, Miss. I'll love you always.

John

"Touching," Yocum said.

"I thought you'd like it. So, you happy, now?"

"This isn't bad," Yocum said, tapping the paper with the back of his fingers.

"Not bad?" The man leaned forward, resting both elbows on the table. "I'd say it's pretty damn good, considering you couldn't find anyone else to give it to you."

"I know, it's great stuff. Page one. But . . ."

"But . . . ?"

Yocum leaned forward so their faces were inches apart. "Got anything else?"

The source shook his head. "You are such a whore."

Yocum grinned. "It's part of my charm."

The man leaned back, stuffing both hands in his coat pocket. "No. I don't have anything else. I don't think . . . Wait. I do have another little nugget you can track down." The source put his fingertips together in front of his chin. "So, tell me what you guys think, is Hanson dead or alive?"

Yocum looked at Candisky. "I think he's alive," she said.

Yocum nodded. "He's definitely alive. Or maybe dead. I don't know. Why?"

The source leaned closer to the table again. "I heard he's alive and has had plastic surgery to change his looks."

"Where did you hear that?" Candisky interjected.

The source looked at Candisky, but didn't answer her question. "Do either of you two know Hawkins's old roommate, Erik DeSando?"

"Cathy does," Yocum said. "She interviewed him the other day, and spent a little time with him out in Las Vegas. Why?"

"I hear DeSando knows about the plastic surgery. Ask him."

"So, Hanson's alive? Erik told me there was no doubt that he was dead," Candisky said.

The source shook his head. "The last I knew they weren't performing plastic surgery on dead people," he said, getting up from the booth. "Maybe DeSando was being a little less than honest with you. So, are you straight with the letter?" the source said, looking at Yocum and then Candisky.

They looked at each other and nodded. "We're straight," Yocum said.

"Good," he said. "Just make sure you keep me out of it." He took three steps toward the door, then turned back. "One more thing. You know your hero from Golden Rule?"

Yocum frowned. "My hero?"

"The guy who said he couldn't believe Farmers paid on their policy, and that Golden Rule would never pay."

"I remember."

"Well, they paid, they just didn't get burned."

"I don't understand," Yocum said.

"Golden Rule sent Hawkins a check for a half million dollars. They sent it certified mail to his old apartment, but Hawkins had moved and hadn't left a forwarding address, so the check sat at the post office for a couple of days, maybe longer. Golden Rule finally got word of the scam and cancelled payment on the check before Hawkins could pick it up. If Hawkins would have been smart enough to leave a forwarding address, Golden Rule would have been out the cash."

24

"Cheese or no?"

"No, just plain," Candisky said, taking the foil-wrapped Wendy's burger Yocum handed her.

"How's it going?" he asked, setting a bag of fries and sodas on the desk.

"Take a look," Candisky said, pushing the computer screen toward Yocum's desk. He began proofing the story she had put together on the stun-gun attack.

"The copy desk ought to have a field day coming up with a headline for this one. I vote for, 'Crazed stun-gun-toting gay doctor zaps would-be lover to bag first million.' "

Candisky grinned. "I like it. Did you bring any ketchup?"

"In the bag," Yocum said around a mouthful of cheeseburger.

It was just after noon on Saturday, September 3, and Candisky and Yocum had set up camp in a corner of the newsroom, comparing notes and trying to determine which leads to pursue. Candisky was thumbing through a stack of pink "While You Were Out" telephone messages that Yocum had stuffed in an envelope.

"A reporter from the *New York Times* called?" Candisky asked, holding up one of the messages. "Did you call him back?"

"No. Screw him. They call in here wanting all kinds of information and think you should drop everything to help them. Let them track it down themselves."

"How about if I call him back?" Candisky suggested. "You never know when you might need a favor."

"Suit yourself. The last time I helped one of them they took the information and ran it as if they'd generated it themselves. They're no better than the TV whores. I'm getting a little tired of watching the six o'clock news and seeing our stories rewritten and run as their exclusives."

Candisky ignored the tirade and held up another pink sheet. "The *Globe*. The supermarket tab?"

Yocum nodded. "I may call him back."

"You won't return a phone call from the *New York Times,* but you will for the *Globe*?"

"Granted, the *Globe*'s a shameless rag, but that's all it claims to be. I can respect that," Yocum said.

Candisky rolled her eyes. "What's this one?" she asked, holding up an illegible note scribbled on a half-sheet of yellow legal pad.

Yocum squinted past the computer terminal. "Oh, some guy, he wouldn't give me his name—surprise—said Hanson went to Texas and filled a $3,000 prescription for some kind of hormone pills."

Candisky studied the note. "He's a woman," she said. "I'll bet you he's a woman."

"What?"

"A sex change. It fits. He was taking the hormone pills because he's had a sex change. We were just told he's had plastic surgery. It's the perfect cover. Everyone's looking for Gene Hanson, and he's living somewhere in sunny California as Gene Hanson's long-lost sister, Gina."

Yocum laughed. "Ten days ago that would have seemed farfetched, but now . . . I still can't figure out why a guy like Hawkins—young, good-looking, bright—gets mixed up with a couple of old queens like Hanson and Boggs."

"I know. It's weird. It must be for money, or maybe drugs." She shrugged. "What else could there be?"

"Beats me." Yocum crinkled up his hamburger wrapper and fired it in the general direction of a trash can. "Have you talked to Jackie Cirian lately?"

"No. But I was going to give her a call this morning and see if she's heard from John. She works nights and I didn't want to call too early."

Cirian was up fixing breakfast for her daughter, Kari. No, Cirian told Candisky, she hadn't heard from her son, but she had received two unnerving telephone calls from the "vacationing" Dr. Boggs.

"What did he want?" Candisky asked.

"He wouldn't say," Cirian said, sounding nearly in tears. "He said he was looking for Johnny. He called me at home and again at the casino. I'm worried. I called Austin Wildman and asked him what I should do, and he told me to stay away from Boggs. Austin said Boggs is under investigation by the FBI for dealing drugs to Hollywood tough shits."

"Tough shits? Like who?"

"He didn't say and I was too upset to ask." Cirian was now sobbing. "What does he want with Johnny?"

"I wish I could tell you, Jackie. We've tried to interview him a couple of times, but he won't talk to us. He apparently thinks John and Gene set him up."

"Set up! He said he was set up? My son was the one who was set up. Is that what Dr. Boggs told the police?"

"No, but that's what he told a couple of reporters from Los Angeles. Hold on a minute." Dr. Boggs had consented to brief interviews with two California papers, the *Glendale News-Press* and the *Daily News,* and Yocum and Candisky had picked them up through the *Dispatch's* electronic library. Candisky motioned for Yocum to pass her the computer printouts of these stories. "Boggs said, 'I been averaging between $200,000 and $300,000 a year. Something like this, I don't need it. I'm making a comfortable living. All I can do is continue to practice and hope they find Mr. Hawkins and find some answers as to what happened to the money and who it was who was in my office. If it wasn't Hanson, I was set up.'" Cirian did not respond, so Candisky continued. "He told this other reporter pretty much the same thing. 'The gentleman said he was Mr. Hanson. My job is to treat medical ailments, not to check into peoples' backgrounds. If he isn't who he said he was, I don't know who he is. Hanson still owes me $1,000. We billed Mr. Hawkins back in May and I was told by his office he was on a trip. I do feel I have been set up. If it was a scheme, it was an elaborate one.'"

"Cathy, I haven't heard from Johnny in three weeks, not since he left Las Vegas. I'll be real honest with you, I don't think he's in a clinic. I think he's gotten scared and left the country. I fear for his life. I don't know where he is. I think I've lost my son."

Cirian had finally realized that her son was in trouble, Candisky thought as she hung up hung up the phone. "I feel sorry for her," Candisky told Yocum. "She really thinks the world of John."

"A mother's love." Yocum's phone rang. "She'll never allow herself to believe he did anything wrong."

He picked up the receiver on the second ring. "Yocum."

"Rob, Sol Sokol here. Didn't know if I'd catch you in on a Saturday. Have you seen next week's *Business First?*"

"No, but it sounds like you have."

"I get mine in the mail and it gets here a couple days early."

The weekly business tabloid didn't hit the newsstands until Monday mornings, but Sokol's mail subscription bought him the paper on Saturday. "They have a story on Just Sweats. Did you and Cathy know about the police report one of the part-owners filed with Whitehall police?"

They didn't. In fact, neither reporter realized that the Just Sweats headquarters wasn't in Columbus, but was actually situated just inside the small east-side suburb of Whitehall.

"We knew there was a silent partner, but we didn't know he filed any complaint with police," Yocum said.

"Well, he did, and he says Hawkins embezzled money from Just Sweats."

"You mean Hanson? Hanson embezzled from the company before he blew town in February."

"No, this says Hawkins. It was sometime in July. Do you want me to Xerox a copy and run it down to you?" Sokol asked.

"You're a prince, Sol."

"I'll be there in fifteen or twenty minutes."

"Damn," Yocum said, throwing the handset back on the telephone. "They filed the report with the Whitehall cops. Just Sweats isn't in Columbus, it's in Whitehall, and that's why the Columbus police had no reports. Why didn't I think of that? I was out at the Just Sweats headquarters. I thought it was still Columbus."

"It's a Columbus mailing address, but it must be within the jurisdiction of Whitehall police," Candisky said. "The municipal boundaries are screwy in this town. It's impossible to keep them straight."

Candisky called the Whitehall police, who confirmed the existence of the report. Reporter Scott Powers volunteered to retrieve a copy of the two-page report, while Candisky and Yocum waited for Sokol.

According to the complaint, Michael A. Guglielmelli, who owned 10 percent of Just Sweats, claimed Hawkins had embezzled about $200,000 from company accounts. On July 20, officials at Fifth Third Bank contacted Just Sweats and said the company accounts were empty. According to bank records, Hawkins, who owned 90 percent of the company, began writing checks to himself and for cash. As Hanson had done six months earlier, Hawkins drained company accounts on July 15 and on July 16, the day he fled from Columbus.

Guglielmelli, a 40-year-old New York clothier who lived in West Windsor, New Jersey, filed the complaint on July 29.

Yocum tried directory assistance for northern New Jersey. The operator found only one listing for a Michael Guglielmelli. When Yocum called the number he got no answer.

"Did you read this part about the car?" Candisky asked Yocum.

"Skimmed it. Why?"

"This says that eleven days after Hawkins left town they found his blue Mercedes with the top down and the keys in the ignition in the parking lot at the airport."

"Let's see if we can track down Laramee and ask him about the car and the embezzlement," Yocum said.

Ed Laramee wasn't difficult to find. Every Saturday since Hawkins's abrupt departure he was busy in the office. Laramee never seemed particularly thrilled to hear from the reporters, but he was always cordial and answered their questions. Of the police report, he said, "That's accurate. Based on our calculations, John took about $200,000 from our account."

"What about John's car being found at the airport—top down, keys in the ignition?"

Laramee chuckled. "Missy found John's car. She went to the airport to look for it and found it in the short-term parking lot. It was like a fish pond. It had been raining and he'd left the top down and the back was filled with water."

"Was there anything else in the car?"

"No, not really, but there were the carbons of several checks John wrote."

"Who'd he write them to?"

"Himself."

Laramee said shortly after Hawkins left town on July 16, company checks began bouncing. "At first, we just figured John was buying merchandise, but then we got a call from the bank, which was very anxious due to cash withdrawals. And I want to stress the word 'cash.' That was our first inkling that there might be a problem."

Guglielmelli, Laramee explained, was a silent partner who originally wanted to buy a Just Sweats franchise. Hawkins wasn't interested; instead, he convinced Guglielmelli to invest in the company. The clothier paid $50,000 for 10 percent ownership in the company.

Candisky called Cirian to ask her about Guglielmelli's complaint. Cirian became enraged. "How dare he," Cirian yelled. "Johnny paid him $60,000 for his share of the company. I personally delivered the check to Johnny's lawyer to have the money wired to him."

"You took it to John's lawyer?"

"Personally. Johnny asked me to deliver the check because he wanted to make Mr. Guglielmelli whole. Mr. Guglielmelli got his money."

25

Austin Wildman sat hunched over his desk, elbows dug into the blotter, intently working on straightening a paper clip. He looked at the two reporters sitting before him, then out his window overlooking the Scioto River, all the time twirling the paper clip between his thick fingers. "The thing I'm most worried about," Wildman began, "is violating a lawyer-client privilege. I'd like to help you, but I don't know how I can without getting myself in trouble."

"We don't want you to get in trouble," Candisky insisted. "But, at the same time . . ."

"You'd like to know what the hell happened?"

"Exactly."

"I don't see the conflict," Yocum said. "You represent Just Sweats. Hawkins ripped off your client. Why can't you talk on behalf of your client? Hawkins isn't associated with the company anymore."

Wildman winced. "True, but technically, he was my client when he took the money."

"You know, Mel Weinstein showed us an addendum to the lawsuit that spells out the amounts of the withdrawals," Candisky said. "Couldn't you just elaborate on what we already know?"

Wildman smiled at the reasonableness of the suggestion. "That wouldn't violate any confidences." He walked across the room and dug under a heap of papers on his couch until he found the object of his search—a slightly battered manila folder. "We called this 'Hawkins's Mad Dash for Cash,' " Wildman said, showing the reporters the folder. "Let's do it this way, you ask me the questions. If anyone asks, I didn't offer it up freely. Fair enough?"

The reporters referred to their notes and the copy of the Farmers Insurance addendum. "On Friday, July 15, Hawkins withdrew $135,000 from the Just Sweats account at Fifth Third Bank. Can you give us any details about these withdrawals?" Yocum asked.

Wildman smiled. "As a matter of fact, I happen to have some of that information right here. And, yes, your information is correct. He made three withdrawals that day. He wrote three checks, all made out to cash, for $5,000, $30,000, and $100,000. At the bottom of each check he made the notation, 'inventory purchase.' "

"And this inventory he supposedly purchased, it arrived at the stores when?"

"Curiously enough, we haven't received it yet and we don't really expect to."

"What about the following day?" Candisky asked. "July 16. The day he withdrew $84,000. Do you know anything about that?"

"Oh, most definitely," Wildman said. "Three checks. All to cash. He left about $3,000 in the Just Sweats account."

"How did he get all that money out of the bank on a Saturday?" Candisky asked.

Wildman leaned back in his chair and shook his head. "The only thing I can figure is that he simply charmed them out of it. John's a great talker. I'm sure he went in there and somehow convinced them that he absolutely had to have that money, and they got it for him. You figure it out. He walks into a bank wearing shorts and one of those flowered Hawaiian shirts, carrying a suitcase—which, I might add, he bought earlier that morning with a check that is still bouncing— and he tells them he needs his money, and please put it in the suitcase." Wildman laughed and tossed the wire that had once been a paper clip into the trash. "You figure it out. I've got no explanation."

"I didn't even think a bank would have that kind of money laying around on a Saturday," Yocum said.

"They didn't," Wildman said. "That's the best part. He went to one bank branch, and when they couldn't cover the check, they called ahead to a couple of other branches so they could finish giving him the rest of his money. Then he skips to the airport, $219,000 in company money tucked under his arm plus the money from his personal accounts he had already wired out of town, and hops a plane to St. Louis. Good night, Irene."

26

Michael W. Jones pushed open the glass door and looked up and down the aisles of the tiny pharmacy. An elderly lady, with a worn cane and a black purse dangling from her elbow, inspected a bottle of witch hazel through her bifocals. She looked at Jones, then walked to the counter with the bottle.

Riley's Pharmacy occupied much of the first floor of the medical building at 540 North Central Avenue, the same building where Boggs's had reported the death of Melvin E. Hanson. It was a modest pharmacy, carrying only medical items and primarily serving the thirty doctors who rented offices in the building. Once the old woman had taken her bag and left, Brian Archambault turned to Jones. "Can I help you sir?"

Jones approached the counter while reaching into his breast pocket. "Yes, my name is Michael Jones, I'm an investigator with the California Department of Insurance," he said, showing his badge and identification.

Archambault, a pharmacy technician, looked at the badge and nodded. "Let me get my boss."

"Fine. I'd like to talk to both of you."

Alan Genter, a pharmacist and owner of Riley's, came from the back room.

"Are you gentlemen familiar with any of the patients of Dr. Richard Boggs?"

Both men nodded. "A lot of them get their prescriptions filled here. I'd say I know most of them," Archambault said.

"Are you familiar with a patient by the name of Gene Hanson?"

"Sure," Archambault said. "He's a customer."

Jones handed Archambault three photographs of male corpses, including one of the man who had died in Boggs's office. "Do you recognize any of these men?"

Archambault studied each of the photographs, but finally shook his head and handed them back to Jones. "Uh-uh."

132

Jones handed him three more photos, including a driver's license photograph of Hanson. "That's Mr. Hanson," Archambault said, handing the photograph back to Jones.

"You're sure?" Jones asked.

"Positive."

Jones repeated the photo array with Genter, with identical results. The investigator then walked out into the first-floor hall and scanned the directory for Boggs's office. He jotted down "Room 201" in his notebook, then made his way up the stairs to the office. The investigator introduced himself to Jean Walker, the doctor's receptionist, and again showed his badge and identification. Jones waited several minutes before Walker ushered him in to see the doctor.

Boggs put down a pen and stood up from behind his desk. Jones nodded. "Dr. Boggs's, Michael Jones. I'm with the California Department of Insurance."

Boggs shook Jones's hand and waved his left palm toward an empty chair. "Please, sit down. What can I do for you?"

Jones opened his notebook. "I'd like to ask you a few questions about the death of Gene Hanson."

Boggs nodded. "Gene Hanson, huh? I haven't heard that name in a while."

"He was a patient of yours, wasn't he?"

"That's right. Had been for several years. You know, Mr. Jones, I've already given several statements to the police and the fire department."

"Yes, I know. But if you don't mind I'd like to go over the morning of his death once again, just so I have it straight."

Boggs shrugged and arranged some papers on his desk. "Not much to tell, actually," he said, avoiding eye contact with the investigator. The doctor methodically recounted the events of the morning of April 16, explaining how he had received a phone call at home and met Hanson at the office where his patient collapsed and died. "In retrospect, the emergency room would have been a better place for him, but he was afraid of hospitals."

"Would you mind letting me take a peek at Mr. Hanson's medical file?"

"Not at all," Boggs's said, picking up his phone. "Jean, would you bring me Gene Hanson's file, please."

Jones inspected the file, noting that Hanson had signed several documents. Jones continued to thumb through the file as though preoccupied with its contents. "You know, Dr. Boggs, a fingerprint comparison has shown the corpse was not Gene Hanson." He watched Boggs for his response.

Caught off guard, Boggs's swallowed and muttered, "No comment."

"We've had people look at the picture on Hanson's driver's license, and they've identified him as your patient. Those same people looked at the corpse and said they'd never seen him before."

"I have no comment. I've told you everything I know."

"Well, you must have known the real Gene Hanson, since the information on the insurance policies and the information on his medical files is identical."

"All I can tell you," Boggs's said, "is the gentleman who died in my office was known to me as Gene Hanson." Boggs stood up and opened his office door. "Is that all, Mr. Jones?"

Jones closed his notebook and stood. "For now, Dr. Boggs."

On Monday, August 29, Los Angeles Municipal Judge David S. Milton granted Jones's request for a warrant to search Boggs's office.

In his affidavit for the search warrant, Jones wrote that Boggs's misidentified a corpse as Melvin E. Hanson in order for John Hawkins to collect $1.5 million in life insurance. "Farmers New World Life Insurance and Golden Rule Insurance Company are the victims of a fraudulent scheme perpetrated by Dr. Boggs's misrepresenting the identity of the deceased body in his office on April 16, 1988, as the true Melvin Eugene Hanson. As a result, Hawkins received a $1 million check and has not been located."

Milton signed the warrant, authorizing investigators to seize Hanson and Hawkins's medical and billing record files, including ledger statements, appointment calendars, patient information cards, address books, and any correspondence between Boggs, Hanson, and Hawkins.

The next morning, August 30, 1988, Jones and three investigators from the department of insurance and the coroner's office returned to Boggs's office. That afternoon they walked out of the office with a .32-caliber revolver and a foot-high stack of documents.

On Tuesday, September 6, 1988, Franklin County Common Pleas Court Judge Dale A. Crawford extended a temporary restraining order issued in response to the lawsuit filed by the Farmers New World Life Insurance Company on August 23, 1988. Judge Crawford ordered John B. Hawkins not to spend any of the $1 million he had received from Farmers. Crawford's ruling in effect froze the money until the mystery surrounding the reported death of Melvin E. Hanson could be unraveled. The judge gave Hawkins until September 22 to respond to the allegations in the lawsuit. To no one's surprise, neither Hawkins nor an attorney representing Hawkins attended the hearing.

Following the brief hearing in courtroom 5-A, Crawford sat in his chamber and chuckled with reporters at the effectiveness of his order. Hawkins and the money were nowhere to be found. He had, in all likelihood, already spent a healthy chunk of the cash. "We have no debtor's prisons anymore," Crawford said, hanging up his robe. "But Farmers can attach whatever he has for years and years."

Melvin Weinstein, Farmers counsel and a former assistant Ohio attorney general, appeared anything but confident that the money would be recovered. He acknowledged that he had hired a private investigator September 6, but said that with no criminal charges pending against Hawkins, there was no possibility of detaining or arresting him. Still, Farmers was anxious to know where Columbus's newest millionaire was spending his time and their money.

Speaking to the reporters, Weinstein selected his words carefully. "If all the money is gone, it certainly makes the issue more interesting. Our philosophy is to recover the money," he said. "We're going to pursue Mr. Hawkins as vigorously as we can. If the money has been spent, we'll consider our options. We intend to get the money back."

About noon the next day, Wednesday, September 7, Priscilla Lee called Candisky with news that authorities in Los Angeles had searched Boggs's medical office. "How'd you find that out?" Candisky asked.

"Our court reporter stumbled on to it. It's about a week old."

"Who did it? Glendale cops?"

"No. It was an investigator with the . . . wait a minute, here, the state department of insurance."

"Terrific. What's it say? What were they looking for?"

"Oh, nothing great, I don't think. I didn't look at it that close. Medical records and stuff, I think. I can fax you a copy of the search warrant if you'll give me your fax number."

"Hold on a minute," Candisky cupped the receiver. "Run down to three and get the number for the fax machine in advertising," she told Yocum. "Priscilla's faxing us a copy of a search warrant for Boggs's office." Candisky went back to the phone. "It's going to take a minute, Priscilla. I know this is hard to believe, but we don't have a fax machine in the newsroom. Rob went down to get the number. So, I've been scanning the wire, but I didn't see anything on this. Have you run it yet?"

"No. We probably won't. Until they file charges, we probably won't write anything else. What happens if he never gets charged? He could sue us. Aren't you guys worried about that?"

"Not really. He's a public figure and a lot of what we've been writing has been public record—the lawsuit, police reports, autopsy, now the search warrant. He'd have a hard time suing us."

Yocum ran up the stairs, puffing, and gave Candisky the fax number. A copy of the search warrant arrived fifteen minutes later.

"When did they do the search?" Candisky asked.

"This says, Tuesday, August 30. But they were out snooping around the medical building the previous Friday."

"Monday. That was the day I tried to get a copy of the autopsy and the file was empty, remember? That's also when I called Boggs's office and they told me he was on vacation."

"I love this," Yocum said, "They let the thing sit for almost five months. Then, as soon as we call, they start falling all over themselves. I'll bet the Glendale cops didn't even know about the search warrant."

27

A few days earlier, on August 27, Yocum had received a call from Tim Martin, the man who had offered to set up an interview with Blizzard, Hawkins's girlfriend. It wouldn't be easy, Martin said from a phone at his job at the Columbus airport, since Hawkins had convinced Blizzard that the paper, for whatever reason, was printing blatant lies about him.

The meeting was arranged for eight o'clock on the evening of September 7. Martin had suggested the Chi-Chi's on Route 161, which he said was just a few blocks from Blizzard's apartment. The reporters munched on the restaurant's complimentary snacks while they waited for the couple to arrive.

Yocum scraped up the last of the hot salsa on a scrap of chip and popped it in his mouth. The final swallow of his first beer washed it down.

"Think she's going to show?" Candisky asked.

Yocum shrugged. "He said they'd be here at eight." The reporter looked at his watch. It was five after eight. "He'll show."

Both reporters wondered about Martin's motivation for arranging the interview. "I think he's got the hots for her and he wants someone else to tell her Hawkins is a liar and into this up to his ears," Yocum said.

"Makes sense," Candisky said. "Whatever the reason, we're biting."

Yocum pointed toward a woman in her late twenties with blonde hair that obviously got its fullness from a half a bottle of mousse. "How about her?"

Candisky shook her head. "Not Hawkins's type. too old."

The blonde walked to the bar and sat down with two friends. Yocum was 0 for 3 in finding Amy Blizzard among the happy hour crowd at Chi-Chi's Restaurant on Columbus's north side.

A young man casually dressed in a polo shirt and jeans walked up to the table. "Are you Robin and Cathy?"

The three found a quieter table and waited for Blizzard. Martin said she was running a few minutes late. "She's really uptight about talking to you guys. She's afraid of getting Hawkins in trouble. I don't know why, the guy treats her like dirt and she . . ." Martin rose from the table. "There she is."

Amy Blizzard was, as Candisky had predicted, a thin 24 year old with long blonde hair. She walked timidly toward the table, diverting her eyes so as to avoid looking at the reporters. She forced a smile as Martin pulled out a chair and ordered her a margarita.

"Tim said you're pretty nervous about talking to us," Yocum began. "You don't need to be. We've been writing these stories about John, but we haven't been able to talk to him, and we're relying on people like you and his mother to give us his side."

She nodded.

"A lot of people are saying a lot of bad things about John. We were hoping you could shed a little light on what he's really like and what he's going through right now."

Blizzard hesitated, glancing at Martin. "Go ahead," he told her.

"The articles don't show the good side of John. He did a lot of good for a lot of people," Blizzard said softly, selecting each word carefully. "He gave them jobs, money, but now no one has anything nice to say about him. I would like for people to see him through my eyes. Every article about him says he's guilty. I don't know whether he's guilty or not, that's for the courts to decide. I just want to say something nice about him. I think he's a nice guy or I wouldn't have stayed with him."

While Candisky asked Blizzard about her trip to California, Yocum jotted notes on a cocktail napkin, afraid the sight of a notebook would make her even more uneasy. "So, this was your first trip to L.A.?" Candisky asked, trying to draw Blizzard out.

She nodded.

"Where did you and John go when you were out there?" Candisky continued.

Blizzard looked at Martin again. "It's all right," Martin said, stroking her forearm. "Go ahead and tell them."

"Did you get to the beach?" Candisky suggested. "When I was there I went to Venice Beach. It's a pretty wild place."

Amy smiled. "John took me to Venice. We walked on the boardwalk and he worked out at Muscle Beach."

"Did you make it over to Hollywood?"

Blizzard sipped her margarita. "Uh-huh. We spent an afternoon walking around."

"Pretty disappointing isn't it?" Candisky said. "I thought it was really trashy."

Blizzard nodded. "It's not like you see in the movies." Appearing a bit more at ease, Blizzard confided that they spent a few days in Los Angeles, and one afternoon pricing boats. Hawkins, Blizzard said, was interested in starting a charter business. Her admission echoed DeSando's statement that Hawkins had wanted to be the captain of a booze cruise in Hawaii.

Hawkins suggested that he and Blizzard leave Los Angeles and drive up to San Francisco. They took their time, she said, following scenic Route 1 along the Pacific coast. They spent their first night on the road at a cheap motel in Santa Barbara. Blizzard said she paid for the motels and breakfast, and Hawkins paid for lunch and dinner. Despite his use of an alias, Hawkins didn't want to pay for the motels because he was trying to avoid signing his name.

The next day they drove to Carmel and spent the day at the beach. Unable to find a motel, they drove to nearby Big Sur and slept on the beach. Another night they slept in Hawkins's rental car.

During the trip, Blizzard said, Hawkins would stop at pay phones and make calls.

"To . . . ?" Yocum asked.

"I don't know."

"Didn't you ask?"

"I didn't think it was any of my business."

After one such call, en route to San Francisco, Hawkins told her that some damning stories about him were appearing in the *Dispatch*. He told her to call home to assure everyone that she was all right.

"So what did John have to say about those articles?" Yocum continued.

"He said they weren't true, but I think he was worried about them, because when we were in San Francisco he stopped at a couple of newsstands looking for copies of the *Dispatch*."

"He was looking for *The Columbus Dispatch* in San Francisco?" Yocum asked.

Blizzard's nod showed her embarrassment for her boyfriend.

"He didn't find one, did he?" Candisky asked.

"No."

Blizzard said she had seen a noticeable change in Hawkins. He was no longer the brash, carefree man she had known in Columbus. He had cut his hair short and was growing a beard. While he had once been free with his money, he was now quite frugal, as though he was keeping track of each penny. Blizzard said Hawkins didn't have a permanent address: he had been living out of three suitcases he toted around in a beat-up rental car.

"The insurance company said he left Columbus with a million dollars, but based on what you're telling us, it doesn't sound like he has nearly that much," Yocum said.

"He told me he had about $200,000, enough to live on for a little while," she said. "He said he sold the company for a million and a half, but had put most of it back into the company."

Yocum gave Candisky a smirk, which she returned with a beneath-the-table, "don't-piss-her-off" kick to his shin. Like most of his friends, Blizzard never questioned Hawkins.

"Tell them about the accident," Martin urged.

"Well, we were driving around Los Angeles and we got sideswiped by a bus on Hollywood Boulevard. It wasn't bad, but I got out of the car and said I was going to call the police, and John took off."

"He drove off and left you?" Yocum's tone revealed his disbelief.

"Yes. He drove around the block or something. I mean, he wasn't gone a real long time. He came back a little bit later and yelled for me to get in the car. He didn't want the police," she answered, defensively.

"Don't you think that was a little odd?" Yocum asked.

Blizzard shrugged. "I don't know, maybe. He's always been good to me and I figured he had his reasons."

"What reasons could he possibly have for leaving you on the street in Los Angeles?" Yocum asked.

"I don't know," she snapped.

Yocum backed off, not wanting to anger her further.

A waiter set down a round of drinks, and Candisky used the break to sway Blizzard to an easier topic. "So, how long have you known John? From what you've said, you two must be pretty tight."

Blizzard said she had met Hawkins in April 1987 at The Continent, a north-side commercial-residential complex where Hawkins had a condominium. They had dated on and off ever since. Hawkins had been generous, showering her with clothes and jewelry, including a pair of diamond earrings. She conceded that the relationship had always been on Hawkins's terms. He continued to date other women, but Blizzard always made herself available when he called. "John is a 'me' person and I accept that," she said. Blizzard's only demand was that Hawkins be tested for AIDS. She made him take the test because Hawkins had lived in New York and had numerous sex partners.

Late on July 15, 1988, the night before Hawkins fled from Columbus, Blizzard found a message from Hawkins on her telephone answering machine. He said he was leaving town the next day and wanted to see her. "He begged me to come over," she said. Blizzard said she had been out on a date that night and didn't get home until early the next morning. When she heard the message she immediately drove to Hawkins's Ellerdale Drive condominium. "He told me he had sold Just Sweats. He said he just couldn't take the pressure any more. He said he had to leave," Blizzard recalled. "I believed him. It sounded like something John would do, and I had no reason to think he was lying. But he was real emotional and upset about leaving that night. The next morning he got into his Mercedes and said, 'I'll see you in a year.' "

"And you didn't see him again until last week?" Candisky asked.

"Yeah. The night before he left he told me he probably wasn't coming back to Columbus and he wanted to meet me in another city, but he didn't say where. A week or so later he called me a couple of times to come out to the West Coast, but I wasn't able to get away from work. He said he was really lonely and he missed me. But, I . . . I didn't know if I wanted to see John anymore. When I finally told him I'd come, he sent me a plane ticket a week later."

Blizzard left for Los Angeles on August 23, the same day Farmers filed suit against Hawkins.

Yocum was having a hard time understanding why Blizzard would continue to see Hawkins: it seemed obvious she wasn't that important to him. She rationalized much of what he was doing; what she couldn't explain, she ignored. Candisky understood perfectly.

Blizzard was in love, mesmerized by the powerful charms Hawkins's mother had described. When they were together, Hawkins made Blizzard feel as if she was the most important person in his life. Her life began and ended with John Hawkins and his sporadic displays of affection. Despite repeated warnings from her friends and family that Hawkins was incapable of being loyal, Blizzard clung to her passion. Her instincts told her that he would break her heart, yet she desperately hoped that someday he would change and settle down.

"I went to California because he wanted someone to be with, someone he could trust and talk to. I thought he needed me," Blizzard said.

"When you care for someone and think they need you, what are you going to do?

"He was depressed in California. He hid it a lot, but every once in a while you could tell. He told me that I would see stories about him in the paper when I got back, but not to believe them."

Candisky wanted to know if he had told her about the lawsuit.

"No. He told me there were some questions about Gene's death, but that it was okay because his roommate and his attorney had identified Gene's body."

"But Amy," Yocum said. "Erik DeSando and Austin Wildman were here when Gene died. They weren't in L.A."

"All I know is what John told me."

"Amy, does John realize he's in a lot of trouble?" Yocum asked.

Blizzard looked into her lap for several seconds, then finally nodded. "He's not absolutely innocent, but he's not as guilty as everyone thinks he is. If someone gave you a million dollars, you might question how you got it, but you still might take it."

"Are you trying to tell us that John didn't kill anyone?" Candisky asked.

"No. He didn't kill anyone. He didn't have anything to do with that man's death."

"What man?" Yocum asked.

"I really don't know any more about it. But I'll tell you one thing. He said he'd kill himself before he goes to prison. He couldn't handle prison. He's such a free spirit, he just couldn't handle prison. He wouldn't survive in there."

Blizzard and Hawkins had talked about prison when they toured Alcatraz Island while in San Francisco. Blizzard said Hawkins stood looking up at one of the prison walls and vowed: "I'd never go to prison. I'd kill myself first."

"He talked about faking his death. He was thinking if he rented a helicopter he could go up and jump out with a parachute. Then he would be listed as missing at sea and no one would be looking for him."

"He said he wants to fake his own death? Who's the beneficiary of his insurance policy?" Candisky asked.

"I don't know, but I know what you're thinking and you're wrong. He's just scared."

"Tell them about Mexico," Martin said. He turned to the reporters. "He wanted her to bring a passport with her to California."

"Is he going to leave the country?" Yocum asked.

"He wanted to go to Mexico, but I wouldn't go."

Blizzard said Hawkins was trying to obtain several sets of identification and had developed a scam to obtain them. He would run a newspaper ad that said he could get credit cards for people with bad credit. When people called, Hawkins would take down their names, social security numbers, and birth dates. He had gathered about fifty different names and he planned to use them as aliases.

"Does he seem to be holding up under the pressure?" Yocum asked.

"Kind of, but John wasn't acting like himself and he said a lot of strange things. He kept asking me to marry him, but I never gave him an answer. Then he kept telling strangers that we were going to get married. That isn't like John at all. And he was really upset with Erik DeSando. He knew Erik had been talking to you guys and John said if he was any kind of friend he'd keep his big mouth shut."

"John told his mom that he was checking into some sort of clinic for stress. Did he mention that to you?" Candisky asked.

"No. He didn't say anything about that, and I don't think he did."

But, Blizzard admitted, she was getting scared and told Hawkins she wanted to fly home from San Francisco.

"What were you scared of?" Candisky asked.

"John was acting strange and he obviously wasn't telling me everything. I didn't understand what was going on and I didn't want to embarrass my family."

Blizzard said her return ticket was nontransferable, so she agreed to wait until they returned to Los Angeles.

After traveling up and down the coast, Blizzard was nearly out of money. She said that they spent her last night in California in an Inglewood motel, where this time Hawkins checked in under the name Jerry Anthony Green, the brother of a boyhood friend. Blizzard said she left the next day, August 29, a few days earlier than planned. As she boarded her flight, Hawkins told her he would be leaving Los Angeles the next day. He didn't say where he was going, and Blizzard didn't ask. Hawkins merely told her that he would be in touch.

"Why'd you leave early?" Yocum asked.

"I felt something was weird; I thought I better leave," Blizzard recalled. "He was acting funny, acting different. It kind of scared me." Blizzard pulled the sleeves of her sweater over her hands and hunched over at the shoulders. "He's lost a lot of confidence. He used to tell me he was a genius, but when I was out there, he said it doesn't take a genius to open a clothing store. He does things without thinking of the consequences. He used to go to high schools and give talks to classes about his business. Now, he's worried about what those kids are thinking of him. He had the world at his feet."

28

Late the next afternoon, September 8, Yocum and Candisky were giving the final read to a story based on their interview with Blizzard. Across the newsroom, a reporter held up a telephone. "Which one of you guys wants to take this?" Candisky grabbed the receiver.

The caller identified himself as Mike Merritt, Amy Blizzard's roommate. It was urgent that he and Blizzard meet with the reporters. Blizzard, he said, was very upset over a message left on her telephone answering machine, and the story Yocum and Candisky were planning could put her life in danger.

"In danger? What do you mean?" Candisky gave Yocum the "wait-one-minute" signal with her index finger.

"Hawkins is back in town and he's been involved in seven murders. Amy's afraid he's going to kill her for talking to you guys."

"Seven murders!" Candisky exclaimed. She quickly grabbed a pen. "Okay, we can meet you tonight. When and where?" She scribbled down the information, but before she could ask for more details, the buzz of a dial tone ended the conversation.

Yocum dropped into a nearby chair. "What?"

"That was Amy's roommate. He said John's killed seven people."

In the early evening on September 8, Yocum and Candisky drove up I-71 toward the Burger King on Route 161. "Why are we doing this?" Yocum asked. "You know, I know, the world knows John Hawkins didn't kill seven men."

"I know. But . . . Merritt—is that his name?—Merritt's obviously a screwball, but we better humor him if we don't want to alienate Amy."

"True. Maybe she believes anything anyone tells her about Hawkins. Who knows, maybe she'll 'fess up to something new."

They pulled into the Burger King parking lot at eight-thirty. Blizzard and her roommate were already seated at a booth. He was short and slender, in his early twenties, with blond hair cut short on the sides but bushy on top. Blizzard took a nervous drag on her cigarette. Already, four butts crowded the aluminum ashtray on the table. When the reporters sat down, Blizzard said nothing. She let Merritt do the talking.

"Like I told you on the phone, John's back in town and he's killed seven people," Merritt said dramatically.

"What? Who told you that?" Yocum asked.

"It's true. There was a message on our answering machine from Erik DeSando. He said John's back in the area and he's responsible for the deaths of seven men. Erik was warning us."

"For all the oddball things we've heard about Hawkins, his being a homicidal maniac was not one of them," Candisky said. "Have you talked to Erik?"

"No. We tried, but his phone's been disconnected. Do you know how to get in touch with him?" Merritt asked.

"Well, I know his dad. Maybe I can give him a call," Yocum said. He went outside to a pay phone and first tried the number he and Candisky had for DeSando. It had been disconnected. DeSando's father taught at Franklin University, where Yocum was an adjunct journalism instructor. The university operator gave Yocum John DeSando's home number in Delaware, Ohio. The professor answered on the third ring.

"John, this is Robin Yocum. I'm sorry to bother you at home, but I'm trying to find Erik and his phone's been disconnected. Do you have a new number for him?"

"No. He's moving and I don't think he has a new one yet. What's up?"

Yocum took a deep breath. "Well, it's a little hard to explain, John. But Erik left a message with one of Hawkins's girlfriends that supposedly said—and I'm only telling you what she told me—that John is back in the area and he's killed seven men."

DeSando laughed for several minutes before he finally regained his composure. "I guess I need to have another talk with Erik. Killed seven men, huh? If I hear from him, I'll have him give you a call."

Inside the restaurant Candisky was trying to calm Blizzard's fears about the next day's newspaper story. Blizzard believed Hawkins would be angry with her for talking to reporters. Candisky reassured her that the story was going to be one of the few the reporters had written that would cast him in a good light. Somewhat relieved, Blizzard asked Yocum for the senior DeSando's telephone number. Yocum, who knew he had to face DeSando before their respective eight o'clock classes the next morning, reluctantly gave her the number and a quarter to make the call.

While Blizzard made the call, Merritt took advantage of his private audience with the reporters. He explained that Amy knew a lot more about Hawkins than she had let on, but, like Martin, Merritt was very protective of Blizzard.

"John's a son of a bitch and he's using Amy. She knows he's fucked up and in a lot of trouble, but she won't admit it. Don't tell her I told you this, but she said John had a book in California on how to change your name, and he's using three different aliases. He used Amy's name to send some stuff Federal Express." He took a long and overly dramatic draw on his cigarette. "He also told Amy that his family has ties with the mob and drug dealing."

"How do you know all this?" Yocum asked.

"She told me everything when she got back. She trusts me."

Blizzard returned acting much calmer. John DeSando had assured her that, in all probability, John hadn't killed seven men and wasn't going to kill her, either. Yocum suggested that they all go next door to Victoria Station, thinking a few drinks might settle Blizzard's nerves.

The four grabbed a booth and suddenly it was Blizzard who dominated the conversation. Yocum and Candisky had seen it happen before. They had interviewed people, crime victims or grieving relatives, who were reluctant to talk at first, but found themselves somehow relieved afterward. The reporters' interview worked as a kind of therapy session. Blizzard was apparently beginning to have her doubts about Hawkins.

"You said you talked to John's mom, right?" she asked Candisky.

"When I was out in Vegas I spent about six hours with her."

"What did you think about her?"

"She's crazy about John."

Blizzard smirked. "Do you think that relationship is unusual for a mother-son relationship?"

Candisky again recalled the statue of the embracing nudes. "Maybe a little," Candisky teased, hoping Blizzard would respond. "Why?"

"Oh, nothing, I just thought it was sort of a strange relationship. He told me once he really liked my body because it reminded him of his mother's." Blizzard waited for the reporters to react. "Don't you think that's strange? A couple of times they'd be talking on the phone and he'd say, 'I love you.' Not like you tell your mom 'I love you.' But he said . . ." Blizzard dropped her voice to a seductive whisper. " 'I love you.' "

With Blizzard speaking more freely, Yocum dared to broach a topic that had been bothering him. "A lot of people have been telling us John is bisexual. Do you . . ."

"John! No way," Blizzard interrupted. "That's one thing I can be sure about. If you ever met John you'd know he wasn't gay." She turned to her roommate, as if to prove her point. "Everyone thinks Mike is gay, but he isn't."

Yocum and Candisky instinctively looked at Merritt for some kind of response. He happily obliged them. "If people ask me if I'm gay, I say, 'No, I'm straight.' If they ask me if I'm straight, I say, 'No, I'm gay,'" Merritt said, running his fingers through his blond hair. "My family always thought I was gay. And some people wonder about me and Amy, but we're just roommates. We're friends. We both worked at Max & Erma's together."

Merritt ground out his cigarette and headed for the restroom. When he got around the corner, he motioned for Yocum to follow. Although Yocum was still trying to decipher Merritt's proclamation of sexual preference, the reporter reluctantly followed. "I've got to tell you something," Merritt said as he edged up to the urinal. "But you can't tell anyone, not Cathy, not anyone, okay?" Merritt's conspiratorial tone reasserted the overly dramatic nature he had displayed earlier on the phone. Before Yocum could agree to the conditions, Merritt blurted out, "Amy thinks she's pregnant with John's baby. She's late on her period."

Yocum doubted Blizzard was pregnant, but he didn't want to stand in a public john debating the possibility, either. Yocum said he hoped Amy wasn't pregnant and started out of the restroom.

"Don't tell her I told you," Merritt said.

"Count on it."

The next day, Yocum called DeSando after getting his new number from his father. "Erik, why did you tell Amy that John had killed seven guys?"

DeSando laughed. "It was a joke," he said. "I didn't think she'd go vertical. That's pretty funny but, you know, I did hear John was back in the area."

"Who told you that? Where's he at?" Yocum asked.

"I can't tell you who told me. But he's staying somewhere down by Lancaster, Ohio. He's living with a bunch of gay guys, male strippers. All I know is one guy is named Tom Thunder and one is named Dallas.

I'm sure John's poking all of them. Track them down, one of 'em will squeal."

Yocum hung up and turned to Candisky. "Erik says John's living in Lancaster with a bunch of male strippers. You'll love these names—Tom Thunder and Dallas."

"Dallas?" she asked, blushing. She searched through her desk and pulled out a package of recently developed photographs. She handed Yocum a shot of a muscular blond clad in a black jockstrap. "I think this is Dallas."

Yocum was chuckling. "And how, dare I ask, do you know Dallas?"

She snatched the photograph from him. "We hired a stripper for a friend's bachelorette party and he showed up. I just remember the name because it was so unusual."

The company that had sent Dallas to the party would provide just about anything to entertain a crowd or to embarrass a co-worker—belly dancers, singing gorillas, balloons, strippers. Candisky called the company. Dallas was working and told Candisky that he didn't know Hawkins. However, he did know Tom Thunder.

"Could you give me his address?" she asked.

"No. Sorry. I can't do that."

Candisky hung up the phone and turned to Yocum. "His name is Tom Thunder, but I don't have an address or phone."

"Let's look in the phone book," Yocum suggested.

Candisky grimaced. "I really doubt we're going to find Tom Thunder in the phone book. I mean . . ." The name jumped off the page. "Tommy Thunder, here it is. Unbelievable. Let's hit it."

The phone-book address led them to a narrow, tree-lined street on Columbus's far north side. The homes were modest and the lawns were neat, except for one, which was adorned with beer cans and a black Camaro. "Nice parking job," Yocum said, stepping around the automobile to the front porch. He rapped on the screen door. The two reporters heard heavy footsteps pounding through the house. An obese woman with frizzy, flaming-red hair appeared in the door. "Yeah?"

"We're looking for Tom Thunder," Yocum said.

She gave the two a half sneer and turned away, screaming, "Tim, it's for you."

In a minute a man with bleached blond-and-black streaked hair came to the door. His large belly spilled over the red bikini swimsuit he was wearing.

"Are you Tom Thunder?" Candisky asked.

"No, I'm Tim Thunder."

"We're reporters from the *Dispatch*. We've been working on the Just Sweats case and we were told a Tom Thunder was a friend of John Hawkins."

"Well, Tom Thunder is my stage name. I'm in a rock band."

"We heard you knew John Hawkins." Candisky said.

Thunder shrieked. "No! I'll die. You heard I knew him? That's so wild."

"We'd been told that he was staying with some friends who were dancers. Do you dance?" she asked.

"Yes. Well, not much, but once in a while."

"But you don't know John Hawkins?"

"I wish I did. The stories I could tell."

29

The Tom Thunder lead had fizzled. Either Thunder truly didn't know Hawkins, or, if he did, he wasn't telling.

DeSando's story was just bizarre enough to be believable: John Hawkins was staying with male strippers in Lancaster, a city about twenty miles southeast of Columbus. Perhaps he wanted to send messages to some of his friends, like telling DeSando to shut up. However, Hawkins had no rational reason to come back to the area. His friends were afraid to be seen with him. There was no way he could regain control of Just Sweats. Although no formal charges had been filed against him, that nasty business with the insurance money had not been cleared up. But then, John Hawkins had never been famous for rational thought.

During a telephone interview the morning of September 9, DeSando told Candisky, "The last time I talked to John I warned him not to come back, and I haven't heard from him since I was in Vegas. He told me he thought it would be funny if he just showed up at the Elephant Bar or the R 'n' R, but I don't think he'd be that stupid."

"Look, Erik, if you hear anything, give us a yell, okay?"

"I will, but you can't tell anyone I'm talking to you anymore. My attorney says I'm not supposed to talk to you guys anymore."

"Since when do you have an attorney?"

"My dad thought it would be a good idea. He's afraid I'm going to take some heat for this . . . he's probably right. He said the smartest thing I can do is cooperate with the Feds."

"Feds? What Feds?"

"The FBI."

"Since when? We've checked with the FBI and they said they aren't doing anything with this."

"Then they lied."

DeSando, Candisky had learned, liked to be coaxed into sharing his information. He never hesitated to tell what he knew, but he seemed to enjoy dangling the carrot for a while—a moment, two at best.

"I'll bite, Erik, what did they lie about?"

"They're investigating this thing. I don't know how they got involved, but they're looking into it. My attorney gave them this letter from the guy Oleg who's been running around with John."

"Oleg? Oleg who?"

"Mendyuk."

"What? Erik! How did all this come about?" Candisky asked.

DeSando paused, as if weighing how much to tell the reporter. "It's kind of hard to explain, but it involves this Russian chick named Nelly, who is a cheerleader for Ohio State," DeSando explained.

"Erik?"

"No, I'm serious."

"A Russian lady named Nelly?"

"Right."

Candisky laughed. "Do you think she's KGB?"

"I know it sounds weird."

"Let's hear it."

DeSando said he was sitting alone at the Elephant Bar one night, nursing a drink and wishing he had never heard of John B. Hawkins. The *Dispatch* stories about his association with Hawkins had caused a lot of people to question DeSando's sexual preference. Some old friends simply didn't want to get near him for fear of being connected to the insurance scam. Others merely stared and whispered, "That guy was John Hawkins's roommate." DeSando had become tired of the unwanted attention and was about ready to go home. As he was ready to leave his stool, an attractive woman in her twenties sat down next to him. She introduced herself as Nelly Mendyuk, speaking with an accent that DeSando thought might be Russian. The two began talking. Mendyuk said she was in medical school at Ohio State University. Their conversation drifted toward Ohio State football and Coach Earle Bruce. Mendyuk claimed to be a cheerleader and said she didn't care for Coach Bruce because he referred to the cheerleaders as the Whore Corps. "He even spies on us," she said.

"Yeah, I know how that feels," DeSando agreed.

"What do you mean?"

DeSando told Mendyuk that he had been questioned by investigators because he used to be John Hawkins's roommate. To DeSando's surprise, Mendyuk said she knew Hawkins; her brother Oleg was his lover.

"Right!" DeSando said, rolling his eyes.

"It's true," she insisted. "He's with John right now."

DeSando leaned closer. "You know John?"

"Yes."

"Okay, here's a little test to see if you're telling the truth. How many straws does John put in his drinks?"

She didn't blink. "Six." Right. Hawkins always put six swizzle sticks in his drinks because he thought it brought him good luck. "I have a letter from my brother that will prove I'm not lying."

DeSando's attorney told the FBI about the conversation and the letter, and they asked DeSando to set up a meeting with Mendyuk. The two met at the Denny's Restaurant on Route 161, a few miles from the Elephant Bar. She showed him the typed, unsigned letter that read:

Dear Sis!

Hi! How are you? I'm to the point where I don't exactly know how I feel and that's why I'm writing you this sad letter.

I know that you are probably disgusted with me at this point and I don't blame you. John and I are scared to death because it looks like everything is blowing up in our faces. It wasn't supposed to [be] like this. Nel, he asked me to get him a simple birth certificate and a death certificate so he can get a lot of money and we can leave Columbus and be together. I believed him because I love him and he [loves] me. But things went wrong. John did some awful things as you can already imagine and now I don't know what to do. The doctor and John killed that guy behind my back and now I'm in the middle and there is no way out. God I feel like a criminal and I'm not. I'm just an idiot that fell in love with a man that I shouldn't have trusted.

If you talk to John or anything do not mention this letter please. He might hurt me. Pray for me, I need it.

P.S. We'll be leaving the country soon I hope, but I'll write again. Love you a lot.

Mendyuk said her brother had worked in a funeral home and had access to birth and death certificates, which Hawkins needed to change his identity. DeSando said Mendyuk told him she feared for her brother's life. Hawkins also had a $1.5 million life insurance policy: if he had killed once, he wouldn't hesitate to kill again. Oleg Mendyuk might end up being the next corpse.

Nelly Mendyuk had not considered that scenario. She panicked and began telling DeSando all she knew about Hawkins and his relationship with her brother. Mendyuk claimed she had traveled to Atlantic City a few weeks earlier to meet them. Hawkins had been carrying the insurance proceeds, which he was converting into gambling chips and placing in a safe-deposit box. She also repeated a story that had been circulating about how Hawkins, dressed as a mailman, personally delivered a $100,000 payoff to Boggs at his Glendale office. Mendyuk said she had heard the story from her brother.

DeSando didn't believe Mendyuk until she produced a photograph of her brother. Then DeSando admitted recognizing Oleg Mendyuk as the same man who had been with Hawkins at their apartment the morning he left Columbus.

Yocum had been reading over Candisky's shoulder as she talked to DeSando and typed her notes into the computer. He ran down to the sports department on the fourth floor to find an Ohio State football program that contained a photograph of the cheerleading squad. "There is no cheerleader named Nelly Mendyuk," he said, handing Candisky the program. "Besides, what would a med student be doing cheerleading?"

Candisky called the student registration office at Ohio State and found Mendyuk registered as a freshman. "Do you think any of this is worth checking out?" she asked.

"It's just what this story needs, a good communist-bloc connection." Yocum scanned her notes again. "I don't know. It all sounds too bizarre, but I'd hate to ignore it and get burned. I think we have to follow it."

Yocum had a friend at the police department who obligingly ran a driver's license check on DeSando's female friend. The trace yielded one Nelly Mendyuk, who had an east-side address. The reporters drove out that afternoon but found no one at home. They left their business cards and a note asking Mendyuk to call them. When they returned the next day, the reporters could hear someone inside, but no one would answer the door. Yocum and Candisky made one more trip, but again no one was home.

Yocum called a source at the FBI who, as DeSando had said, confirmed that the agency was looking into the case. However, like the reporters, the source didn't put much stock in Nelly Mendyuk's wild tale. Agents found Oleg Mendyuk living in Columbus, and Yocum interviewed him by telephone.

"I've never met John Hawkins," said Oleg. "I'd never even heard of his name until I read it in the newspaper. You wouldn't believe all the trouble I went through over this. The FBI was out here. They told me I was gay, they said that I liked little boys. They told me I was Hawkins's lover. It's embarrassing. I've tried to forget the whole thing. I just want to pay my taxes and be left alone.

"The FBI agents, I think, hoped that I could lead them to Hawkins. The letter is bogus and no doubt the work of my sister's vivid imagination. Nelly likes to imagine things. I don't know why she does these things. She was probably trying to get this guy to like her."

30

The reporters' long, exasperating Friday was finally drawing to an end. After retreating from the futile Nelly Mendyuk story, Candisky and Yocum had spent most of the afternoon making telephone calls, but they had failed to produce a single lead. The reporters were preparing to use their "get-out-of-jail-free" card: a story on the prosecutor's promise to take the allegations of embezzlement to a Franklin County grand jury. It would be a throwaway, a story that really didn't say much. But they rationalized that after more than two weeks of hammering on the Just Sweats case, a freebee was overdue. They had sat on the grand jury story for days, waiting to use it when they couldn't find anything better. Today they had drawn a blank; today they would tap their reserves.

Candisky called James Lanfear, a Columbus police detective in the organized crime squad. She had first contacted him a week or so earlier to see if the organized crime squad was involved in the case. Lanfear told Candisky that Farmers had solicited the help of a Columbus private investigator, Vince Volpi, to find Hawkins. Another man, whom Lanfear described as a "free-lance bounty hunter," also was looking for Hawkins in hope of a reward for his capture. Beyond that, there was nothing new on the case. His department hadn't heard anything new about Hanson since the drug investigation in early 1988.

"Excuse me," Candisky said. "What drug investigation?"

"Oh, we had Hanson and his boyfriend Dr. Boggs under investigation for selling a growth hormone. Protropin, it was called. It was supposed to be some underground treatment for AIDS. You two didn't know about that?"

The reporters remembered they had heard rumors of Hanson running drugs that he obtained through prescriptions from Boggs. Perhaps the two were peddling a bogus AIDS treatment. Perhaps Hanson really had AIDS?

Candisky wrote "Protropin? AIDS treatment?" on a sheet of legal pad and passed it to Yocum, who ran to the *Dispatch* library to research the drug. He made a call to Children's Hospital and found a doctor who was familiar with Protropin. The physician said Protropin is an injectable drug that promotes bone growth and is most frequently used on children who suffer from a growth-hormone deficiency. Treatments of three to four injections a week for one year can cost up to $12,000. The drug is popular among athletes trying to delay the aging process. Also, AIDS victims use it in the belief that it can fight the HIV virus. Prescribing Protropin to adults is illegal; an injection off the streets could cost up to $500.

Lanfear said Boggs had written prescriptions for the drug in the name of Hanson's nephew, a minor. For unknown reasons, Hanson traveled from Columbus to Dallas to have at least one prescription filled. Another was filled in Glendale. Acting on a tip, detectives began investigating the allegations in June, believing Hanson was still living in Columbus. After learning Hanson had died April 16 in Boggs's California office, detectives contacted the Glendale police and told them to check autopsy results for traces of the drug.

"Did they find anything?" Candisky asked.

"Evidently not. I never heard back from them," Lanfear said.

"So, what happened to your investigation?"

"When they told us Hanson was dead, it didn't seem like time well spent to continue investigating when it would be extremely difficult to get a conviction on a dead guy."

"What about now?"

"Well, if this Hanson is alive, it seems to me that he has bigger problems than filling illegal prescriptions."

On Monday, September 12, Assistant Prosecutor Robert Smith told Yocum and Candisky that he was hoping to present evidence in the Just Sweats insurance scam to a grand jury within two weeks.

Smith said authorities investigating the case were relying on a time-consuming document search to gather evidence, since neither Hawkins nor Hanson was around to answer any questions. "Obviously we'd like to talk to them, but frankly, neither of them has shown any inclination of coming forward," Smith said, "and I'm not that hard to find."

Later that day, Yocum and Candisky received a call from a woman who said she was a former girlfriend of John Hawkins. She wanted to talk. The reporters arranged to meet her in a fast-food restaurant on Bethel Road on the northwest side of Columbus. She was quite direct. "What do you want to know about John?" asked Linnette Woda, a lean woman in her early twenties, with sandy-brown hair. "I hope they catch him and I hope he gets what's coming to him. He's hurt a lot of people."

Woda didn't hide her hatred for Hawkins. She explained that Hawkins had hired Woda and her then-boyfriend, Dan Norris, away from Agler-Davidson, a competitor just up High Street, and employed them at the Just Sweats store near campus. Shortly after she began working at the store, Hawkins began asking her out. Three weeks later, Hawkins promoted her to store manager. His interest in her resulted in an uncomfortable working relationship, but eventually, Woda said, she broke up with Norris to begin dating Hawkins.

Hawkins had once suggested that she increase the number of dependents on her W-2 form to save taxes. "He told me to say that I was a single mother with seven dependents." Woda felt that what she had read in the newspapers only confirmed her opinions about Hawkins.

"I don't have any trouble believing John was involved in something like this," Woda said. "There were only three things that were important to John—himself, women, and money."

Woda recalled talking to Hanson about insurance after she had been involved in a minor car accident. Hanson tried to convince her that she should exaggerate her claim. "You can get thousands out of them," Hanson told her. "He got really stressed out when I wouldn't do it," she told the reporters.

Woda said she wasn't interested in being the focus of a story, but she put the reporters on to two people who wouldn't mind talking. One was Norris, who had quit the company, but could give the reporters a lot of insight into it. The other was Tim Green, a childhood friend of Hawkins. The two had grown up together in St. Louis, and their mothers remained close friends.

Yocum telephoned Dan Norris's office, but he was out. Yocum asked a secretary to have him return the call. "What company are you with, sir?" the secretary asked.

"Oh, it's personal," Yocum said, hoping to avoid drawing any undue attention to Norris at work.

Yocum had no trouble reaching Tim Green and the two spent almost an hour on the phone talking about Hawkins. The 23-year-old Green said he had lived in Columbus with Hawkins for a while and worked briefly for Just Sweats. He last heard from Hawkins in July 1988 when he called to ask for a favor. After spending a few minutes catching up on each other's families, Hawkins asked to borrow Green's driver's license, social security number, and a credit card.

"I said, 'John, what do you need this stuff for?' and he said something about renting a safety-deposit box. Then he told me, 'There's a possibility I'm in a lot of trouble,' " Green told Yocum.

"Did you give the stuff to him?" Yocum asked.

"No. I told him I was sorry, but he was getting a little out of my league," Green admitted. "I'd help him under normal circumstances— he's my best friend in the world—but this was too scary. He was acting too weird."

"Scary? What did he say when you told him 'no'?"

"He blew up. I told him, 'I don't know what kind of trouble you're in, but I can't get involved. I'm not sending you my ID' He got mad at me. He acted hurt, but a true friend wouldn't have asked me to do that."

"Did John say anything about the trouble he was in?"

"Not really," Green said. "But I'm sure he realizes the magnitude of this. I'm sure he'll grow a beard and be on the run the rest of his life. It seems like this time he went too far."

31

The silent partner in Hawkins's sweat-suit empire finally tossed in the towel.

In a brief, mid-September communication to Richard L. Innis, the Columbus attorney he had retained, Michael Guglielmelli surrendered his 10 percent of Just Sweats stock in an effort to disassociate himself from the company, John Hawkins, and Melvin Hanson. The letter stated, in part, "The stock seems worthless. Certainly the bankruptcy is a further source of embarrassment. Please tender it back to the corporation." He signed his directive, "A sadder but much wiser Michael Guglielmelli."

The stockholder, who had never been involved in the daily operation of Just Sweats, was at his office when Yocum called. Guglielmelli appeared eager to put his relationship with Hawkins and Hanson behind him, but agreed to explain his involvement with the men. His only direct contact with the company occurred when he flew to Columbus in July to file a police report after Hawkins had skipped town with $220,000. Guglielmelli now felt only acute embarrassment at his sudden notoriety, for his association with two men he now considered con artists, and at his loss of a $50,000 investment.

"I truly feel that my professional judgment and reputation are tarnished," Guglielmelli said. "I am abashed at being so easily hoodwinked in an industry were I am supposed to be knowledgeable. I feel it would be best to take my lumps and try to repair my career without further association with HHG Inc." (HHG, Hawkins, Hanson & Guglielmelli, was the parent company of Just Sweats.)

In a September 15 interview, Yocum told Guglielmelli that Cirian was claiming that she had used an intermediary to pay Guglielmelli $60,000 to buy back his stock: "Hawkins's mother told my partner that she delivered the money to a Las Vegas attorney who wired it to you."

The claim amused Guglielmelli. "Well, she may very well have delivered the money to the attorney, but rest assured I did not get a dime of it."

Yocum and Candisky wondered who was telling the truth. If Guglielmelli had received $60,000 for the stock, Yocum reasoned, why bother with the letter and disassociating himself from Just Sweats? Candisky didn't believe Cirian had lied. "I just think she was telling the truth. Why would she make up something like that?"

Perhaps Cirian had delivered the money to the Las Vegas attorney believing he would send it to Guglielmelli, but Hawkins had instructed the attorney to do otherwise. Yocum opened the Just Sweats computer file and entered a note reminding the reporters to track down the $60,000. Cirian would no longer be of help. For several days she had refused to return the reporters' telephone calls. DeSando said she had received the articles Candisky had sent and felt she had been betrayed.

Now, Dan Norris could laugh.

Linnette Woda's sometimes-boyfriend returned Yocum's phone call the morning of Friday, September 16, and said he would be delighted to talk to the reporters. John Hawkins was going to get his due at last. Norris could finally find some humor in losing both his job and his girlfriend, courtesy of John Hawkins.

Candisky and Yocum met Norris in his northside office. Since leaving Just Sweats two years earlier, he had now become successful in a job selling promotional gadgets—keychains, pens, mugs.

"Linnette tells us there's no love lost between you and John," Candisky said.

"I think that's pretty accurate," Norris agreed, grinning. "He stole my girlfriend. That doesn't particularly endear someone to you. All this stuff that's come out on him in the papers doesn't surprise me in the least. And, frankly, I'm rather enjoying it."

Hawkins had hired Norris, an assistant manager at Agler-Davidson, in 1986. Norris said he had felt stymied at Agler-Davidson, an established store with established practices, and Hawkins had offered him a chance to manage the campus store with a free hand. A week later, Hawkins hired Woda and assigned her to work in the campus store also.

Hawkins became immediately infatuated with Woda, an attractive, brown-eyed dance major at Ohio State. He pestered Woda to dump Norris, but she rebuffed Hawkins's advances. In a thinly disguised plan to get Norris out of the way, Hawkins sent him to Kentucky for a week to, in Norris's words, "learn to fold sweat-suits."

"You mean to learn the business, or how to run it?" Yocum asked.

"No," Norris replied. "To learn to fold sweat-suits. He said he wanted them folded a certain way, and he wanted me to spend some time down there learning how to do it."

"Did he pay for your expenses?"

"Everything."

Norris majored in business at Ohio State and Hawkins's scattershot method of running a business drove him crazy. "That company is a gold mine," Norris said. "The guy had a great idea, but he didn't have the discipline to follow it through. Someone's going to take that business and make a fortune." Hawkins only kept records of daily sales. He maintained no financial records and filed his list of suppliers only in his head. He hadn't filed an income tax return for two years. Norris said he tried several times to organize the business, but Hawkins continually refused, satisfied with the way things were running.

Norris believed Hawkins's problem was simple; he couldn't keep his mind off women long enough to concentrate on the business. One evening before an audit, Norris recalled, he and Hawkins planned to spend the entire night taking inventory at the campus store. As they worked, Hawkins couldn't stop staring out the window at the passing co-eds. "He says, 'Oh God, the women are out tonight. I can't stand it. Dan, you finish up.' And he dashes out the door, leaving me to pull an all-nighter counting sweat-suits. He was clueless. He liked the idea of being president of a company, and he liked the perks that came with it, but he lacked any discipline. He treated Just Sweats more like a toy than a business. He'd disappear for weeks at a time. It was like he got bored. And I'll tell you something: the entire time I worked for him, I never saw him take the blame for anything. It was always someone else's fault."

"For example?" Candisky asked.

"I'll give you a good one. The company started losing money, and rather than look at the possibility that it was mismanaged, he thinks his employees are stealing from him and makes them all take polygraphs. He was the only one stealing from the company."

Norris said his relationship with Hawkins disintegrated shortly after he and Woda broke up. Hawkins had wooed Woda for months, and she finally broke up with Norris to date him. The day after Woda agreed to go out with Hawkins, Norris said he received a scathing, impromptu evaluation from Hawkins, an obvious attempt at convincing Norris to bow out. By this time, Norris was happy to oblige, and he

resigned a few days later. Norris admitted to feeling a certain amount of satisfaction a few months later when Hawkins broke up with Woda, telling her, "You're just too nice."

As for the insurance scheme, Norris was convinced that Hanson and Hawkins began planning it years ago. Norris recalled that one day at work in 1986 Hanson said he would never buy life insurance because he would never benefit from it. Yet, in September of the same year, Hanson bought his first policy for $450,000 from Golden Rule. In 1987, he bought two $500,000 term policies from Farmers.

Norris expressed his surprise at learning Hanson had insured himself so heavily.

"Why?" Yocum asked.

"Well, he'd be sitting at his desk and we'd be talking about something, then all of a sudden he'd say, 'I don't know why people buy life insurance. I'd never buy it. Why would you buy life insurance when you wouldn't be around to get any of the money?' He'd say these things out of the blue. I didn't say, 'Hey, Gene, what do you think about life insurance?' "

As Yocum came back into the newsroom from lunch, September 16, Betty Skain, the front-desk receptionist, slipped a telephone-message sheet into this hand, saying, "He said he needs to talk to you right away. It's about Hawkins and Hanson."

"Albert MacKenzie. L.A. County District Attorney's office," the slip read. "Did he say what he wanted?"

"No, he didn't. He just said he needed to talk to you or Cathy."

Yocum put a call through to California. Albert MacKenzie picked up the phone after the first ring. "Robin. Thank you so much for calling me back. I would like to ask a favor of you."

"Sure. Shoot."

"I'm reviewing the death of Melvin Hanson. You're familiar with Melvin Hanson?"

"Yeah, I'm familiar with Mr. Hanson."

"Yes. I've seen a few of your stories. You and Catherine have been doing such marvelous work. I'd wondered if you'd mind sending me copies of your articles."

MacKenzie had piqued Yocum's interest, even though his monotone delivery conjured up images of an undertaker greeting a bereaved widow. His flagrant blandishments amused the reporter.

"Well, I suppose. What exactly are you investigating?"

"It's a little soon to call it an investigation," MacKenzie said. "We're looking at the evidence surrounding Mr. Hanson's death and the insurance fraud that has been alleged by Farmers Insurance."

"So you're looking at Boggs and Hawkins, too?"

"Oh yes, and anyone else who might have been involved."

"So, what have you learned so far?"

MacKenzie forced a laugh. "Nothing yet, that's why I'd like to see all your articles. I'm just starting to collect some background information."

"Okay, no problem. I'll send you the articles, but how about returning the favor?"

"What would that be?"

"Not much. Just call us first if you have something."

"Deal."

32

Yocum and Candisky felt as if they were tap dancing around the big stories. Where was Hanson? Candisky had spoken to everyone living at Hanson's former apartment building on Poinsettia Place in Hollywood. No one admitted to have even known Hanson. Yocum had made calls at Hanson's more recent address at the East Broad Street condominium building where he had lived until early 1988. Residents there said they had only seen Hanson in passing. The reporters had spent hours trying to track down Hanson's only known acquaintance—Cecil Tanner. Navarre told Candisky that the elusive Tanner lived in Atlanta, but they couldn't find him there. The reporters also spent several hours on the phone with directory assistance in Los Angeles and New York, hoping to get lucky. They didn't.

There were still so many unanswered questions.

How did the scheme evolve and unravel? Possibly, Just Sweats was never meant to survive. The chain's birth and growth might have all been part of a grand scheme that would ultimately lead to a man lying dead on Boggs's examination room floor. More likely, however, was that Hawkins and Hanson tired of the responsibilities of the business and concocted the plan as a way out. Its unraveling seemed to start when paramedics arrived at Boggs's office. Hawkins and Hanson had come very close to pulling off the scam. But ultimately, it was Shelly Navarre, the Farmers Insurance claims adjuster, who initially exposed the fraud when she asked for Hanson's California driver's license photo to compare to that of the corpse.

Who was the dead man? The reporters surmised it was a homeless person who had the misfortune of having made the acquaintance of Dr. Richard P. Boggs and had the equal misfortune of bearing a physical resemblance to Gene Hanson. If he was homeless, there was less chance he would be missed.

The reporters had a hunch that DeSando knew the answers. He

had been evasive, still unwilling to think the worst and fully implicate his former roommate and friend. Despite everyone's warnings, he still seemed somewhat blind to the seriousness of the entire affair.·

Yocum and Candisky asked DeSando to meet them for lunch at the Old Mohawk—the Mo—on Thursday, September 22. DeSando's deck business was booming, and he wanted to squeeze in as many jobs as he could while the weather was good, but he said he could break away for a few hours.

DeSando began lunch with his usual "This is all off the record, guys." He had mastered the phrase after seeing how damning his words looked in print. He worried that Hawkins might be upset with him for some of the things he had said that had already appeared in the paper. "Hopefully, John realizes that was my way of letting him know what I told the police," DeSando said. "I know someone has been sending him the paper, so this way he knows what's going on."

"Well, what is going on, Erik?" Candisky questioned.

"*Rolling Stone* is working on an article about this. I've been working with this freelance writer from Chicago. He gave me $500."

"What's his name?" Yocum asked.

"Gus. I don't remember his last name. I just call him Gus the Musk. You know I'm not supposed to be talking to you guys anymore. That's part of the deal," DeSando said. "But don't worry. He doesn't have to know."

"We'll be sure to keep it hush-hush around Gus," Candisky said.

DeSando acted as if the magazine and newspaper reporters alternated as interchangeable best friends. While he pretended to confide only in Candisky and Yocum, they assumed Gus the Musk was privy to the same information.

"So what are you guys working on now?" DeSando asked.

The reporters wondered if DeSando asked out of his own curiosity or at the suggestion Gus the Musk.

"We're still trying to track down some of the company background," Candisky said. "Have you ever heard of a store in L.A. called Pure Sweats?"

DeSando nodded. "Sure. Why?"

"We heard that's where John got the idea for Just Sweats," Candisky continued. "Is that right?"

"Beats me," DeSando said, shrugging. "I've heard that, but John never told me. John always said it was his idea."

"What did you hear about John and Pure Sweats?" Yocum asked.

"I don't put much stock in it, but they say John paid off some accountant to teach him how to set up his own company. The guy helped John and, in return, he promised to keep Just Sweats east of the Mississippi. Supposedly the guy told him he needed to set up near a campus. I guess this Pure Sweats started up near UCLA in Westwood. So John put his first store in Lexington near the U of K."

"How did he end up in Columbus?" Candisky asked. "Just another campus?"

"Kind of. He told me he broke down in Columbus on his way to visit Missy Hughes. He had this big old boat of a Buick and it took them a couple of days to get it fixed. So anyway, while he's here he's hanging out on High Street and he falls in love with it. He told me he'd never seen so many good-looking women in his life. It reminded him of UCLA and he started looking for a place to put a store."

The waitress set a plate of steaming potato skins in front of DeSando. "Have you heard anything about the guy who died in Boggs's office?" Yocum asked.

"Like what?"

"Like that he was murdered."

DeSando shoved half a potato skin in his mouth. "Murdered?" he said through the food. "No way. John's pulled some crazy stunts, but he would never kill anyone. He's not capable of murder." He took a hit of iced tea. "They got the body from a hospital or maybe it was the morgue. Yeah. I think John said Dr. Boggs had connections and they got it from the morgue. John said it was a guy who died during heart surgery."

"Couldn't be," Yocum said. "We've got the autopsy and there was no mention of chest scars or a recent surgery."

"Maybe that was wrong, I don't know. But I know John. You guys never met John, but believe me, he just couldn't be involved in murder."

"So Gene's alive?" Candisky asked.

DeSando looked puzzled as he spit the ice cube he had been sucking back into the glass. "Hmm. I don't know. I really don't know. I never asked him."

"You mean he told you the dead guy wasn't really Gene and you never asked where Gene was?" Yocum asked.

DeSando rolled his eyes. "You guys act like I sat down and interrogated him or something. I really didn't want to know about it."

DeSando appeared irritated, so Candisky tried to lighten the mood.

"Are you still harassing Amy Blizzard, or has John stopped killing people?"

"Very funny. Ha-ha. She deserved it. John was crazy to get involved with her. She's a ditz."

"Speaking of Amy," Yocum said. "Is it true that she made John get an AIDS test?"

"She wouldn't have to make John. He got an AIDS test every three months. He was paranoid about it. It was the only thing he was really afraid of. He used to brag about having had every sexual disease in the book, but he didn't joke about AIDS. Of course, it didn't stop him from screwin' anything that moved, either."

"Have you heard from John since the time he called you in Vegas?"

"No, and I really doubt I'll ever see him again," DeSando said.

"If he's so innocent, then why is he hiding?" Yocum asked. "Why doesn't he defend himself?"

"He's scared and he doesn't want to turn on Gene. He'd do anything to protect Gene."

"Why?" Candisky asked.

"That's just the way John is. Like I said, you'd have to know John to appreciate this, but he's really a great guy. He'd do anything for his friends, and he's very generous. He used to compare himself to Robin Hood. He said he wanted to find ways of taking from the rich—like insurance companies—and give it to the poor."

Yocum and Candisky exchanged glances. They both saw the opening. "Wait a minute, Erik," Candisky started. "What do you mean, 'like insurance companies'? We've heard this wasn't the first time John ripped off an insurance company."

"Aw, come on, guys, I can't tell you that."

"Did you ever hear that he and Gene faked a robbery in New York City?" Yocum asked.

"How did you guys find out about that?"

They smiled at DeSando. "Now, Erik, if we revealed our sources how could you ever trust us," Candisky toyed.

"Good point."

"So?" Yocum continued. "What do you know?"

The story DeSando gave was very similar to the one Yocum and Candisky had heard from Hawkins's former girlfriend and employee, Linnette Woda. Hawkins and Hanson had faked the robbery of some furniture and scammed an insurance company for "about a hundred grand."

Hawkins, DeSando conceded, was no amateur in the insurance game. Hawkins and some guy from New York had faked a pedestrian-car accident out in Los Angeles with Boggs's help. According to DeSando, Hawkins's friend rented a car and took out full insurance. He then drove to a specified location. As the car approached, Hawkins crossed the street and pretended to be hit. The friend admitted full liability, and Boggs performed Hawkins's medical examination. "John said he was able to pull it off with the greatest of ease because he had the doctor in his back pocket," DeSando said. Boggs diagnosed severe neck and back injuries. Through the bogus medical claims, Hawkins collected $25,000.

"Now you guys aren't going to print that, are you?" DeSando asked. "Seriously, I can't be your source."

"Don't worry. We'd have to confirm it before we could use it, anyway," Candisky said. "Do you know when this happened?"

DeSando shrugged. "Sometime before he started Just Sweats. It was his first scam."

"Can you believe it?" Candisky chuckled. "These guys could have made a living just doing insurance scams."

"They practically did," DeSando interrupted. "I told you guys about the time Gene was stranded over in Europe, didn't I?"

"We heard something about," Yocum said. A small lie, but he didn't want DeSando to think he was giving away too much. "How did it go?"

"I'm not sure why Gene was over there, but I think it was when they had the shoe business together. Gene had gone to Europe to sell shoes or something, and he ran out of money. He couldn't pay his hotel bill or buy a plane ticket back. John went out and bought a beater Porsche for $5,000—I guess the engine was just about blown. Anyway, he got insurance on it and then had someone torch it." DeSando laughed. "The funniest part about it was John had the car torched in front of this gay bar. When he saw it burning he started screaming and throwing a fit, sounding like he was a real flamer. He thought it would be more believable. He got eight or ten thousand for it. He sent some money to Gene so he could get back. Then, he went and gave $5,000 to the car dealer because he had paid him with a bad check."

The three finished their lunch and walked outside onto the red brick sidewalk. "You know, Erik, we heard something else you might know about," Yocum said, saving the most damaging question for the end of the interview. "Somebody told us that you sent John your birth certificate."

DeSando shook his head. "You guys never let up, do you?"

"Is it true?" Candisky asked.

"No. No way. I'd never do anything like that. But I think he took it. It was missing from the desk after he left."

"Why would he steal your birth certificate?" Candisky asked.

"He didn't really steal it. I think he just wanted to set up some bank accounts and he needed it."

"Sounds like stealing to me," Yocum said.

DeSando shrugged. "Where'd you hear that?"

"That's what John told Amy."

"Oh, she's reliable," DeSando said as he walked away. "I've got to get back to work. Catch you guys later."

"One more thing," Yocum said. "That part about John wanting to play Robin Hood, scamming the rich to give to the poor. Did he ever give money to the poor?"

"No," DeSando said, smiling. "But I'm sure he meant to."

The reporters both felt that DeSando knew more about Hawkins than he readily admitted. Each time they interviewed DeSando he came through with a little more information—more facts and previously "forgotten" details—all pointing to Hawkins's deep involvement in a murder-for-insurance scam. The reporters just had to push the right buttons: if Yocum and Candisky persisted, DeSando would usually give them an answer.

33

The unimaginative piece of architecture called the Ohio Statehouse sits like a giant salt lick in the middle of downtown Columbus. The large limestone building has no pristine dome or grand outdoor stairway, only a couple of bronzed, charging doughboys guarding the front entrance. Yocum and Candisky sat in the shadow of the weathered statue of William McKinley on the cement wall that ran in front of the statehouse. The reporters were trying to chart a course of action. After writing several stories on the flight of John Hawkins and retracing his last days in Columbus, Candisky and Yocum found themselves back in a familiar spot: scrounging for a lead. After stories about a doctor assaulting a corpse and attacking his would-be lover with a stun gun, it was tough to keep their editors' interest.

"Ellis said it had to be spectacular, huh?" Yocum asked.

"That's what he told me. If we want it out front, it better be spectacular," Candisky answered.

"Spectacular? What does that mean?"

"I don't know, Rob, he didn't qualify it." Candisky wedged half of her hot dog between two fingers and flipped the pages of her notebook with her thumb. "Right here," she said, pointing to a note she had scribbled during their interview with DeSando at the Mohawk.

Talk to accountant
Colgan
On Gene's disappearance

"This might be worth tracking down," Candisky said. "That's probably our best shot for a story for tomorrow."

Yocum shrugged.

"You're not interested?" she said.

"I'm interested, but why don't we try to track down the New York scam? That would be a real coup if we could pin that down," Yocum asserted. "It would show these guys had a history of insurance scams."

"Fine, but I don't think we can pull all that together in an afternoon," Candisky said.

"I know, but maybe we should start working on the more in-depth stuff. Besides, what are the chances Colgan will talk to us?"

"Slim," Candisky conceded. "Colgan probably won't talk to us, but Bob Smith has interviewed all those guys at Just Sweats and I'll bet he knows the story. Why don't we give him a call?"

"Why don't we just walk down to the prosecutor's office and jump him? I don't want to sit around all afternoon waiting for him not to return our calls."

It was a three-block walk down South High Street to the prosecutor's office at the Hall of Justice. Yocum sidestepped a panhandler in front of Woolworth's. Candisky gave him some change. "What are the chances that Smith will talk?" Yocum asked.

"Very good. Of all the assistant prosecutors, he's one of the least shy around reporters."

Smith's desk occupied most of his windowless office on the fifth floor of the Franklin County Hall of Justice. One of two assistant prosecutors assigned to white-collar crime, Smith sat behind a mound of paper. The lean man had a smallish face that seemed as overwhelmed by his large features and his eyeglasses as he himself was by the mountain of files.

His office door was open and the reporters took that as an invitation to enter. Candisky knew Smith from covering the courts and introduced him to Yocum, who was already settling into a chair. "Any sign of Hawkins or the missing million?" Candisky asked.

"None yet. What have you guys heard?" Smith said.

"Well, Bob, we're always willing to engage in the free exchange of information," Yocum said, smiling. "We hear Paul Colgan has the details about Gene's embezzlement. I guess he got about $1.8 million?"

"That's right. He was their accountant. What else do you want to know?"

"Just all the details. You've interviewed him and we figured you were the best person to talk to."

Smith's brow arched. "What makes you think I interviewed him?"

"We figured by now you would have interviewed all those guys, right?" Candisky asked.

"Actually, the whole thing is kind of funny," Smith said. "Hanson

John Hawkins (*center*) loved to party. While entertaining friends Erik DeSando (*right*) and Jim Connors (*left*) in Hawaii, his scheme of murder and fraud was already well under way. (photo by "Ten Casting")

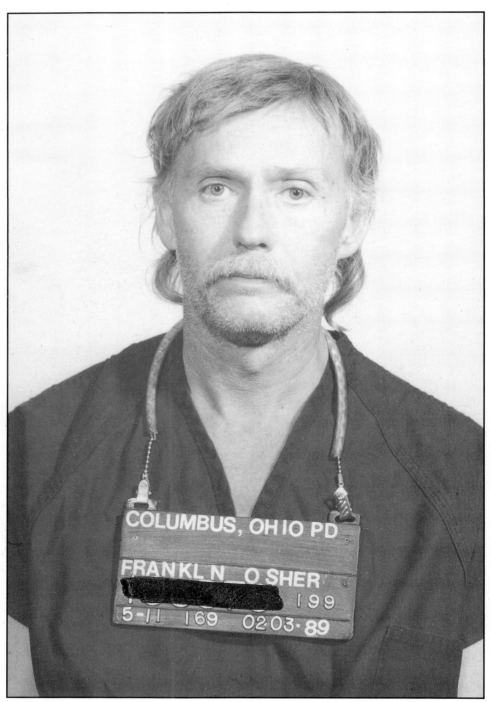

Co-conspirator Melvin Hanson hid out in Mexico, pretending he was dead, until he was forced to return to the United States to sell a piece of property for much-needed cash. He was quickly arrested.

John Hawkins, with a very different look, on the run from authorities. He was finally apprehended on the Mediterranean island of Sardinia, as he was docking his forty-foot catamaran, called the *Carpe Diem*. (AP/World Wide Photos)

Above: Convicted murderer Dr. Richard Boggs, who never let scruples about the Hippocratic Oath stand in his way. (reprinted with permission from *The Columbus Dispatch*)

Right: The victim, Ellis H. Greene, whose corpse was passed off as that of Melvin Hanson, as part of the insurance scam.

was left in charge of the company around Christmas. He was supposed to run this after-Christmas sale for one day, and he ran it for three weeks. He really beefed up the accounts. Of course, there's nothing left in the stores because he quits ordering new merchandise, and then he empties the bank accounts and skips town."

"So how does Colgan fit into this? Was he involved?" Candisky asked.

"Colgan? No. He was duped just like everyone else," Smith said. "Hawkins and Hanson sent him out of the country about a week before all this happened. Colgan had always taken care of the books. They had to get rid of him because he would have known what was going on. It wasn't until he got back that Colgan knew why he had been sent out of the country."

"Where did they send him?" Yocum asked.

"Europe. It was some company-paid thing, a bonus or something."

"So this embezzlement is as much a part of the insurance scam as Gene buying up all these policies and faking his death?" Candisky asked.

"I think so. They had never paid for anyone else's vacation. They didn't usually reward employees for good deeds."

"Then Hanson was supposed to go to California and die with the money before anyone could find him?" Yocum inquired. "What happened, couldn't they find a body quick enough?"

Smith shrugged. "At this point it's anyone's guess. It looks that way, but it won't be easy to prove. This whole thing is going to take a while to piece together. There's just so much paper. I'm still waiting on bank records. I don't know if I'll get them before I leave or not."

"You're leaving?" Candisky asked. "When?"

"The end of October. I took a job with the state attorney general."

"Well, congratulations. So what happens to the Just Sweats case after you're gone?"

"Danny Abraham is taking my place, so I assume he'll take it. But I'm hoping to keep working on it part-time."

The reporters decided that they would have a better shot at talking to Colgan by telephoning him. If they walked into Just Sweats headquarters, Laramee and Mantz would probably try to keep them out of Colgan's office. Candisky had no great expectations when she made the call on the afternoon of Tuesday, September 27.

"Paul Colgan please," Candisky said.

"Speaking."

"Hi, Paul. This is Cathy Candisky at the *Dispatch*. How are you?" She waited to hear a dial tone.

"Pretty good. How about yourself?"

Candisky swallowed, surprised. "Not bad. How are things at the company? Still pretty hectic?"

"Oh, everything considered, not bad I guess. At least it keeps me pretty busy."

The 25-year-old accountant had been with the company for more than two years. Two weeks earlier, Yocum and Candisky had watched Colgan nervously stumble through his testimony at the court hearing to prevent Hawkins from spending Farmers' million dollars. Colgan had brushed off the reporters outside the courtroom, but he spoke with surprising ease while on the phone with Candisky.

"I was talking to Bob Smith from the prosecutor's office, and he was telling me about how you were sent out of the country while Gene drained the accounts. He told me most of the story but thought you might be able to provide a little more detail."

"Mr. Smith told you about that?" Colgan sounded suspicious.

"Yes. He said you'd fill me in on the details."

"He told you to call me?"

"Uh-huh. Do you have a few minutes?"

"I guess so, if he said it's okay."

"Good. Why don't you start by telling me what your job entailed when Hawkins and Hanson were still around."

"During most of that time I kept the books and wrote checks and kept track of the bank accounts."

"Smith said you were sent out of the country before all this happened. Can you tell me what was going on before that? Did you suspect something was up?"

"Looking back on it now I do, sure. Last November, about a month before I left, John ordered me to turn over the company checkbooks to Gene. I mean, one day, out of the blue, John came up to me and told me he and Gene were going to take over the checkwriting."

"I thought Gene was dying?" Candisky asked.

"He was, I guess, but this was before he told anybody."

Hanson had obtained the final life insurance policy in October 1988 and a few weeks later began telling employees at Just Sweats that he was dying. Hanson—normally neat to a fault—began coming to work unshaven and with his hair uncombed. Bags appeared under his eyes.

He told Colgan that he had fluid around his heart and his doctor had told him to change his lifestyle, like his strange diet of pizza and eggs. He told Missy Mantz that the doctor had given him some heart medication to rub on his chest and it was making hair grow there. Hanson told Mantz his doctor ordered him to quit smoking and start exercising. About the same time, Hanson began taking employees to lunch and, in the middle of a conversation, he would seemingly drift into a trance and begin muttering about his dislike for his family.

In the midst of all of Hanson's personality changes, Colgan had to teach him how to maintain the company books.

"It took me about two weeks to train Gene, and then he took it over around the end of November. At the time I thought they did it because they were trying to sell the company and didn't want anybody to know what was going on."

"Do you remember when you went on vacation?"

"I left right after Christmas and was gone for about three weeks."

"Where did you go in Europe?"

"Everywhere. I was on this whirlwind tour of a dozen or so countries. My idea of a vacation is going to a beach and relaxing. This was more like boot camp. They had put me on this one tour and when it got canceled at the last minute, John got me on another one. It was me and about forty Australians."

"Did they make you go?"

"I don't know if I was forced to go—it was never said—but I got that impression. I was really paranoid. I thought they were trying to get rid of me. They said my work had been excellent, but I couldn't figure out why, with Hanson telling everyone he was dying, why they would want him in charge of the books. I didn't think I'd have a job when I got back, but in a way it would have been a relief. For two-and-a-half months before I left all I did was talk to creditors eight-and-a-half hours a day."

Colgan told Candisky he returned from Europe on January 17, 1988, and found the company in dire straits. Not only were the store shelves bare, but vendors were also complaining of long-overdue bills. The company accounts were empty. Before leaving, Colgan had written forty checks and left them for Hanson to sign and mail. No one could understand the complaints since, according to the books, all the bills had been paid. The puzzle was solved when Melissa Mantz found the checks in Hanson's desk drawer.

"John seemed like the hero at the time," Colgan said. "He came back from Hawaii, turned around and went out to California, and came back with almost all the money Gene took."

"Which was how much?"

"About $1.8 million. John got it all back but a couple hundred thousand."

"How'd he get it back?"

"I was never really clear on the details, but we're figuring we're going to have to close the doors, then John shows up with the cash. We were so relieved to have the money that I never asked how he got it back."

34

Yocum and Candisky walked through the back door of the statehouse annex and weaved their way through the corridors that ran under the capitol building, through its parking garage, under High Street, and finally into the basement of the Huntington Center. They took the escalator to the first floor and went through a side door to the Huntington Bank Building, where Austin Wildman had his office.

The reporters wanted the details of how Hawkins recovered the money Hanson had embezzled in early 1988. Colgan had said that Hawkins had managed to get nearly all of the $1.8 million back from Hanson. The reporters hoped Wildman would know how Hawkins did it.

Despite the strain of a divorce, the addition of twenty-five pounds following nicotine withdrawal, and the antics of his former clients, Wildman still enjoyed talking to the reporters and swapping theories on the whereabouts of Hawkins and Hanson. For weeks he had defended Hawkins and insisted Hanson was indeed dead. But by September 28, a month after Farmers filed its suit, Wildman was beginning to feel as if he too had been duped.

Reclining behind his cluttered desk, his fingers interlocked behind his head, Wildman chuckled when Candisky and Yocum asked what he knew about Hawkins's January foray to Los Angeles to recover the money. "It was a scam just like everything else, but at the time I believed him—but he got me too," Wildman said. "I was there when John found out Gene had taken the money and he hit the roof. I didn't think there was any way he could have faked that. I had no idea he was such a good actor."

According to Wildman, in early January 1988, Hawkins was vacationing in Hawaii with his mother, sister, and three friends: DeSando; Jim Connors, a Columbus attorney; and Kenny Powers, a friend from San Diego. They spent their days on the beach and their nights on the prowl in Honolulu's clubs, with Hawkins picking up most of the tabs. When DeSando and Conners returned to Columbus, Hawkins took a side trip to Seattle to spend a few days with Jill Birdwell, a co-ed he had met on vacation.

"He finally gets back in mid-January, around the fourteenth, and Missy tells him Gene's cleaned out the accounts and blown town. He was storming around the office, slamming drawers and swearing. He had tears in his eyes he was so upset. It's hard to believe that was all an act, but I guess that was all it was. He was acting crazy, yelling at everyone. He wanted to know how everyone could let Gene get away with such a stunt. But Christ, he was half-owner of the company. They couldn't have stopped him."

Wildman leaned forward in his chair and took a swallow of coffee. He started talking again before the liquid had cleared his throat. "Missy told him that Gene had beefed up company accounts by extending a half-price, day-after-Christmas sale for three weeks. She said she confronted Gene, asked him what the hell he was doing, but he ignored her. A few days before John got back, Gene abandons his condominium and his Porsche, empties the company accounts, and disappears."

"How did he get the cash?" Candisky asked.

"No big trick. He was still the company VP. He withdrew some of it in cash; the rest he wrote out as checks to himself, which he converted to bearer bonds."

"Didn't the bank say anything?" Yocum asked.

Wildman looked toward the ceiling and tried unsuccessfully to suppress a grin. "Oh yeah, plenty. Our loan officer at Fifth Third, David Kessler, was mega pissed. Jesus, was he pissed, and demanding an explanation."

"What did you tell him?" Yocum asked.

"I told him the truth. We didn't have one. We were scared. We figured the company was headed for bankruptcy. You can't take that kind of money out of a company the size of Just Sweats and expect it to survive."

"So what happened?" Candisky pressed. "How did you get it back?"

"At first, John's really upset, but he's not making any attempts to find Gene. He's acting like it's a lost cause. Then, Dick Curtin told John that the embezzlement had to be reported to the FBI. Evidently that got John's attention. He pleaded with us to give him a few days to track Gene down. He kept saying it wouldn't be difficult. He said, 'I know right where I can find him. I know right where he hangs out in Los Angeles. I'm sure this is all just some kind of misunderstanding, and if you give me a couple of days I'll find him.' He said he didn't want to get Gene in trouble because Gene was dying and obviously not thinking right."

"So you guys agreed?" Yocum said.

Wildman shrugged, two palms up. "What did we have to lose? We were already out $1.8 million. Besides, we were having enough problems. We weren't real anxious to have the FBI snooping around to boot."

"How did he even know where to start?" Candisky questioned.

"Missy had found a receipt from a UPS package Gene had shipped to Los Angeles before he left. John took the receipt and jumped on a plane for L.A. Everyone's back here trying to put out fires. Fifth Third is going nuts. Creditors are screaming to be paid. We don't even have enough money to meet the payroll. Then John calls one day— he's been gone about a week, I guess—and he says he's got almost all the money."

"That's it?" Yocum asked. "He just said he had gotten the money back. He didn't offer any kind of explanation?"

Wildman smiled and slowly nodded his head. "Oh yes, and a beaut it was."

"Care to enlighten us?" Yocum asked.

"Sure. Fasten your seat belts, race fans, this is where it gets good. John comes back with a suitcase stuffed full of bearer bonds. He has all the money except . . . hold on, I've got the exact amount, here." Wildman reached for a manila folder on the corner of his desk. "All but $243,580. That's how much he said he gave Gene for his share of the company. So, I asked him how he got the money back, and he gives me this wild-ass tale of how he tracked down Gene and convinced him to return the money. He said he gets to Los Angeles and the first thing he does is check out a safety-deposit box that he and Gene shared at some bank. That's where he found the woe-is-me note from Gene." Wildman read the blank looks on the reporters' faces. "You've seen that note, haven't you?" Wildman asked.

"No," Candisky said. "This is new to us."

"Do you have it?" Yocum asked.

"Yeah, somewhere," Wildman said, rubbing his hand over his face as he leafed through the heaps of papers in his office. He began searching a stack of binders that lay on the couch. After several minutes he pulled a sheet of paper from a pile. "The only thing is, I don't know if I can show it to you. This might be client privilege. Let me give Ed

Laramee a call and see if it's okay."

"You won't be violating any confidences," Candisky said. "Besides, we won't tell anyone where we got it."

"I better check," Wildman said as he dialed the telephone. He then placed the note on the desk—clearly visible to both reporters—and leaned back in his chair.

As he explained the reporters' request to Laramee, Wildman didn't seem to notice Yocum copying the note onto a pad on his lap.

About five minutes later, Wildman hung up the telephone and shook his head. "Sorry. No go. Ed's not comfortable letting it go."

Candisky smiled. "Well, thanks for trying."

Glancing over toward Yocum, she scanned the letter from Hanson to Hawkins that her partner had transcribed.

> John:
> By now you will have found the safety deposit box and this letter. I left the money to someone I have cared for—for a long time. I never told you, because you would never understand, you never approved of my lifestyle. I wanted to give him something for everything he has put up with in the last three mo's. He took care of me when no one else cared. I'm sorry about all I put you thru [sic], but you have the business now and I know you will be a success in everything you do. Please forgive me for everything. Your [sic] the only family I have.
>
> Love,
> Gene

"So, what happened after he found the note?" Candisky asked.

"John checks into the Beverly Hills Hilton, because he says that's Gene's favorite hotel and he figures Gene might be there."

"Why didn't he just call and ask?" Yocum suggested.

"I don't know. I wasn't trying to understand his logic at the time. Anyway, John somehow finds out that Gene is renting a room one floor up from his, so he starts staking it out, wandering the halls and loafing in the lobby waiting for Gene to return. A couple of days pass, but no sign of Gene. So, John says he gets a new idea. He waits until a maid was cleaning Gene's room, then he walks in pretending to be Gene. When she leaves, John searches the room and finds an address of a condominium where he believes Gene might be staying."

"So why . . ."

" . . . would Hanson be renting a room while he was staying in a condo?" Wildman said, completing Candisky's question. "I don't know. John didn't say and I didn't ask. At the time I didn't think anything of it. John said he went to the condo, but no one was home and none of the neighbors knew Gene. Now, John said, he was getting desperate, so he goes to a print shop and has a couple hundred missing-persons posters made. They say something like, John is looking for his business partner, Gene Hanson, and it's an emergency. If anyone knew of Gene's whereabouts would they please call him at the hotel. Supposedly, he put them up all over town."

"Do you have any of the posters?" Yocum asked.

Wildman shook his head. "I never saw them. John just told me about it. So, anyway, two days later, presto, Gene calls and agrees to a meeting."

"Hanson rips off the company for almost $2 million, then agrees to meet with Hawkins?" Candisky asked, incredulously.

Wildman nodded. "Yep. But to hear John tell the story, that didn't sound that unusual. According to John, Gene took the money because he wanted out of the business and believed that $1.8 million represented his share of the company. He and John had talked about selling Just Sweats to a shoe company in late '87. Apparently they wanted $4 million for the company, which they obviously didn't get, but that was the figure Gene used and he thought he was due half of it."

"Of course, Hanson truly believes that's his fair share, but he takes it when no one is around to stop him," Yocum points out. "So, how does our hero get the money back?"

"John said he convinced Gene that the company wasn't worth near that much, and that it was going under if he didn't get the money back. Gene starts crying and says he's sorry, and gives John all but the $243,580, which they somehow felt was a more accurate reflection of Gene's share. The next day John's back in Columbus with this suitcase stuffed with $1.6 million in bonds."

"So, Hawkins just decided this is what Gene should get and gave it to him?" Candisky queried.

"As you have probably discerned, they didn't stand on formality," Wildman said.

"And you believed all this?" Yocum asked rather bluntly.

Wildman laughed. "Every bit of it . . . then. At the time we were just so happy to have the money back that I didn't give much thought to how he got it. It was bizarre, but believable. If it was a giant scam—

and I'd thought of that—why did he come back? John could have collected Gene's insurance money and put Just Sweats into receivership. But Curtin was threatening to go to the FBI. John said he didn't want to get Gene in trouble, but apparently he was afraid if the FBI got involved it would ruin the entire scheme, so he volunteered to go look for Gene. My bet is that Gene was supposed to be dead before John returned from Hawaii, but evidently they couldn't find a body and that screwed things up. With Gene dead, John would go on a vain search for the money, but all he would ever find would be the note in the safety-deposit box. They must not have been able to find someone to play dead for Gene."

35

At first, it seemed like the type of insignificant prattle that reporters scribble in a notebook and file away. Erik DeSando had told Yocum and Candisky a little about the New York scam the day they had lunch at the Mohawk, but his information was sketchy at best. He said Hawkins and Hanson had pulled off an insurance fraud in New York City in the mid-1980s. It involved faking the theft of some furniture and paintings, but DeSando had no other details.

The reporters had heard that Hawkins and Hanson were no strangers to insurance frauds. Hanson had even given a Just Sweats employee tips on how to bilk money from an insurance company. While documenting other insurance scams of theirs held the possibility of making a good story, the reporters didn't have time to go chasing after past history when so many other immediate questions remained unanswered. Besides, even if it were true that they had collected on a fraudulent insurance claim, that act seemed somewhat insignificant compared with Hawkins and Hanson's other misdeeds. The reporters simply jotted the allegations down in their notes for later reference.

But during the restaurant interview with Linnette Woda, Yocum had asked if she had ever heard of Hawkins pulling an insurance scam involving a fake theft in New York City. Woda nodded. "He used to brag about that all the time," she said. "That's where he and Gene got the money to start Just Sweats. John locked Gene in a truck somewhere in New York, and when the police came Gene said he'd been robbed of a bunch of stuff. They got over a $100,000 from the insurance company."

"They were living in New York City at the time?"

"They had some $5,000-a-month apartment in Manhattan. They filled it with all this expensive furniture and paintings, all rented. That's the stuff they said got stolen."

"How'd they pull it off?" Yocum persisted.

183

"He told me they rented two moving vans, then hired these movers to put the stuff in one truck. Right before they were finished, John offered to take them to lunch, and while he was gone Gene switched vans. I guess they had a bunch of junk—boxes and stuff—in the back and he covered it with a tarp so the movers couldn't tell it wasn't the same truck."

Candisky called Amy Blizzard, who was growing tired of the reporters' calls, but seemed more receptive to Candisky than Yocum. "I really don't want to talk about it," Blizzard said. "It'll just make things look worse than they already do."

"So, it's true?" Candisky asked.

"Yeah, I guess. John told me about it right before he left Columbus. He said, 'I can tell you about it because the guy I did it with is dead, and there is no way they can get us.' "

"Who did he mean by the dead guy? Hanson?"

"I guess."

"We heard that's where he got the seed money for Just Sweats. Is that what you heard?"

"Yeah. He and Gene faked a robbery—they had two vans and they switched them to make it look like a robbery, or something like that. Gene had this insurance policy that covered all the furniture. John said it was easy. The insurance company never asked any questions. I just really don't want to talk about it."

It was 6:30 P.M. on Thursday, September 29, when the *Dispatch* operator placed a call to DeSando and hooked up a three-way conference connection with Yocum and Candisky. "Jesus Christ, get a life" was DeSando's greeting. "Don't you two have anything better to do?"

"We're the ever-vigilant press, Erik. We don't have a social life," Yocum said.

"Yeah, yeah. Spare me."

"We just want to ask you a few questions," Candisky explained. "It won't take long, I promise."

"Well, it can't take long, because I'm getting ready to get out of here. What's up?"

"Remember you told us about John and Gene faking a robbery in New York?" Yocum asked.

"Yeah. Old news."

"We need a refresher," Candisky said.

"That's all you want?"

"That's it," Yocum promised.

"Okay. The best I can remember, here it is. John said Gene leased this apartment—a real expensive place—and filled it with rental furniture and paintings. They've had the place a month or so, and they go out and rent two panel trucks. They hire these movers to come over and put the stuff in one truck. Then they went to lunch or John took them to lunch, I can't remember, but while they were gone Gene switched trucks."

"Couldn't the movers tell the difference?" Candisky asked.

"Before they left to eat they covered the furniture with a paint tarp. John said they threw the tarp over a bunch of boxes in the second van and you couldn't tell the difference. They had another guy involved and . . ."

"Who was . . ." Yocum began.

"I don't know. John never said who he was. I didn't ask. But whoever he was, he returned the furniture and paintings while John and Gene drove the other truck to a secluded area and dumped out all the junk. So then John locks Gene in the back and drives to a bad part of town and abandons the truck. John goes and sits in this parking lot and watches, and Gene starts screaming for someone to help him. About fifteen minutes later the cops come and get Gene out, and John books. Gene tells the cops that these two gunmen commandeered the truck, shoved him on the floor with a gun to his head, and drove to a warehouse where they unloaded it. John said they collected a hundred grand from the insurance company."

"But why such an elaborate plan?" Yocum asked. "Why did they hire movers?"

"John said they needed the movers to corroborate Hanson's story. Everything was rented, so they didn't have receipts. But when the insurance company called to question the movers, they said they loaded all these expensive paintings and furniture into the truck."

DeSando paused a moment. "Anything else?" he asked with a tone of impatience.

"That ought to do it," Yocum said. "So, what's on the agenda for tonight? Where are you going?"

"I don't know, but it'll be somewhere where you can't get a hold of me. See ya around."

Yocum hung up the phone, then began spreading the notes from the three interviews out on a desk. There were too many similarities among the accounts for the story not to be basically true. "What was the name of that company Hawkins and Hanson had before they started

Just Sweats?" he asked his partner.

"The shoe company?" Candisky asked. "Hawkins & Hanson Enterprises. Cirian said they sold it a few months before John opened the first Just Sweats. Supposedly that's where he got the money."

Yocum scanned the notes again, then turned to Candisky. "Wrong again, Jackie," he said.

"Look, this all fits. They pull the scam in New York City in early 1985, collect the cash, make up the story about the sale of Hawkins & Hanson Enterprises, and use the insurance money to start Just Sweats in June. They run the company for a year, build up some cash, and then start buying insurance policies in late 1986." Yocum nodded toward a timeline the reporters had been keeping on the case. "When did they buy the insurance policies?"

Candisky ran her finger across the sheet. "Hanson bought the first policy from Golden Rule—the one for $450,000—on September 24, 1986. He didn't get the next one until May of '87. That was the first Farmers policy for $500,000. He got the second one from Farmers in October, same year."

"The second Farmers policy was for what, another $500,000?"

Candisky nodded. "They got the last policy about the time Gene started telling everyone he was dying. He changed his will in November, bought the Porsche in December, and left town in January."

"And was dead by April. How convenient. They never intended for Just Sweats to succeed," Yocum said. "Hawkins & Hanson Enterprises was just a paper company, a cover for the New York scam, and Just Sweats was a cover for this scam."

"This fits the pattern. Bob Smith said he was positive these guys had pulled off smaller scams and built up to faking Hanson's death."

Yocum nodded, slipping the notes into his top desk drawer. "It would be great if we could show a history of insurance fraud. That would make a hell of a story. So, how do we document it? We can't write a story based on their word."

"If he collected insurance money, Hanson must have filed a police report," Candisky suggested.

"Yeah, but how do we find it? We have no idea when this happened or where," Yocum said. "But if they used the money to start Just Sweats, we can probably assume they did it, say, maybe as early as six months before opening the first store."

"They opened the store in Lexington in June 1985. So with your theory, we'd be talking January to June of that year," Candisky said.

36

Yocum phoned the New York City Police Department the next morning. His call was transferred nearly a dozen times before he reached an officer willing to listen to his story.

"I know it's a long shot, but I'm looking for a robbery report that was filed during the first six months of 1985. I don't have the exact date or an address, but it was filed by a Melvin Hanson, or he may have used the name Gene Hanson," Yocum said.

"No date or address, and this report was filed three years ago?" the officer asked.

"Correct."

After a few moments of silence the officer started laughing. "It's impossible. The reports are filed by precinct, and without an address, I can't even tell you where to look. We have seventy-five precincts here," he said.

"Isn't there someone I could call who could punch the name in a computer and pull up a report number or something?"

"We aren't computerized that way," the officer said. "Why don't you call Lieutenant Kelly? He likes dealing with out-of-town reporters and maybe he can help."

Yocum turned to Candisky. "That was worthless," he said. "Unless we can find an address, we're screwed."

All night, Yocum thought of little other than how to track down that address. The next morning, the reporters went to the public library to check old New York telephone books and city directories for Hanson's former address. Yocum also asked a source at the police department to run a computer check for a New York driver's license in Hanson's name. Despite their efforts, the reporters could come up with nothing that showed Hanson had ever lived in New York.

That afternoon, Yocum suggested that Candisky try the cop who liked out-of-town reporters. "I think you might have better luck," he said.

"How do you figure?" she said.

"Well, you know Allison Ash, the reporter over at Channel 4?" Candisky nodded. "I was covering a chemical spill on the southwest side one time. I asked this cop what was going on and he wouldn't tell me anything. Nothing. Ten minutes later, Allison Ash walks up and says hello to the guy and he turns into a babbling idiot. Tells her everything."

"So, what are you saying?"

"Cops love skirts."

"Not being too stereotypical here, are we?"

Yocum handed her the phone receiver. "Prove me wrong."

"If I get it, you're buying lunch for a week."

"You got it."

Candisky had no trouble reaching Lt. John Kelly and spent about fifteen minutes explaining how Hanson and Hawkins seemed to have faked Hanson's death for insurance proceeds. Kelly was intrigued by the story. "I don't think I'll be able to help you on this one," he said. "You really need an address for me to track it down, but I'll tell you what I'll do. I'll make a few calls and if I hear anything, I'll let you know. What agency is investigating this in Ohio?"

"The Franklin County Prosecutor," Candisky said.

"Okay. I probably don't have to tell you what a long shot this is, but I'll see what I can do."

Late in the afternoon of Friday, September 30, the reporters hauled their notebooks and files down to the canteen in the basement of the *Dispatch*. They needed to hash over theories, to review some leads, and to decide what to focus on next. If they could pin down the New York insurance scam, it would show a history of insurance rip-offs. Candisky and Yocum knew that for Hawkins and Hanson to have collected any insurance money, they would have had to have filed a robbery report with the New York City police. But without having either a date or an address for the incident, the reporters knew they had a slim chance of ever finding the report.

"The only thing better than that New York story would be an interview with Hawkins—or Hanson, if he's still alive," Yocum said.

"I want to know who masterminded the scam."

"Hanson."

Candisky winced. "Hanson? Why do you think that?"

"He's older, been 'round the block a few times. Hawkins seems like a nickel-dimer to me. Hanson would be more likely to think through a big plan. Why? Do you think it was Hawkins?"

Candisky nodded. "Sure. He was always looking for the quick buck. Gene was just a player in the scam. He was in love with him and would have done anything for him."

Yocum shook his head. "Hanson."

"You're wrong. Hawkins."

"Either way, what was Boggs thinking? He's left holding the bag while Hawkins and Hanson are out sipping margaritas."

"Doesn't make sense," Candisky said, gathering up her notebooks. "I'll bet he didn't get his cut of the money. Why else would he have been calling Jackie Cirian looking for John?"

The two reporters started toward the elevator. "You know, I hate to beat this horse to death, but . . ."

Candisky finished his thought. "Erik?"

Yocum nodded. "Every time we talk to him he gives us something new. Let's try him again."

37

The reporters had had enough of DeSando feeding them bits and pieces of the story: they wanted to hear it all. Other reporters had begun sniffing around; Candisky and Yocum couldn't afford to play DeSando's games any longer. They decided to try a more aggressive approach with DeSando when they paid him a visit on the morning of October 3.

As Yocum pounded on the door of the townhouse for a second time, the jamb shook and the mailbox rattled.

"I know he's home," Candisky said. "He never gets up this early. Knock again. He's probably still in bed."

"I'll knock all day if that's what it takes. I'm getting tired of him jacking us around all the time," Yocum said, continuing to hammer on the steel door.

Yocum knocked again and a moment later they could hear movement inside. "All right. All right. I'm coming," a voice yelled. DeSando opened the door and shielded his eyes from the sunlight with the sleeve of a blue terrycloth bathrobe. "You guys?" DeSando looked up and blew out a long breath. "I should have figured. What time is it?"

"Practically noon," Yocum said, slipping past DeSando and into the living room.

"Christ, really?" DeSando asked.

"It's almost ten o'clock," Candisky said, eyeballing the stub of a half-smoked joint in the ashtray. "Rough night?"

"Oh, that . . . Well, you know. What can I say?"

They walked into the dining room. DeSando cleared a week's worth of mail and magazines from the table. "Do you guys want some cereal or something?" DeSando said, rubbing his eyes.

"Got any Coco-Puffs?" Yocum asked.

"Sorry, no. How about . . ."

"I was kidding, Erik."

"Oh, yeah, well it's early," DeSando said, drawing a chair out from

190

underneath the table. "So, what do you guys want now? I thought I gave you enough to keep you busy for a while?"

"Erik, you've been telling us that Gene was dead," Candisky started, approaching DeSando head-on. "But you said John told you the body wasn't Gene's, and it was some corpse Boggs had picked up. It seems pretty obvious that these guys pulled a scam. What else did John tell you about it?"

DeSando took a deep breath to clear his head. "You guys got to understand. John told me a lot of things before he left that didn't make much sense. But now, after certain things have come out, a lot of what John told me is starting to fit. I didn't realize a lot of this until recently."

"Fair enough," Yocum said. "Like what? When did he tell you all this stuff?"

"The night before he left Columbus." DeSando backcombed his hair with his fingers. "I hope this doesn't sound a lot worse than it is. I didn't know John was going to leave, I really didn't. He came home that Friday and said he had rented a limo and we were going to go out. That wasn't that unusual. John rented limos every once in a while, just to go out and make a show.

"Anyway, the limo picked us up and we went to the Just Sweats over on Morse Road. John went in and got a couple of hundred bucks out of the cash register, and then we went over to the Elephant Bar. It was packed. We had a couple of drinks and then drove over to the R 'n' R. John was usually wild whenever we went out. But I remember on that night he wasn't saying much at all. He'd been smoking some grass and drinking, and he got drunk real fast, and he was real emotional. He was being real mellow and reminiscent, you know, talking about what a good friend I was, talking about things we used to do, how much he liked Columbus. He was talking about stuff John just never talked about. So, I don't know how long we had been there—maybe an hour, I remember it was after midnight—and John pulled me away from the bar and over by this big popcorn machine. His whole face was a puzzle; he was almost crying. He said, 'I've got something to tell you. I'm in a lot of trouble. I'm leaving tomorrow and I'm not coming back.' He didn't say anything for a few seconds, then he looked me square in the eye and said, 'Gene's alive.'

"I couldn't believe it. I fell down. Really, fell down. My knees buckled. John had to help me up. I didn't figure it out at first. All I could think about was that my best friend was leaving. I tried to talk him into staying. I asked John, 'Why do you have to leave? Why don't you just return the money and stay?' But Dr. Boggs had tapes that incriminated him. John said, 'He taped all our telephone conversations.' "

Candisky and Yocum looked at each other, then at DeSando, then at each other again. For the first time, they thought that DeSando was being totally honest with them. "Why has it taken you this long to level with us?" Yocum interrogated.

DeSando shrugged. "For a long time I was trying to help John. He was my best friend. Hell, I didn't want to hang him out."

"So, why now?" Candisky asked.

"I never realized how much trouble John was in. I'm not going to lie for him anymore. The FBI thought I was involved. They were going to arrest me." DeSando smiled. "You can only take friendship so far."

"So Hanson's alive. Did John tell you where he's living?" Yocum asked.

DeSando shook his head. "I really don't know. He's had a hair transplant and plastic surgery and he was in Florida, but I don't know if he's still there. John told me he went down to give Gene $20,000 for the surgery and they were walking on the beach. John said, 'The old guy looked pretty good.' I guess he looked a lot younger."

"So he's living on the coast?" Candisky asked.

"I don't know. All John said was they were on the beach."

"And you didn't ask him where Gene was living?" Candisky continued.

"Nope. I didn't want to know."

"Do you know the name of the doctor?" Yocum asked.

"No. I didn't want to know that either."

"When was it?" Yocum persisted.

"Well, I'm not sure of the date, but a couple of weeks before John left—sometime in June—he went to Florida to visit his dad, or at least that's what he told me at the time. That's probably when he went to see Gene."

"Okay, back to the night at the R 'n' R," Candisky said. "He told you Gene was alive and living in Florida. Then what?"

"That was about it. John took the limo and left right after that."

DeSando said he remained at the R 'n' R until almost closing time. He went out and got something to eat and afterward hitched a ride home with a friend. When he walked through the front door, DeSando said he found Hawkins curled up on the living room floor, sobbing.

"What did you say to him?" Yocum wanted to know.

"Nothing. By that time I was pissed at him for pulling such a stupid stunt. I went upstairs, slammed the door, and went to bed. I guess he called Amy Blizzard and she came over later that night, but I didn't see her."

"What about John? Did you ever see him again?" Candisky questioned.

"Yeah, the next morning. John was up before me and he came into my room. He was apologizing for everything he had said the night before. He said he felt a lot better and he had overreacted. He kept saying everything was going to work out, and he asked me not to tell anyone what he had said, especially his mother."

"Now, just so I've got this straight," Yocum said. "We're talking about the morning of Saturday, July 16. Correct?"

"Right," DeSando said.

"What else did John do before he left?"

"Well, about an hour or so later I came downstairs and he was fixing breakfast. Then he left. He told me he was going to the bank." Hawkins returned to the condominium several hours later carrying a duffel bag full of money—tens, twenties, and fifties. "I had never seen so much money. The duffel bag was just stuffed. And there was this guy out in the car that I'd never met. I thought, 'Who in the fuck is this guy?' John said he had to catch his plane and he had to run. He said he would call, but I'd probably never see him again."

"So you've only talked to him on the phone since then, right?" Candisky asked.

"Right," DeSando said. "Thank God. I don't need another surprise visit from his dad. What a psycho master."

Candisky and Yocum glanced at each other again. DeSando had a knack for letting information fall out of his mouth.

"When was John's dad here?" Yocum asked.

"Didn't I tell you guys about that?"

"No, but please go ahead."

About a week after Hawkins left town, his father called DeSando in a fit of rage. DeSando had spoken with Hawkins's mother, Jackie Cirian, and told her that John "was in big trouble." Cirian had evidently called her ex-husband.

"He calls one night and tells me he's three hours away and he's on his way. I have no idea where he was calling from," DeSando said. "So about midnight, he calls and tells me to pick him up at a motel near the outerbelt and High Street. He gets in the car and immediately blasts the radio. He thinks the car is bugged. He'd driven his car to the parking lot at the Continent, then took a cab to the motel. He thought he might be followed. Then we go back to my place, but he wouldn't talk inside, so we are walking down my street and he's whispering. He told me something like 'They have sensors that can pick up sounds outside.' "

"Who's . . ." Candisky began.

"Don't even ask. I don't have any idea who 'they' are."

DeSando said Hawkins, Sr., told him that "John was in a lot of trouble and murder might be involved."

But what perhaps distressed DeSando the most was learning that his best friend was bisexual.

"How the hell did that come up?" Candisky demanded.

"I don't know, he just sort of blurted it out, like it was some kind of excuse for everything John had done. He said something about how John really needed his friends right now and that there was something else I might as well know about him," DeSando replied. "Then he told me John swung both ways. Blew my mind."

"Sounds like John's dad thought his kid was having a meltdown," Candisky offered.

DeSando nodded, getting up from the table. "I'd heard the rumors about John, they were all over the place—even my sister said he was gay—but I'd never believed them. Once this guy at work was spreading rumors about John, and John was going to pay someone to break his legs. He went nuts."

Hawkins, Sr., DeSando continued, arrived in Columbus carrying his clothing and other personal belongings in a plastic garbage bag, and DeSando gave him one of his son's suitcases. The morning after he arrived, the senior Hawkins asked DeSando to arrange a meeting with some Just Sweats officers so he could explain the situation. Ed Laramee, Melissa Mantz, and Paul Colgan met at DeSando's apartment. Without going into too much detail, Hawkins, Sr., told them that his son was in trouble and wouldn't be coming back. "They were all very solemn," DeSando recalled. "It's like they knew it was coming."

Later that afternoon, DeSando drove Hawkins, Sr., back to his car. As they parted, he warned DeSando to keep his mouth shut. He also said he was heading to California to "have a talk with Dr. Boggs."

"He didn't take any of John's stuff with him?" Yocum asked.

"Not really."

"And all John had taken with him was that duffel bag full of money?"

"Pretty much. John didn't own very much personal property. He took some clothes, but he left a lot of stuff here."

"Like what?"

"Everything. Clothes, furniture, paintings, personal stuff. And this great leather coat. I've still got it and . . ."

"Excuse me, Erik. What kind of 'personal stuff' are we talking about?" Yocum inquired.

"I don't know, lots of papers and stuff. There's one you guys might be interested in. I think the insurance company has it now. Missy Mantz found a note in John's desk after he left, and it said what he was going to do with the insurance money," DeSando explained.

"Like, what he was going to spend it on?" Yocum asked.

"No, it was more like how he was going to divvy it up. It said something like: Just Sweats—$500,000; Gene—$50,000; and I think there were initials like M for his mom, F for his father, and B for Boggs. I don't remember all the figures, but this note showed how he planned to split the money."

"You've been sitting on this for a month?" Yocum asked.

"I don't remember exactly when," DeSando explained. "Besides, I'm never sure what I should be telling you guys."

"Any other notes lying around that you want to tell us about?" Candisky asked.

"There was one other one that was kind of weird. John made lists for everything. There were always lists around here. Anyway, one of them said, like, pick up the laundry, go to the bank, call Amy, and cut all ties with Wolfgang."

"Wolfgang?" Yocum said. "Who's that?"

DeSando snickered. "Who do you think?"

"Hanson?" Candisky asked.

"Maybe," DeSando said.

Yocum scoffed. "Wolfgang! Who would use a name like Wolfgang? If the guy is trying to hide, why wouldn't he use something a little less conspicuous?"

"I'm just telling you what the note said," DeSando said.

"Why would he be so stupid as to put that in a note and leave it where you could find it? It's a setup. He put that there to throw people off, blowin' smoke. No one is that stupid."

"Do you have that note?" Candisky asked.

"No. I turned it over to my attorney."

"Can we take a look at the rest of his stuff?" Candisky continued.

DeSando was tiring of the interview. "Maybe next time you come up. I put all his stuff in one of those storage places when I moved out of the old place. I'll try and get over there and get it sometime."

"Where's the locker at?" Yocum asked.

"It's over off of Schrock Road. But I know what you're thinking and forget it. I'm not going over there now. All that stuff is in a garbage bag and that place is a mess. I don't know where it is."

It took five minutes of badgering before DeSando relented. "You're not going to leave until I go get it, are you?"

The reporters smiled. "It's a nice apartment Erik, we could get to like it here," Candisky said.

He ran upstairs to change his clothes.

The storage locker was a five-minute drive from his apartment. DeSando pulled up to the gate and punched in his security number. It didn't work. He tried it two more times before remembering he hadn't paid his bill. He also remembered he hadn't brought his wallet, so Candisky had to loan him thirty dollars so the reporters could get into his bin.

The inside of the garage-sized locker looked as if Hawkins's belongings had arrived in a dump truck. Furniture, paintings, garbage bags full of clothes were strewn everywhere. DeSando tunneled his way to the back, climbed over a table, and spent several minutes digging through the rubble before emerging with a green garbage bag. "This is it. But you guys have got to give it back when you're done."

"No problem," Yocum said, taking the bag from DeSando. "We'll have it back to you in a day or two."

DeSando nodded. "So, how about you guys returning the favor?"

"How so?" Candisky asked.

"Write a story that says I'm not gay."

Yocum burst out laughing. "What?"

"I'm serious. Ever since my picture with John was in the paper, these guys are calling me up in the middle of the night."

"For what?" Yocum tried to choke back his laughter.

DeSando looked away for a minute, then back at Yocum. "They want to come over and suck my dick, okay?"

"So, what do you tell them?" Candisky asked innocently.

"Oh, hilarious. You guys don't understand. I can't go to the R 'n' R or the Elephant Club or anywhere. They stare at me."

"Who?" Yocum asked.

"Everybody! Women won't come near me and everybody thinks I'm gay. I'm through in this town."

38

Back at the *Dispatch* office, Yocum and Candisky took over the mail-room, spreading the contents of the garbage bag all over the floor, on the copy machine, and in mail slots. They began sifting through the stuff, trying to sort, categorize, and Xerox everything that had been in the bag before a bolt of consciousness struck DeSando and he demanded the return of Hawkins's belongings.

The items in the bag displayed the personal, the inane, and the bizarre sides of John Barrett Hawkins: a VIP pass to the R 'n' R USA nightclub; business cards from Columbus attorneys Alec Wightman and John P. Connors; a love letter from actress Missy Hughes; Gene Hanson's account statement from the Imperial Bank; a canceled check for $5.13, drawn on Hawkins's account at The Bank of Beverly Hills; an American Airlines Advantage Program Mileage Summary, a foil-wrapped, lubricated condom.

"How about unopened mail?" Yocum asked.

"Open it."

Yocum slid a finger under the flap of a square, white envelope that had a printed return address:

Colt

P.O. Box 1608

Studio City, California 91604

He winced at the material he pulled from the envelope. "I guess this leaves little doubt as to where Mr. Hawkins's sexual tendencies run." The literature advertised a collection of homosexual bondage and S & M videos, magazines, and calendars. One brochure bore the title, *Buckshot, All Male Videos, The Leather Report.*" Another was called *A Leather Tour de Force.*"

"Hey Cath, 'Enter the domain of the mighty and the yoke of the servile as powerhouse men cram the pages of this sensational leather essay,' " Yocum read. "Quality literature, huh?"

"Secret lives," Candisky said. "Everybody has them. He must have been a pretty frustrated guy, trying to perpetuate this image of the macho womanizer while keeping all this a secret."

"People had to know. I don't care what they tell us, Amy, Erik, Melissa Mantz. Especially Erik. Look, this stuff was delivered to the house—he must have seen some of it. How about this?" Yocum said, holding up another brochure. " 'Big Al delivers, and so do these photos! This is a mouth-watering man who enjoys being appreciated, so we keep him happy.' " Candisky leered at Yocum. "Okay, back to the mundane."

The reporters continued to rummage: a letter from friends in New York; a note containing the work and home phone numbers of Just Sweats silent partner Michael Guglielmelli; the Denver phone number of Bob "Stud Cool" Farrell; a rate card from the Waikiki Shore Apartments in Honolulu; a taxi receipt; a withdrawal slip for $15,000 from Fifth Third Bank in Columbus.

"Look," Candisky said, holding up an American Airlines ticket for flight 599 from Columbus to Chicago to Los Angeles, April 16, 1988. "It's the ticket he used to get to Los Angeles the day this all started."

Yocum didn't react. He was engrossed in a find of his own. "I've got something," he said.

"More leather on parade?"

"Better. Look. Another life insurance policy."

Yocum held up a letter to Hawkins from the Globe Life Insurance Company in Chicago, apparently written in response to a claim Hawkins had made on the policy.

Estate of Melvin Hanson
1620 E. Broad St.
Columbus, OH 43203

Re: Insured: Melvin Hanson
    Claim #C88295281
    Cert. #AW36908

Dear Sir/Madam:

We are in receipt of a claim on the above named insured who passed away on April 16, 1988. We extend our condolences to the family. In reviewing the claim, we note that we do not have the completed information that is necessary for us to process the claim. At the present time, we have hired an outside service to obtain this information. As soon as we have received the information from the outside service, we will further be able to evaluate the claim. If you have any questions regarding this matter, please feel free to contact our office.

Sincerely,

Belinda Standefer
Claims Agent

The garbage bag contained other treasures from the life of John B. Hawkins: a speeding ticket from Kentucky; a 1984 ownership certificate for a Porsche; an overdue bill for $127 from the Continental Athletic Club; a December 1987 notice from the Internal Revenue Service informing Hawkins that he owed $147.62 in back taxes; various airline tickets; a J. C. Penney credit card; a Farmers New World Life drug card; a card from Studio 54 announcing a preview opening of the newly renovated nightclub on November 22, 1985; an Eastern Airlines frequent traveler bonus program; a Howard Johnson hotel receipt; a municipal court filing by Lazarus department store against Hawkins for failing to pay a $463.77 debt; dry cleaning receipts.

The inventory continued. An overdue bill for $42 from St. Ann's Hospital; an envelope from Mountainview Mortuary in Altadena; a notice from a collection agency trying to recover an overdue dental bill of $115.55; a book of blank checks from Fifth Third Bank; a receipt from Ruby Tuesdays restaurant; a B-D, 3cc22g1 Syringe and PrecisionGlide Needle; a parking receipt; more letters from Missy Hughes; a receipt from the Uptown Restaurant for $12; a Christmas card from Missy; a script for a Just Sweats television commercial.

Candisky emerged from the mailroom with a copy of an affidavit made out by Hanson on December 17, 1987. It stated:

The undersigned, Melvin E. Hanson, being of sound mind and first duly sworn, hereby leaves the following instructions to my Executor, John B. Hawkins, regarding the arrangements to be made for my funeral:

1. I direct that my body be cremated.

2. I direct that no relatives, whether by blood or adoption, shall be notified of my funeral or death unless a subsequent probate proceeding requires it.

"It was just his parents and siblings. He was never married," Candisky observed.

"Beats me. He doesn't appear to be the marrying type," Yocum replied.

"But he was the insuring kind—look here," Candisky said, handing Yocum a scrawled note that read, "$15,000 policy, Farmers."

"Now that I think about it, Shelly Navarre told me about this before. Hawkins tried to collect it, but he wasn't named beneficiary for some reason," Candisky said. "We've got to get a hold of Farmers."

"Be my guest," Yocum said. "I'll take my turn in the landfill."

The reporters needed several days to track down this latest—and fifth— insurance policy. Navarre, the claims agent who handled Hanson's policies, was no longer returning their telephone calls. Yocum and Candisky assumed she had been told to let the attorneys handle the press.

Candisky pulled her notes from the August 25 interview with Navarre. She had said the $15,000 policy was a death benefit included in a health insurance plan carried on employees of Just Sweats. Unlike Hanson's other policies, the fifth one named as beneficiary Cecil Tanner, a longtime friend from Atlanta. When Hanson rewrote his will in November, he named Tanner as secondary executor and beneficiary.

Navarre had said Tanner never filed for the money. However, Hawkins tried to collect the $15,000, saying he was entitled to the money as executor of Hanson's will.

Weinstein confirmed the story. The attorney told the reporters that when Farmers refused to process the claim, Hawkins complained. After being told that he had no right to the money, Hawkins made no further attempts to collect on the policy.

DeSando called a few days later to retrieve Hawkins's belongings. The Franklin County Prosecutor wanted to inspect the contents of the bag, Hawkins's friend told Candisky and Yocum. The reporters returned all the documents, except for a book of John Hawkins's checks.

"I don't know if holding on to them is such a good idea," Candisky said. "I don't want to be accused of tampering with evidence."

Yocum threw the checks in his desk drawer. "They'll never miss 'em. Besides, what a great souvenir."

39

Yocum crossed the newsroom wearing a smug smile on his face. He put on Candisky's desk a scrap of notebook paper bearing the name "Ellis Henry Greene" in block letters. "Who's this?" he asked, interrupting her phone call.

She cupped the receiver and frowned. "I don't know. Who?"

"Guess."

"I don't know!" She hated it when Yocum played these games, and she went back to her phone conversation.

"Okay, if you're not interested," he said, turning to walk away. "But it's the corpse. The would-be Melvin Eugene Hanson."

Candisky quickly terminated her conversation. "I'll have to call you back," she said, slamming the handset into the phone. "How did you find that out?"

"Albert."

Albert MacKenzie had been good to his word. Since first contacting the reporters two weeks earlier, the Assistant Los Angeles County District Attorney had called regularly requesting copies of their stories and asking questions about their contacts. He had been very complimentary of their work, though Yocum and Candisky took the praise at face value. After all, MacKenzie was an investigator stroking his sources.

Yocum had just finished copying the contents of Hawkins's garbage bag when MacKenzie called. The assistant district attorney said investigators had identified the corpse as Ellis Greene, whom he described as a 31-year-old alcoholic drifter. They had identified the body the previous Thursday, but hadn't released the information until they had performed another search of Boggs's office and apartment.

"What were you looking for? Did you find any link between Boggs and Greene?" Yocum asked.

MacKenzie declined to discuss the investigation any further, citing the constraints of his position. However, that afternoon he faxed the reporters a copy of the press release.

> The body of a man who reportedly died April 16 of this year in the office of a Glendale physician has been positively identified as Ellis Henry Greene, of North Hollywood.
>
> The body was originally identified by Dr. Richard P. Boggs as Melvin E. Hanson, 46. Boggs, who summoned police to his Glendale office at approximately 7 a.m. on Saturday, April 16, said Hanson had been a patient of his for seven years. He also told police that Hanson had died in his office after complaining of chest pains.
>
> A joint investigation by the Los Angeles County Coroner's office and the fraud division of the California Department of Insurance determined the following:
>
> —The fingerprints of the corpse and the real Melvin Hanson do not match.
>
> —The corpse was claimed and quickly cremated by John B. Hawkins, a business partner of Melvin Hanson.
>
> —John Hawkins is also a patient of Dr. Boggs.
>
> —John Hawkins collected $1 million as the beneficiary of a life insurance policy carried by Hanson.
>
> —Authorities have not been able to locate either Hanson or Hawkins.
>
> On September 29, investigators confirmed through a relative and several friends that the corpse was Ellis Greene. It was also determined that Greene was last seen on April 15, the night before his body was found in Dr. Boggs's office.
>
> Investigators are now requesting the assistance of the public in determining Greene's movements during the night of April 15. It is known that he was last seen at approximately 10 p.m. leaving the Bullet Club Bar, 10522 Burbank Blvd., North Hollywood. Mr. Greene, who witnesses say was in a highly inebriated state, is believed to have left in a cab and may have been en route to the Oak Lounge, 11518 Burbank Blvd., North Hollywood.
>
> Greene was a 31-year-old white male. He was 5 foot 10 inches tall and weighed approximately 135 pounds. He had a small build, thinning brown hair, a light beard and blue eyes. He was last seen wearing a striped pullover shirt and blue pants.

Candisky called Ron Warthen, the chief investigator with the Fraud Bureau of the California Department of Insurance, to whom she had talked several of times before. "Congratulations. You guys didn't waste any time identifying this guy," she said.

"We got lucky. We were looking through missing persons reports and this one just jumped right out. I think we'd only been through about 150," Warthen said. "This is a major breakthrough. We have taken Mr. Greene to within seven hours of when he was found dead on the floor of Dr. Boggs's office. All we have to do is close those missing seven hours, then we should know a lot more about what went on that night."

"Do you think he was murdered?" Candisky asked.

"Don't know and I don't really want to speculate."

"Fair enough. How about Ellis Greene? Can you tell me any more about him? What did this guy do? Did he work? Have a family?" Candisky asked.

"Evidently not. H ɛ ppeared to be a vagabond. He was known to be a heavy drinker; he didn't keep many jobs too long," he said.

Warthen said there was no indication that Greene was a patient of Boggs or that he knew either Hanson or Hawkins.

"Okay. Just so I have this straight. There are two departments involved in this investigation—the Department of Insurance and the District Attorney. Correct?"

"Correct."

"What about the Glendale police? Are they working this, too?"

"No. Just us and the DA at this point."

Yocum decided to try MacKenzie once more to see if he had any other tidbits they might work into their story.

"Well, I don't know if this would be of any interest to you, but there is an unusual coincidence," MacKenzie said. "He used to live in a place called Portsmouth, Ohio. Are you familiar with that town?"

Yocum was.

Portsmouth was a dying industrial town on the Ohio River, about two hours south of Columbus. For years Portsmouth had been a major producer of steel and shoes, but both industries crumbled during the recession of the early seventies. Yocum had been to Portsmouth several times working on stories and was familiar with the city.

"Do you have his parents' names?"

"Yes. Harry and Darlene Greene. We talked to his aunt, a Cleo Fasulo, who lives in North Hollywood. Apparently Ellis lived with her sometimes. She filed the missing person report and identified his photograph."

Yocum felt there had to be a connection between Greene and Hanson and Hawkins. The Portsmouth phone book listed two Harry Greenes. "Why don't you call his parents and I'll see if I can find the number for the Bullet Club," Yocum said. Candisky looked at Yocum as if he had asked her to shoot a puppy. "You don't want to call them?" he asked.

"I'd rather call the Bullet Club."

Four years on the police beat had somewhat hardened Yocum to interviewing the relatives of murder victims. He estimated he had covered about a thousand violent deaths—murders, suicides, traffic fatalities, plane crashes, drownings. The most dreaded task in the newspaper business is knocking on a door and soliciting an interview from a father whose only son has just been killed in a motorcycle accident, or a mother of three widowed through a soured drug deal. As a rookie reporter on the police beat, Yocum would often sit for a half-hour in a car outside the targeted house, trying to summon the courage to knock on the door. Those death interviews never became easy, though experience had made him pretty good at them. He had learned the importance of being the first reporter to the door—before the family could be besieged by other reporters or paralyzed by the reality of the death. Yocum almost always managed to talk his way inside a house. He had developed a nonthreatening manner of easing into questions and bringing out details of the victim's life.

Some, however, could never be convinced to grant such an interview. They considered the request the ultimate invasion of privacy and bad taste. Yocum had been called "ghoul" and "leech" and had been chased away with dogs and ball bats.

Yocum remembered the lessons of those days that afternoon as he called one of the two Harry Greenes in the Portsmouth phone book. A woman with a slow, southern-Ohio twang answered the phone. "Ma'am, this is Robin Yocum, I'm a reporter with the *Columbus Dispatch*. I'm trying to track down the parents of Ellis Greene."

"This is Darlene Greene; I'm Ellis's mother."

"Mrs. Greene, have you talked to anyone about Ellis lately?"

"No."

"The authorities in California haven't contacted you?"

"No."

Her slow, terse manner of speaking made Yocum realize that she didn't know what the reporters did. "Mrs. Greene, oh my, uh, there isn't an easy way to tell you this, and I'm sorry I have to be the one, but your son is dead."

"Oh God, oh God, no, no . . ." Darlene Greene began to sob and pulled away from the phone. "It's a man from the newspaper," she told her husband. "He said Ellis is dead." She cried for several moments before regaining her composure enough to talk to Yocum. He was patient, allowing her to ask the first questions. How and why? Yocum didn't know the how, but he told her it appeared that Ellis had been killed as part of a murder-for-insurance scam. Yocum read the press release to her and relayed what MacKenzie and Warthen had told the reporters.

"Mrs. Greene, I know this is a rough time for you, but we'd like to have a little background information about Ellis for our story. Could you tell me a little bit about your son? When was the last time you talked to Ellis?"

"Oh, it was a few months back, before Mother's Day. I remember because he didn't call me on Mother's Day and that wasn't like Ellis. He always called me on Mother's Day. The last time we talked he said he was coming to visit in June on vacation. I hadn't seen him since he moved to California and that was, oh, about four years ago."

"Had you followed this story on Just Sweats? Do you know if Ellis knew Hawkins or Hanson?"

"I don't know that he did. I've read some of the stories, but I don't think Ellis would associate with people like that," she said.

"In one of our earlier stories we ran Ellis's photograph. You evidently didn't see that one?"

"Now that you mention that, I did see that paper. One of my friends knew Ellis was missing and she brought over the paper, but I didn't think it was him. It didn't look anything like him. I told her, 'That's not my Ellis.' "

Greene, his mother said, was not the ne'er-do-well the California authorities had claimed. He wasn't a vagabond. He worked as an accountant and was simply between apartments. He had been living with his aunt, but she had sold her house and he had been staying in an extra room at the office. "Ellis was a good boy. He would never hurt anybody. I just can't imagine how he got mixed up in this mess," she said.

Ellis Greene had spent nearly all his life in the eastern Ohio village of Powhatan Point. He dropped out of high school and joined the army, but was discharged after one month because, his mother said, "Ellis just wasn't suited for the army. He thought the army was a good idea at first, but once he got in he just couldn't adjust."

Greene returned home and worked a string of odd jobs—cook, street cleaner, hospital aide. When the family moved to Portsmouth,

Greene followed and met JoAnn Rawlins, whom he married in 1979. The marriage began to crumble when the couple moved to Los Angeles in 1982. Greene loved the carefree California lifestyle, but JoAnn felt out of place and was upset over her husband's increased drinking. The couple separated without animosity.

"He was a heavy drinker," JoAnn told Candisky in a telephone interview. "That's the main reason why we separated. I came back to Columbus and our divorce became final in June 1986."

"So you didn't stay in touch?" Candisky asked.

"No, not really. I hadn't seen Ellis in years. He went his own way and I went mine."

"Do you have any idea how he might have gotten mixed up with this bunch?"

"He was the type of person who would do anything for you," JoAnn said. "He might have met those guys in a bar and they gave him a hard-luck story, and he would have done anything for them."

Like Greene's mother, Joann had seen the photograph of Greene in the paper but failed to recognize her former husband. "I was really drawn to that story for some reason. I told my girlfriend at work that this picture looked so familiar to me, but he had a full head of hair when I last saw him. There was some reason why I was drawn to that story and that picture."

After moving to California, Greene pursued a preferred homosexual lifestyle and quickly became a fixture in the gay bars around Hollywood, such as the Rawhide and the Bullet Club.

Candisky interviewed Charles "Chip" Suntheimer, a friend of Greene's who was with him several hours before he was found dead on Boggs's office floor. Suntheimer said Greene was a loyal friend, but he carried a lot of emotional baggage.

"He'd do anything for you," said Suntheimer, who had known Greene for three years. "He was carefree and outgoing, but he had some problems, too. He liked his drugs—cocaine and crystals, mostly; he liked his alcohol; he liked to have fun."

Suntheimer said Greene would prostitute himself when money was tight. For a time he sold pornography and sex toys in a West Hollywood shop. Despite having watched several friends wither and die from AIDS, Suntheimer said Greene never altered his promiscuous lifestyle. It wasn't unusual to find him with a new lover each week. (Blood samples taken from Greene during the autopsy tested positive for the HIV virus.)

"We had a love-hate relationship," said Suntheimer, who stressed that he and Greene were good friends, but not lovers. "If it involved drugs, Ellis wouldn't share it with me. He knew that was a part of his life that I wasn't happy with. I didn't approve. I told him, 'Don't come to me when you're fucked up, expecting me to listen when you're having an emotional experience, crazy on drugs.' There were long periods of time where we wouldn't speak at all, then he'd get upset about something and he'd call me. He was sort of zany."

Candisky and Yocum conducted interviews with several of Greene's friends, his employer, and a co-worker. Through those interviews, the reporters could reconstruct how Ellis Greene spent the last day of his life.

On Friday, April 15, 1988, Parker Martin was already at his Burbank accounting office when Greene arrived about seven that morning. The men had been working long hours in the weeks before the tax deadline. Greene had quit his job in a convalescent home two months earlier to take a part-time job helping Martin around the office during tax season. Martin had promised to teach his employee bookkeeping after the tax-season crunch.

They finished their last tax return about 1:30 P.M., well ahead of the midnight deadline. Martin closed the office for the week and paid Greene his weekly salary of $240 in cash.

Greene's final task for the day was to drive to the post office and put some completed tax returns in the mail. He then planned to meet Martin for a drink at the Rawhide to celebrate the end of tax season. As Greene left the office he kissed the office secretary Brenda Zisovic, who asked him what he was going to do over the weekend. Greene replied that he and several guys were going to a party in Long Beach.

Zisovic chided him. "Ellis, you're a waste. There are all those beautiful girls out there. They'd love a nice-looking guy like you."

"You've got your life and I've got mine," Greene said as he opened the door. "Be happy for me."

As Greene disappeared out the door, Zisovic shook her head and said to Martin, "He scares me the way he's always out running around."

Although Greene was known to have many sex partners, Martin reassured Zisovic that Greene "had a new beau, some rich guy from Glendale. Ellis said this guy was going to back him in a business venture."

Zisovic arched a brow. "A business venture? Ellis?"

Greene had told several people about wanting to start a business, but no one had ever taken him seriously. Martin thought that this time Greene might have a chance at success. Martin continued, "Ellis wants to start a business making cheesecakes. He's been making some for a caterer and he thinks he can make a go of it. He got this recipe from his mom. I had him make some for a party once, and they were heaven."

Greene finished his errands at the post office at about 2:30 P.M. and entered the Rawhide through the back door. Martin and Zisovic were seated at a table, and Greene stopped to talk for a few minutes. He told Martin about his plans to go to Long Beach for the weekend, then left. They never saw him again.

About 7 P.M., Greene went to the Bullet Club where he ran into Suntheimer and a friend, whom Suntheimer knew only as Billy Ray. Suntheimer was on his way to mail his tax returns and Greene asked if they had been typed. When Suntheimer said "No," Greene insisted on typing them. The three men went to Martin's office and grabbed a beer from the refrigerator as Greene began typing the tax return.

Greene had his own key to the office because he had been sleeping there on the couch for several weeks. He left the bungalow he had been renting from his elderly aunt, Cleo Fasulo, when she decided to sell her property. The buyer—a church—planned to raze the buildings for a parking lot. Greene moved his belongings into storage and promised Martin that the sleeping arrangement was just temporary.

About an hour after the trio arrived at the office, they piled back into Suntheimer's 1984 Mustang GT and drove to the Van Nuys Post Office, open late that night for the tax deadline.

After mailing the tax forms, Greene, Suntheimer, and Billy Ray went to a nearby Arby's for sandwiches and a drink. Sunthemier treated. The men sat in the restaurant and talked until about 10 P.M.—listening to Greene boast that he was dating a doctor—then headed to The Mag, a gay bar at the corner of Laurel Canyon and Magnolia. Before they had finished their first beer, Suntheimer told Greene he could only stay for a half-hour because he had to work in the morning. Suntheimer and Billy Ray got up to leave about ten-thirty and they offered Greene a ride. "I told him I had to go, but we would take him wherever he wanted," Suntheimer recalled. Greene asked to be dropped off at the Bullet Club. The bar wasn't in the best of neighborhoods so Suntheimer waited until he saw Greene go inside before pulling away.

Suntheimer maintained that Green was "stone, cold sober" when he arrived at the Bullet Club. But Tony White, the bartender at the club, said he refused to serve Greene because he was too intoxicated. "His speech was slurred and he was having a real hard time walking. I knew Ellis pretty well. He used to come in two or three times a week.

He was a heavy drinker. I told him I wasn't going to serve him alcohol. I gave him a Coke, instead. He wasn't too happy with me." (The autopsy conducted on Greene's body showed a .29 blood-alcohol level, nearly three times the legal limit.)

About thirty minutes after arriving at the club, Greene attempted to make a phone call, but was apparently too drunk to dial the number. He asked White to call him a cab and handed him a business card bearing Russell Leek's name and phone number. Taxi dispatch logs show that Leek picked up a fare at the Bullet at 11:15 P.M. and drove him to 2221 West Olive Street in Burbank, the address of Martin's accounting office. Greene didn't have any money and stiffed Leek for the fare.

The taxi driver was the last time person to see Ellis Greene alive.

Just after midnight, Suntheimer and Billy Ray were awakened when the telephone rang. Suntheimer let his answering machine take the call. "Chip." Suntheimer recognized Greene's voice, but by the time he snagged the phone, Greene had hung up. "He sounded really stressed," Suntheimer said. "I got dressed and got back in the car and drove from my apartment in Studio City back to the Bullet." He made the four-mile trip in about ten minutes, but Greene had already left. Suntheimer went to the Rawhide, then the Job Site on Vineland Boulevard in Burbank, and finally to the In Touch East across the street from The Bullet.

"I didn't get worried when I couldn't find him because sometimes Ellis would call me, upset over the littlest thing," Suntheimer said. "Whenever he got drunk, he got really depressed. It was a funny thing about Ellis, he didn't handle the little pressures well. But if someone was having a major crisis in their life, like someone found out they had AIDS, Ellis was always there. He could talk with the person and really handle it well. But the little things used to really stress him out."

When Greene failed to show up for work Monday morning, Martin wasn't overly concerned, assuming the party in Long Beach had delayed Greene. But when he hadn't returned by Tuesday, Martin called Fasulo, who said she hadn't seen her nephew either. "The first week we just thought he was out having some fun," Martin said.

On Saturday, April 23, Martin drove Fasulo to the Los Angeles Police Department to file a missing person report on Ellis Greene.

40

On Friday, September 30, the day after they identified the man who had died in Boggs's office, investigators conducted simultaneous raids on the physician's medical office and his apartment at 519 South Street. The search warrants were sealed in Los Angeles Municipal Court and MacKenzie refused to reveal their contents. All he would tell the reporters was that investigators spent more than six hours that Friday night searching for evidence linking Boggs, Melvin Hanson, and John Hawkins, and any connection between the men and Ellis Greene.

Candisky and Yocum did, however, learn from a source that investigators seized a stun gun found in the pocket of a faded denim jacket in Boggs's bedroom closet. The search yielded ordinary items, such as Pacific Bell records, but it also shed some light on the doctor's extraordinary bedroom manner. Investigators found whips, chains, and sadomasochist photographs of his live-in lover of three years, a 27-year-old Swede named Hans Jonasson. When Boggs and Jonasson returned home during the raid, investigators snatched an address book from the briefcase the physician was carrying. They also confiscated six cassette tapes that had their ribbons pulled out. The source told the reporters that investigators suspected that the missing tapes held the telephone conversations Hawkins had claimed Boggs had recorded.

With the Los Angeles County District Attorney stepping up the investigation, attorneys for Farmers began positioning themselves for Hawkins's arrest. If he had any money when the authorities apprehended him, Farmers wanted to be first in line for it. On October 4, Farmers' attorneys Robin Hoke and Larry McClatchey filed an involuntary bankruptcy suit against John Hawkins in United States Bankruptcy Court in Columbus. The move was designed to give the insurance company a better chance of collecting its money—if and when Hawkins was found. Farmers acknowledged that most of the money was probably gone, but the involuntary bankruptcy put Farmers at the front of the line for any assets Hawkins might have.

While investigators and attorneys maneuvered within the legal system, Yocum and Candisky explored all avenues for a link between Greene, Hawkins, and Boggs. During her telephone interview with Candisky, Greene's ex-wife had said that he had lived briefly in Columbus while he was working at the state mental hospital in Orient, Ohio. The reporters thought that some kind of connection might have resulted from this.

After learning that Greene had worked for the State of Ohio, Yocum and Candisky requested his employment records from the department of administrative services.

The state's employment file on Ellis Greene contained an accurate work record, but nothing sexy—as the reporters liked to say.

In early 1980, Greene had injured his hand. One document in the folder contained a letter from a Jackson, Ohio, physician, Dr. Robert Williams. The name jogged Yocum's memory. "What's the name of that doctor in southern Ohio who is under investigation for handing out prescriptions to those kids in exchange for sex?" he asked.

Candisky frowned. "Something common. Like Jones or Smith . . ."

"Or Williams?"

"That's it. Why?"

"Look who was treating Ellis," Yocum said, passing the letter to his partner.

The reporters had been trying to find a connection between Greene and Boggs, Hawkins, and Hanson. It was too coincidental that Greene had once lived in Columbus. Now Candisky and Yocum thought Dr. Williams might be that connection.

Boggs, Williams, and Greene were all homosexuals. Williams had been Greene's physician. Greene ended up dead in Boggs's office. Perhaps the doctors were friends and Williams had introduced Boggs to Greene. Boggs was known to be "loose with the scripts." Williams, according to investigators, had also been free with his prescription pad. Yocum called Williams's office to ask if he could see Greene's medical records.

The woman who answered the phone in Williams's office refused to put the doctor on the phone. "He's not taking any calls," she said quite curtly. "What do you want?"

Yocum explained that he was doing a background piece on Ellis Greene, choosing his words carefully so they would not give away his belief that he thought Williams might be involved in the whole Just Sweats debacle. "So, what I would like," Yocum said, "Is to come down and take a look at Ellis Greene's medical records."

"We can't do that," she said. "That would violate the patient's privacy."

"Ordinarily," Yocum persisted. "But the patient is dead. It would be pretty hard to violate his privacy now."

"Well, we're not going to give it to you. The only person we'll release it to is a family member."

Yocum called Darlene Greene and explained the situation. "Cathy and I think there may be a connection among the men," Yocum told her. "If we can get Ellis's records, maybe they will show something." Darlene Greene agreed. Yocum said he and Candisky would pick her up the next morning, October 5, and drive her to Williams's office.

The Greenes lived not far from the Ohio River, in an old frame house in the shadow of a cement factory. The red-eyed, beer-bellied Harry Greene met them at the door. "Darlene can't see you today," he bellowed in a deep, raspy voice. "She's sick."

"Sick!" Yocum said. "Why didn't you call and tell us that before we drove two hours to get here?"

Greene smirked and appeared amused.

"Mr. Greene, we really need to see her," Candisky said softly. "We really need those medical records."

Greene shrugged. "We've heard some television shows want to do stories on this and they'll pay for their interviews."

Harry Greene didn't beat around the bush. He wanted money.

Candisky saw Yocum's eyes widen. Afraid that his next words would immediately conclude the conversation, she asked if they could talk to Mrs. Greene.

"She's too sick," he said.

It was no use. He wasn't going to budge unless they pulled out their checkbooks. As they stepped off the porch, Yocum turned back to Greene. "You know, I've gotten calls from a couple of those television news shows. They told me they were paying a couple thousand dollars for interviews, but I didn't know if I should give them your phone number or not."

Now it was Greene's eyes that widened. "That would have been okay," Greene said.

"Really. Damn. I wish I'd known that. I don't think they need the interviews now."

The reporters climbed back in the car and headed out of town.

"There weren't any shows offering money," Candisky said.

"He doesn't know that. Let the greedy son of a bitch stew over that one for a while."

MacKenzie sent Candisky and Yocum a copy of a photograph taken of Greene a few months before his death. The reporters began carrying it with them to show to anyone to whom they talked about the case: employees of Just Sweats, Wildman, Curtin, Weinstein, DeSando, Woda, Blizzard. No one recognized the man in the picture.

The reporters even took the photograph to some of Hawkins's hangouts, the Elephant Bar and R 'n' R USA, but with no luck.

The Greenes hired an attorney and stopped talking to the reporters. Darlene Greene always sounded polite over the phone, but she wouldn't give up the medical records. If any connection existed between Ellis Greene, Boggs, Hawkins, or Hanson, the reporters couldn't find it.

41

Tom Tornabene, the media liaison in the prosecutor's office, loved to wheedle newspeople for confidential details of their stories. He thrived on the sordid tidbits that the *Dispatch,* being a family newspaper, had never found fit to print. Tornebene had the heart of a gossip—or a reporter. When the Just Sweats case broke, the media liaison began grilling Yocum and Candisky for unpublished particulars of the story. Many times he called Yocum with some inane baseball trivia question. On the afternoon of October 5, however, he called Candisky, and he did not want to talk about America's pastime.

"I don't know if this means anything to you, but some guy from the New York Police Department just called asking to talk to whoever is handling the Hanson and Hawkins case."

"Really? This is great, Tom. I owe you," she said.

"Don't hold back on me. What's going on?"

"We'd asked cops in New York to track down another scam these guys supposedly pulled off. I doubt they'd be calling you guys if they hadn't found it."

Candisky waited about fifteen minutes before calling Lt. John Kelly to see if he had had any luck tracking down Hanson's robbery report.

"Funny you should call. I just got off the phone with the prosecutor in Ohio," Kelly said. "A few days after you called, I was having lunch with a buddy and I told him about the story. He remembered it. Turns out he was the one who took the report."

"You're kidding. That's unbelievable. How many officers are with your department?"

"Oh, about twenty-five thousand," he said.

"And you happened to have lunch with the one guy who took the report?"

"Pretty fortunate, huh?"

"I guess. How can I get a copy of the report?"

"The detective's name is John Miles. Here I'll give you his number."

Miles refused to send Candisky a copy of the report, claiming it was now part of an investigation, but he did agree to answer some of her questions.

"It basically happened just like you said it did."

On February 6, 1985, Hanson claimed that he had been robbed at gunpoint of about $100,000 worth of furniture and personal items. Hanson said he was driving a truck on Manhattan's East Side at about 11:30 A.M., when a man jumped on the side of his truck and shoved a gun in his face. The hijacker ordered Hanson to drive to a warehouse where two other men emptied the truck. Hanson told police he was then locked in the back while the men drove the truck several blocks and abandoned it. He pounded on the door for about ten minutes before a passerby let him out.

Miles told Candisky there was no insurance company listed on the report. Police in New York weren't likely to pursue the case, he said, but he was forwarding the information to investigators in Ohio.

Yocum, who had been reading Candisky's notes over her shoulder, was giving high-fives to an imaginary friend. "Great. Great. This is the best," Yocum said, pacing up and down the aisle, too excited to sit.

With a smirk, Candisky handed Yocum a folded sheet of notebook paper.

"Mario's, Tony's, Nonni's, Lindy's, Skyline Chili. What the hell's this?"

"That's where you're taking me to lunch for the next week."

42

Candisky hung up the phone and spun around in her chair. It was mid-afternoon on October 6, the day their story on the New York scam had hit the streets. "Remember what Rutkoske said about the coroner's ruling?"

Yocum cupped the receiver of his phone. "Yeah. He said it was carved in granite," Yocum said, gathering up notes from another story he was working on.

"Concrete. He said it was cast in concrete."

"Whatever," Yocum said, holding up an index finger. "No thanks, I'll call back later." He hung up the phone and turned toward his partner. "Why?"

"I just got off the phone with Pat Smith, the flack out at the coroner's office. They've changed the cause of death."

"About time. To what?"

"Undetermined."

"Oh, they've really nailed it down, huh? Did you call the Glendale cops?"

"I bet they already know."

Five days after identifying the corpse on September 29, the coroner changed the death certificate of Ellis H. Greene, ruling he died of undetermined causes, rather than the previous ruling of heart failure. "But that's not the best part," Candisky said. "They used the 'H' word. Listen, Smith said, 'The new ruling will allow authorities to begin conducting a homicide investigation. Because of the circumstances surrounding the death, it is unlikely he died of natural causes.' "

"I wonder what Captain 'There-was-no-homicide' Rutkoske has to say about this?"

"Who cares? I'm not dickin' with those guys anymore. I've got a call into MacKenzie. He should be calling . . . ," the ringing of her phone interrupted, ". . . right about now."

"Cathy, I've got sixteen investigators working around-the-clock on this case," MacKenzie said. "We have the entire fraud bureau of the California Department of Insurance working on this, and investigators from the coroner's office, the county sheriff's department, L.A.P.D., and Glendale police."

"Glendale police, huh?" Candisky said, looking at Yocum. "I didn't think they were interested in this case."

"Oh, since it happened in Glendale I asked them for an officer to assist in the investigation."

"Where do you go from here?" Candisky asked.

"We're trying to place Boggs with this man prior to the date of his death," MacKenzie said. "And we're really interested to establish whether Greene was a friend or acquaintance of Hawkins or Hanson."

"I realize it's early in your investigation, but do you anticipate filing charges anytime soon?"

"It's much too early to even speculate on that. First we need to establish Mr. Greene's cause of death. As you know, the body was cremated and our pathologists will only have a small amount of blood and tissue samples to examine."

"So, what will the pathologists be looking for, some kind of poison?"

"That's certainly a possibility," MacKenzie said. "We've got a list of almost two hundred chemicals that could have induced death."

"Did you find any of those chemicals when you searched Boggs's office?"

"Yes, as one would expect to find in any physician's office, we found a number of potentially lethal chemicals."

"Such as . . . ?"

Mackenzie chewed on the question for a few moments. "Let's see if I can remember. Oh yes, they found some oxalic acid."

"Uh-huh," Candisky said, scribbling "o-x-a-l-i-c a-c-i-d" on a sheet of paper and handing it to Yocum. "What else?"

Yocum ran back to the *Dispatch* library to grab the drug and chemical encyclopedia.

"Cathy," MacKenzie continued, "I really don't think it's proper for me to get into specifics at this point."

"Are you looking into any other ways Greene could have died besides poisoning?"

"You might find this interesting. We're looking into the possibility of electrocution from an ungrounded electrocardiogram machine."

"I didn't think I could be surprised by anything these guys might have done, but an ungrounded EKG?"

"It's just a theory, but since there was no obvious cause of death, we have to look at all kinds of possibilities."

"We were told that three sections of the strip of paper that records the EKG test had been cut. Could that have been what Boggs was hiding?"

"Again, Cathy, I simply can't discuss that right now."

"How could you electrocute someone with an EKG machine? They aren't designed to deliver a jolt, are they?"

"No, they're not. I've gathered some literature on the subject and I'll send it to you. I think you'll find it fascinating."

Yocum came back from the library with three medical reference books, one open to "oxalic acid."

"Nasty stuff," Yocum said, sitting next to Candisky. "Sudden death when ingested. Just a few drops can cause internal hemorrhaging. That might explain the blood they found in Greene's stomach."

"Do you know any heart specialists?"

"What's that got to do with oxalic acid?"

"Nothing, but we need to talk to someone about EKG machines. Albert thinks Boggs and Hanson electrocuted poor Ellis with an ungrounded EKG machine."

"What? That's too bizarre. I know a cardiologist up at Riverside. My grandmother baby-sits his kids."

Candisky handed Yocum the phone. "Call him."

The reporters followed politely as Dr. Al Nichols pointed out all the modern life-saving devices on the cardiac care unit at Riverside Methodist Hospital. "What about an EKG machine?" Yocum asked.

"Oh yes, that is what you're here for, isn't it?" Nichols said. "There's one right over here, but I have to tell you, I doubt someone could be electrocuted with one."

"But what if it was ungrounded?" Candisky asked.

Nichols shrugged. "I suppose it's possible, but I've never heard of anyone being electrocuted."

"But if you wanted to electrocute someone," Yocum pressed. "If that was your intention, could it be done?"

"I suppose, but I think you'd have to run the catheter clear to the heart."

"So it is possible," Candisky said.

Nichols nodded. "Possible, just not probable."

43

The reporters produced a quick-hitter for the October 7 paper on how California authorities had changed the cause of death. The reporters then decided to concentrate on tracking down three stories.

Their first lead came from the garbage bag containing Hawkins's personal papers. According to a letter in the bag, Hawkins had attempted to swindle $50,000 from the Globe Life Insurance Company of Chicago by trying to collect on an owner-death insurance policy Hanson held on his Porsche. The reporters had also ferreted out other documents further substantiating the allegation of insurance fraud: Hanson's loan papers with Huntington Bank for the Porsche; title to the Porsche; and a probate filing by the Huntington National Bank, claiming the estate of Gene Hanson owed the bank $56,638.11.

According to county automobile records, Hanson bought a black Porsche convertible from Capital Imported Cars on North Hamilton Road on December 7, 1987—less than a month before he embezzled $1.8 million from Just Sweats and fled Columbus. Although he had told his co-workers he was dying from alleged heart trouble, Hanson applied for and received a five-and-a-half-year loan for $56,350 to purchase the vehicle and an insurance policy that which would pay off up to $50,000 of the car debt.

A week after Hanson's reported death on April 16, Hawkins filed a claim for the money.

Yocum contacted Belinda Standefer, the claims adjuster at Globe Insurance whose name appeared on the letter in the garbage bag. Standefer said that before Globe finished processing the claim, they learned from an officer with the Huntington National Bank in Columbus that Hanson's death may have been a hoax. Huntington held the loan on the Porsche, and at that time was attempting to repossess the vehicle because Hanson had made only one of the $1,177 monthly payments.

"We were lucky," Standefer told Yocum in a telephone interview.

"They just called us out of the blue. We were trying to check out the cause of death, but we hadn't heard it was a scam until we got the call from Huntington."

The Globe loan story ran on Sunday, October 9. By that time Huntington had repossessed the car and scheduled it to be sold at an October 19 Columbus auto auction.

The reporters also tried to substantiate Erik DeSando's claim that Hanson was living in Florida and had had plastic surgery and a hair transplant.

The third story—and the one they wanted the most—required that they determine whether Hanson was indeed using the alias "Wolfgang." Yocum began by telephoning Austin Wildman on the morning of October 11. The lawyer interrupted a meeting with a client to take Yocum's call.

"Sorry to bother you, Austin. Cathy and I are trying to piece together some information on a cryptic note Hawkins supposedly left on his dresser when he skipped town. We think it might refer to Gene."

"Really? What's it say?"

"It was part of a longer note, like a list of things to do. The part we're interested in says, 'Cut all ties with Wolfgang.' "

"Wolfgang?" Wildman laughed. "You think Gene is using the name Wolfgang?"

"Maybe. We don't know. Does it ring any bells?" Yocum asked.

"You know, this is really weird, but I have heard that name. A few days after John left town, his dad showed up here at the office. He was asking about John and the business and how much money he left."

"Yeah, DeSando told us a little bit about that, the old man's visit—really bizarre, huh?"

"You could say that. He was kind of going off on different tangents and then he says, 'You know I'm under investigation by the FBI for selling drugs.' I think he said it was in St. Louis. I told him I didn't know about it and he said the Feds called the investigation 'Operation Wolfgang.' He was bragging about it."

"Operation Wolfgang?"

"Yeah, I'm sure that's what he said. I remember thinking, where did they come up with a name like that?"

"What prompted him to say all this? What do you think he was after?" Yocum asked.

"I don't know," Wildman said. "Maybe he was trying to tip us off to Gene. That's assuming Gene really is Wolfgang."

"Well, we've gotten some information that Gene may be in Florida. Does that make any sense to you?"

"The climate's right," Wildman said. "And I seem to remember John's dad saying something about a car that Gene and John kept in Florida. They would use it when they were down there. I think he said it was a Karmann Ghia."

Later that morning, Candisky and Yocum took a press car and headed up North High Street, knowing there were others trying to track down Wolfgang. DeSando had also told Farmers' private investigator Vince Volpi about the cryptic note. Volpi was the private investigator hired by Mel Weinstein of Farmers to help track down the money and Hawkins. The reporters had first contacted Volpi in late September; they had been exchanging bits and pieces of information with the private investigator for several weeks. Perhaps Volpi wouldn't mind comparing notes with them on Wolfgang as well.

Volpi maintained his office in a nondescript, unmarked brick bungalow nestled among several other homes along High Street that had been converted for commercial use. Watson, a German shepherd belonging to Volpi's girlfriend, guarded the PI's paneled upstairs headquarters.

The reporters' unannounced visit seemed to flatter Volpi more than bother him. Candisky and Yocum had to be careful not to reveal too much of what they had learned. While they didn't mind sharing information, they were never sure of how much Volpi already knew, or how much he was hearing for the first time. Volpi played an equally cautious game with the reporters.

Candisky and Yocum had decided to ask Volpi about Hawkins's note detailing the disbursement of the insurance money before broaching the subject of Wolfgang. The reporters already knew what Hawkins had written and they wanted Volpi to believe he wasn't giving them any new information. If Volpi believed they knew about the insurance money note, he might assume they also knew about Wolfgang and talk freely.

"Erik told us about a note that details how the money was to be divided," Yocum said. "Mantz apparently found it and we've been told that you have it now."

Volpi nodded.

"We're trying to do a story about that note, and we'd like to bounce some things off you. We want to confirm who all of the initials stand for," Candisky said. "Like 'M.' Now we figure that's his mother and 'F' was his father."

"I think you're probably right," Volpi said. He thumbed through a stack of papers on his desk and pulled out a copy of the handwritten note. It read:

JS	$500,000
ME	$50,000
B	$85,000
M	$100,000
F	$30,000

" 'JS' is obviously Just Sweats and 'B' is Boggs. 'ME' might be Melvin Eugene, although maybe it's 'me.' If it was Hanson, he only got $50,000," Candisky said.

"That's strange," Yocum said. "His mom got double that."

"Remember, Hawkins already gave Hanson almost a quarter-million dollars earlier in the year for his share of the company," Volpi said.

"True," Yocum agreed. "But it doesn't seem like much money to give up your identity and your life."

Volpi smiled. "I guess that's a matter of perspective."

"Back to the note," Candisky said. "We know from the bank records that $500,000 went into the Just Sweats account. Any indication that anyone else got any money?"

"I don't know," Volpi said. "We've subpoenaed some bank records, but I doubt that will tell us much. These guys liked to deal in cash."

"Maybe if you can find Hanson he'll tell you," Yocum said.

"Maybe," Volpi said, shoving his pipe into the corner of his mouth. "Know where he is?"

"We've got an idea. We heard Hawkins visited Hanson in Florida in June to give him money for plastic surgery. We also hear he doesn't answer to Gene anymore. He's supposedly passing himself off as a German by the name of Wolfgang. You heard any of this?"

Volpi swirled in his chair, looked at Yocum, then Candisky, then into the bowl of his pipe. He struck a match, lit the fresh tobacco, and drew deeply on the pipe stem. "I'm not sure I can talk about that right now. I'm looking into it and I might be able to talk about it in a few days."

"Let's go off the record, Vince. We don't want you to compromise your position, but we're starting to make lots of calls on this," Yocum said, trying to force Volpi's hand and see if they were on to anything.

"Off the record?"

Both reporters nodded.

"Just for background. You might be right about Florida. I've got a guy down there checking it out, but I really can't tell you any more about it right now. But if this pans out, I'll have a hell of a story for you. It's just going to take a few days."

The story on Hanson's plastic surgery and hair transplant ran the next morning, Wednesday, October 12, under the headline, "Sweats figure said to wear new face." The story included mention of the cryptic notes Hawkins had left behind.

The reporters stopped by Volpi's office before noon that day. Still nothing. When they came by Thursday afternoon, Volpi was sitting in his office, waiting for them.

"I've got a name for you," he said. "Wolfgang Eugene Von Snowden."

"Wolfgang who?" Candisky asked. "You've got to be kidding."

"It's him," Volpi said.

"You know where he's at?" Yocum asked.

"Where he was, but we're closing in on him. We may have him in another day or two."

Volpi said his investigators had picked up the trash in front of DeSando's apartment and traced each of the numbers on his July telephone bill. On July 14, two days before Hawkins disappeared, he made a flurry of early-evening long-distance calls. Three of the calls were to Florida: two to Ft. Pierce, and one, at 7:12 P.M., to Miami. The Ft. Pierce number belonged to Hawkins's father. The Miami number was listed under the name of Wolfgang Eugene Von Snowden.

Melvin Weinstein hadn't been the least bit excited about the Wolfgang lead. He thought that Volpi had spent too much time chasing down peripheral players, such as Nelly and Oleg Mendyuk, Missy Hughes, and Amy Blizzard. Weinstein feared that Volpi's investigation was straying too far from its original objective: locate Hawkins and the missing million. However, when Weinstein's secretary, Marty Highfield, looked over the list of Hawkins's long-distance calls, she immediately spotted the Miami exchange among the telephone numbers. As a former Miami resident, Highfield recognized the number as being from the "high-rent district." She told Weinstein that he should, perhaps, have Volpi check it out.

Volpi told Candisky and Yocum that he had sent one of his investigators, Rick Aeschbacher, to Miami to investigate. Aeschbacher obtained Von Snowden's Miami address, but when he arrived the man was already gone and his telephone disconnected. After reviewing Von Snowden's rental contract and talking with some of his acquaintances, however, Aeschbacher felt almost certain that Hanson was alive and well.

"So, this rental agreement . . ." Yocum started.

Volpi shook his head. "I can't show it to you. It's up to Mel. He calls the shots."

The reporters got back into the press car and headed downtown to the newsroom and began trying to track down Wolfgang Eugene Von Snowden.

"If you were going undercover to hide from the police, what name would you pick?" Candisky asked.

Yocum shrugged. "Jim Smith, John Jones. It wouldn't be Wolfgang Von Snowden."

"Do you think he really picked through the trash for those phone records?"

"More likely he's got a friend inside the phone company, but I don't care how he got it. It's that gift horse thing."

Yocum called information in Tallahassee and got the number of the Florida Bureau of Motor Vehicles. A clerk there told Yocum, "I don't have a Von Snowden, but a Wolfgang Eugene Von Snowde obtained a license in August. This must be the same guy. We don't have many Wolfgangs running round down here."

Yocum jotted down the information the clerk gave him. "Cathy, do you have the Hanson bio we put together?"

Candisky pulled a manila folder from a cardboard box that had become their mobile Just Sweats file. "Right here."

"What's Hanson's birthday?"

"10-8-41."

"Bingo. Same as Von Snowde or Von Snowden, whichever. How about his SS number?"

"263-66-1923."

"Off by one. This guy's is 263-66-1924."

"It's him," Candisky said. "No doubt about it."

Von Snowde's driver's license bore an address at Brickell Shores Condominiums south of Miami. Candisky told the lady who answered the phone at the complex, "I'm calling from the *Columbus Dispatch*, a newspaper in Ohio. Can I speak to the apartment manager?"

"No here," she said with a heavy Spanish accent.

"Okay, maybe you can help me. I'm trying to locate a Mr. Von Snowden. Do you know him?"

"Si. But he no live here now. He move."

"When did he leave? Do you know where he went?"

"I no allowed to say. I no can talk to you."

"Who said you can't talk to me?" Candisky asked.

"I sorry. I go." The phone went dead.

Candisky slammed the phone and turned back to Yocum. "She hung up on me. Either she was scared to talk or Volpi's investigator told her not to talk to us."

"Let's try Weinstein. Maybe he'll give us a copy of the lease," Yocum said.

Marty Highfield met the reporters in the lobby and led them down a flight of stairs to Weinstein's office. "I don't know if he's going to let you see it," Highfield said. "You know Mel."

Highfield escorted the reporters into Weinstein's office. Weinstein stood up from behind a desk of neatly aligned stacks of papers and extended a hand to Yocum. "We need your help, Mel. We tracked Hanson down to Miami and we're trying to get a copy of a lease agreement. Cathy talked to someone in the apartment complex and we understand you have a copy."

"Won't they give it to you?" Weinstein asked.

"We thought this would be quicker," Candisky said. "Besides, the woman I spoke to could hardly speak English."

Weinstein sat back in his chair and clasped his fingers in front of his mouth.

"It can only help," Yocum said after a few moments of awkward silence. "The story could prompt some new leads on where he's gone."

Weinstein nodded. "Marty," he called. Highfield poked her head into the office. "Can you make them a copy of that Brickell Shores lease agreement?" He turned back to Yocum and Candisky. "Just keep my name out of it. I don't mind giving this to you, you obviously knew about it. But just keep my name out of the paper."

"No problem," Candisky said.

It was a one-block walk back to the *Dispatch,* but the reporters couldn't wait. They plopped on a brick planter outside the attorney's office and scanned the lease. "This story is better than sex," Yocum said.

Wolfgang Eugene Von Snowden had signed a one-year lease on January 3, 1988, for Penthouse #4 at the Brickell Shores Condominiums, a housing complex in an area of affluent oceanfront high-rises.

Just as Von Snowden's birthdate and social security number were almost identical to Hanson's, Von Snowden had an employment background similar to Hanson's. Von Snowden listed his most recent job as a nonactive partner with Sweats Inc., of Columbus, Ohio, a position he had held for three years. During the two years before that, he was an active partner with the company and worked in Hamburg, Germany.

The similarities continued. Von Snowden's previous address had been 1620 East Broad Street in Columbus—Hanson's former Park Tower condominium. He also listed two vehicles, a 1988 Porsche and a 1971 Karmann Ghia.

Von Snowden gave his State of California driver's license identification number as C2042656, the same number that was on Hanson's expired license. And, Von Snowden asked that in case of an emergency, John B. Hawkins be contacted at his Columbus telephone number.

But perhaps the most damning evidence of conspiracy came from Von Snowden's two references, both of whom were contacted by condominium management.

"I have had the pleasure of knowing Mr. Von Snowden for approximately ten years. During that time he has always been a friendly gentleman and a very good businessman," Dr. Richard P. Boggs told Brickell Shores employee Maria Del Carmen Lopez.

John B. Hawkins provided Von Snowden's second reference. "I have known Mr. Von Snowden for about seven years. He has always been a very nice and friendly person. He has always canceled his debts on time," Hawkins had said.

Based on the date on which the lease was signed, the reporters surmised that Hanson had gone to Florida after bilking Just Sweats of $1.8 million and telling co-workers he was going to California.

Von Snowden moved into the condominium February 11, 1988. He listed his previous address as the Mutiny Hotel in Hollywood, Florida.

"Why, if you were going to go underground, would you use a name like Wolfgang Von Snowden?" Yocum mused.

"I'd be surprised if he doesn't speak a little German," Candisky said. "Didn't his mother tell us he was stationed in Germany while he was in the army? Then he traveled there as a shoe buyer. He's got to know a little German."

Yocum shrugged. "Still seems farfetched."

The reporters returned to the office and set up a conference call with Volpi. They wanted to let him know that Weinstein had given them a copy of the lease.

"Do you know how long ago Hanson moved out of the condo?" Candisky asked the investigator.

"Sometime in the middle of August. That's when he unloaded all his furniture. He was apparently in a hurry because he sold it real cheap. I guess he took a real wash. Some outfit called the South Beach Furniture Company loaded it up on August 12. Even if he hadn't panicked and left, I guess he wasn't long for that condominium anyway. Rick's been doing some poking around and I guess Mr. Von Snowden had just about worn out his welcome."

"How so?" Yocum asked.

"Some of his neighbors told Rick that he was using some call-boy service and having these guys up to his apartment nearly every night. I guess he liked them young and muscular."

"Was he telling everyone he was from Germany?" Candisky wanted to know.

"I guess so, but I don't think he was very convincing," Volpi said. "The real estate agent who got him the penthouse took him to dinner at a German restaurant and when the waiter spoke to him in German, Hanson just got this stupid look on his face. The waiter told the guy, 'I don't know who he is, but he's not German. That accent is from the Deep South.' "

44

In the late afternoon of October 14, Yocum and Candisky were polishing up a Sunday story on Hanson's living in a Miami penthouse under the alias of Wolfgang von Snowden. It was a typical Friday and the *Dispatch* newsroom resembled a noisy diner as reporters trying to finish their weekend stories fought for computer terminals.

They tried to ignore the confusion around them as they awaited Volpi's call. More than an hour ago the private detective had called to tell the reporters that under orders from Weinstein, he was leaving his office to file charges against Hanson. The insurance company had been reluctant to file criminal charges on its own, but had changed its position at Albert MacKenzie's request.

During a call to Weinstein earlier that day, MacKenzie had said that two of his investigators had flown to Miami to join in the search for Hanson. MacKenzie said he believed that the investigators, acting on Volpi's tip, were closing in on the fugitive.

However, the district attorney's investigation was still incomplete, and MacKenzie wasn't ready to file criminal charges. Nor were the authorities in Franklin County. Once charges were filed, the prosecutors would lose their power to subpoena records and bring witnesses before a grand jury. But without charges on the books, authorities would be unable to detain Hanson. MacKenzie recommended that Farmers file theft charges. The move would allow Hanson to be arrested if he was caught, while prosecutors could continue their investigation unhampered. Company officials at Farmers headquarters in Mercer Island, Washington, gave Weinstein the go-ahead.

Volpi, acting on Farmers' behalf, was to swear out the complaint in Franklin County Municipal Court. The investigator had promised to call Yocum and Candisky as soon as the charges were filed.

By 8 P.M., however, Volpi still hadn't called, and the reporters were unable to reach him at home or his office. They asked Rosemary Kubera, a general assignment reporter covering the police beat that night, to check the clerk of courts office for any charges filed against Hanson. "Don't even ask the guys down there about it, because if they know about it they'll tip off TV," Candisky instructed. "Just sort through the affidavits and see if you can find one for Hanson."

"No problem," Kubera said.

"Even more important," Yocum said. "Don't use the two-way. Either make copies of the warrant or call us on the phone. The TV stations monitor our radio and we don't want to tip them off."

Kubera nodded as she packed the portable scanner and a two-way radio into her bag.

Yocum and Candisky had long finished both their Sunday story on Hanson, aka Wolfgang Eugene Von Snowden, living in Florida and a rough draft on Farmers filing charges against Hanson. To amuse themselves the reporters took turns shooting a Nerf basketball at a hoop suspended above Yocum's desk. When and if the charges were filed, they would fill in the blanks of their draft for the next day's paper. Time passed: Volpi hadn't called, nor Kubera. Candisky started to pace while she nursed a Tootsie-Pop.

"I wonder what's keeping her?" Yocum asked. He flung a shot at the hoop. "It's after nine o'clock." He rimmed it.

Candisky shrugged. "She probably got held up at the police . . ."

The blare of the two-way radio on the city editor's desk interrupted her. "Kubera to city desk."

"What's she doing?" Yocum asked, wincing in disbelief.

"Go ahead, Rosemary," said reporter Grady Hambrick who was closest to the radio.

"Tell her to shut up. Tell her to shut up," Yocum yelled as he sprinted toward the city desk twenty yards away.

"Would you tell Cathy and Robin that a theft charge has been filed against Melvin Hanson. I'm bringing them a copy."

"Okay, Rosemary, thank you," Hambrick said, watching in bewilderment as Yocum ran through a row of copy editors. "Robin, Rosemary says she has your warrant . . ."

"And now the whole goddamn city knows about it," Yocum growled, grabbing the radio. "Rosemary, would you call me at 8521, immediately."

Yocum, who had been nursing a rib he'd cracked playing flag football, thought he had punctured a lung during his dash across the newsroom. He stalked back to his desk. Candisky diplomatically snagged his phone when Kubera called and calmly asked for details from the warrant.

"Tell her she better drop copies off to the TV stations. They might have missed part of her broadcast," Yocum muttered.

Candisky cupped the receiver. "Okay, that's great, Rosemary. Sure, I'll talk to you when you get back. No need to talk about this on the radio anymore."

The reporters pulled their rough draft up on screen to add the details of Farmers' complaint. Hanson was charged with one count of theft by deception, a second-degree felony.

A few minutes later, Volpi called. He told the reporters that he had filed a theft charge, and that U.S. Magistrate Terence P. Kemp had issued a federal arrest warrant for unlawful flight to avoid prosecution. Because of the late hour, Volpi and FBI agent Mark Chidichimo had taken the warrant to Kemp's home for his signature. The federal warrant allowed the charge to be logged in the National Crime Information Computer, which was accessible by law enforcement agencies across the country. Volpi was hesitant to tell the reporters much more. Instead he suggested they call Weinstein, who was at a party at the home of a law partner. Weinstein was expecting their call, Volpi said.

"Do you think you'll have Hanson arrested tonight?" Yocum asked.

After a momentary pause, Volpi answered. "This morning, I would have said yes. But California is screwing it up. I really can't go into it now, but I'll be glad to tell you later."

Candisky telephoned Weinstein at his party. "Mel, I understand the charges, but I still need a quote."

"How about this, 'Farmers is determined to see that those who may have been involved in defrauding it are brought to justice.' How's that sound?"

Boring, Candisky thought. "Fine. Listen, why haven't you filed any charges against Hawkins? Is it because nobody knows where he's at?"

"Um, I can't comment on that at this time."

45

Volpi's comments the previous night had captured the reporters' interest. To slake their curiosity, Candisky and Yocum visited Volpi at his office late Saturday afternoon. Volpi had spent most of the day on the phone with Aeschbacher, who was trying to keep authorities at bay while he searched for Hanson. "If I'd any idea that it was going to turn out like this, I would have never . . ." Volpi slouched back in his chair and ran his fingers through a head of curly hair. "Typical cops."

With an elbow propped up on his desk and his head resting in his palm, Volpi continued. "I called MacKenzie Thursday and faxed him a copy of the rental agreement. I figured we were all on the same team. But our heroes from California had to come in, take over, and screw everything up."

MacKenzie had sent Glendale Police Detective Jon Perkins and Michael W. Jones, with the California Department of Insurance, to meet Volpi's investigator in Miami. Volpi had instructed Aeschbacher to avoid any meeting with Von Snowden until Perkins and Jones arrived.

"They get to Miami Friday morning and Rick meets them at the Brickell Point Hotel . . ."

"Where Von Snowden had been staying?" Yocum asked.

"No. There's a ton of stuff called Brickell whatever, but it was near Hanson's condo. Anyway, Rick told Perkins and Jones all about Hanson's new lover—some massage therapist by the name of Del Bergen—and all about this plastic surgeon who says he gave Hanson a face lift."

"So you've confirmed that Hanson's had plastic surgery?" Candisky asked.

"Yeah, a Dr. Jeffrey Tardiff did it. Rick talked to him and the guy says Hanson looks twenty years younger. Tardiff was getting Rick some post-surgery photographs of Hanson. They were supposed to meet today."

"But?" Candisky said.

"This is what they call a multi-jurisdictional cluster fuck," Volpi said. "Perkins and Jones told Rick to butt out. They'll handle Tardiff. They're going to put the heat on him. They told Rick they were going to threaten Tardiff with aiding and abetting a fugitive. Rick tells them they don't need to muscle him, that they guy's been cooperative, but they wouldn't listen."

"Nice," Yocum said. "First no one wants to investigate this thing, now they're falling all over each other."

"Wait. It gets better," Volpi continued. "Then Perkins and Jones get the FBI to warn Rick that if he doesn't stay away, he'll be arrested for obstruction of justice."

"Is there anything you can do?" Candisky asked.

"I'll tell you what I did do. I called the FBI office in Miami and told them, 'Do you see whose name is on that arrest warrant? Pull another stunt like that and I'll withdraw the warrant. Then you can walk up to Hanson and shake your dick at him.' "

"Withdraw it," Candisky said. "Force their hand. Make them file their own charges."

"I'd like to, but that's up to Mel."

"So has anybody come up with anything on Hanson?" Yocum asked.

Volpi shook his head. "Not that I know of. Perkins and Jones went over to Tardiff's house, but supposedly he couldn't find any photographs of Hanson. I guess the FBI was within ten feet of him but didn't recognize him."

"Back up. Within ten feet of Hanson?" Yocum asked.

"Yeah. He was out on some dock where we heard he was living on a boat. Then they figured it out and went back, but he was long gone."

The activities of Farmers' hired detectives in turn angered the FBI agents and investigators from California. They felt that Volpi wanted to control the entire investigation. Columbus FBI agent Robert Gillespie even cautioned Volpi, "Don't step on my toes." But Volpi remained convinced that he could have apprehended Hanson, if it hadn't been for the lawmen's "quest for the glory."

On Monday morning, October 17, Yocum and Candisky hiked four blocks to the Federal Court Building to pick up a copy of Hanson's federal arrest warrant. They were hoping that the affidavit filed to secure the warrant might have additional details of Hanson's whereabouts. "You want the warrant they filed on Hawkins, too?" the clerk asked.

"Sure," Candisky said, acting as if she knew what he meant.

Yocum leaned toward Candisky so he wouldn't be heard around the room. "They can't file an unlawful flight warrant unless some kind of local charge was filed, can they?"

"No. A local charge has to be filed. Let's see what he's got."

The reporters sat down to read the warrants at a table outside the clerk's office. Like Hanson, Hawkins had also been charged with unlawful flight to avoid prosecution. Federal Bureau of Investigation Agent Mark Chidichimo wrote in his affidavit:

> On 10-14-88, one warrant was issued in Franklin County, Ohio, for the arrest of John B. Hawkins in connection with a $1 million insurance fraud matter. This case has been under aggressive investigation by local authorities for several months. On 10-14-88, investigator Vince Volpi of the (Farmers) New World Insurance Company advised that he has traced Hawkins as he has fled cross country. He spoke with a close associate of Hawkins who advised that Hawkins called the associate collect 9-16-88. Toll records later showed that the call originated in Camden, New Jersey.

"They filed against Hawkins, too. I can't believe Volpi and Weinstein didn't tell us about Hawkins," Candisky said.

"Read me the part about the 'aggressive investigation by local authorities,' " Yocum said, rolling his eyes. "Give me a break."

It was apparent from the information on Hanson's warrant that authorities were much closer to catching Hanson than Hawkins.

> On 10-14-88, a warrant was issued in Franklin County, Ohio, for Melvin Eugene Hanson, in connection with a one million dollar insurance matter. This case has been under aggressive investigation by local authorities for several months.
>
> On 10-14-88, Mr. Vincent Volpi, an investigator for the victim, (Farmers) New World Insurance Company, advised me of the following information:
>
> He had determined, through investigation, that Hanson was using the name Wolfgang (last name unknown). He was then able to determine that two co-conspirators in this matter were referring to "Wolfgang" in written communications and through one of these documents was able to identify Wolfgang as Wolfgang Eugene Von Snowden.
>
> It is noted that both have the middle name Eugene.
>
> Volpi was able to trace Von Snowden to Florida and located

someone who knew him. This individual stated that Von Snowden confided to him that his real name was Melvin Hanson, aka, "Gene Hanson."

On 10-14-88, I was able to determine that one Wolfgang Eugene Von Snowden, date of birth, 10-8-41, had recently obtained a Florida driver's license bearing a Miami address.

It is noted that 10-8-41 is Hanson's birthdate.

Yocum and Candisky walked to the county courthouse for a copy of the theft warrant that had been filed on Hawkins. The reporters had no one to blame but themselves. They had instructed Kubera to look for a warrant on Hanson only.

Early that week, Perkins and Jones returned to California, abandoning their search for Hanson for the time being. Over the next several days, Candisky and Yocum badgered MacKenzie about any leads his investigators had developed in Florida, but the prosecutor would only promise to call when Hanson was caught. The reporters again turned to Volpi, who by now was disheartened and convinced Hanson's trail had long gone cold. The private investigator gave the pair what little new information they had gathered on Hanson.

"You guys were right about the Karmann Ghia," Volpi told them. "He was tooling around in it, but he left it in Miami. And I'm sure he's given up his Von Snowden alias."

"How about John?" Candisky asked. "Is he with Gene?"

"No. Supposedly Gene's with Cecil Tanner."

"Cecil! He's the guy who was the beneficiary on the one insurance policy."

Volpi nodded. "That's him. From Atlanta. He and Hanson were looking at property in Key West. Hanson told some real estate agent he wanted to open a gay bed and breakfast. The cops went to check it out, but Hanson and Tanner were long gone."

46

When the tangled tale of John B. Hawkins and Melvin E. Hanson had begun to unravel months earlier, newly named Just Sweats President Ed Laramee and vice-president Melissa Mantz had asked Yocum and Candisky to write a "positive story" on the company. The reporters thought the executives had a valid point. A week before Christmas they arranged to interview Laramee and Mantz at the company headquarters.

This interview was much more relaxed than their earlier ones. Although he continued to chain-smoke, Laramee seemed much more at ease than Mantz, who never appeared comfortable around the reporters.

Mantz assailed them for what their stories had led the reading public to think about Just Sweats and its employees. "There are a lot of good people out here, struggling to keep the stores open, and it's not fair that they're being lumped in with John and Gene," Mantz said. "This isn't John and Gene's store anymore, but we're still dealing with their mess."

And a mess it was. At a time when the shelves should have overflowed with goods for the Christmas rush, Just Sweats was still dealing with vendors on a cash-only basis. One day, when the Just Sweats staff learned that merchandise wouldn't be delivered until Monday, a group of employees picked up the shipment from the freight company at 2 A.M. Friday so the store would have stock for the weekend.

"When you're operating c.o.d., you're using yesterday's sales to pay tomorrow's bills," Laramee said. "Once that happens, you really have to generate the dollar. A lot of retailers are already working on spring. For us, what was bought last week is being sold today. But sales are pretty strong. Each week has been stronger than the week before. All things considered, we're doing pretty well."

Attorney Austin Wildman said that, under Laramee's leadership, the company was turning a profit, but was still heavily in debt. In mid-September, in an effort to salvage the financially troubled company, Just Sweats had closed four of its twenty-two stores—two in Kentucky and two in Columbus. Management also intended to shave its overhead by closing other stores if their locations proved unprofitable. For example, Just Sweats had placed one Columbus store at Central Point, an outdoor shopping center with a couple of discount stores, a pawn shop, and a liquor store. "You could wonder six ways to Sunday trying to figure out why they put a store in there," Laramee said. Wildman speculated that Hawkins had opened stores such as these with no intention of making money, but simply as a way to show expansion and secure additional bank loans.

David Kessler, vice-president of commercial lending at Fifth Third Bank, had overseen the Just Sweats accounts and approved loans made for the company. On July 15—the same day Hawkins began withdrawing funds from Fifth Third accounts—Kessler resigned his position. Although he refused to talk to reporters, during a deposition taken by Weinstein, Kessler said he had given verbal notice of his resignation two weeks earlier, and it had nothing to do with his association with Hawkins or Just Sweats.

Bank officials also refused to talk to the *Dispatch*. The reporters had even heard that bank personnel were embarrassed about loans they had made to Hawkins and Hanson. In fact, Fifth Third's dealings with Just Sweats had become a joke within the Columbus banking community because other banks had refused Hawkins's requests for similar loans. One source said officers at other banks considered Hawkins an oddball and his loan requests ludicrous.

After Just Sweats had filed for Chapter 11, Fifth Third floated the company a $100,000 loan for merchandise. The amount wasn't enough to deal with the outstanding financial problems, but it was the best Laramee could get for his company. Laramee began stocking quality merchandise—something that had not been done under Hawkins's directorship—in hopes of luring back former customers.

By keeping Just Sweats open, Fifth Third stood a chance of recovering more of their loans. According to Wildman, Fifth Third gave Laramee a loan, but with explicit instructions to keep the bank "out of the paper."

47

Danny Abraham succeeded Bob Smith in the prosecutor's office and so inherited the Just Sweats case. In August, in a moment of bravado, Smith said John B. Hawkins would be in police custody within six months.

Neither Candisky nor Yocum trusted in the accuracy of Smith's prediction. While the reporters had felt certain that Hawkins would be the first to be apprehended, neither believed he would remain at large for up to half a year. Hawkins's own brash, flamboyant nature would surely bring him to justice. He might boast of his crime to an untrustworthy acquaintance or confide the secrets of his past to a soon-to-be-scorned lover. He might even foolishly decide to visit his mother during the Yuletide season, believing himself to be somehow beyond the law's grasp.

From mid-December to January, Candisky and Yocum awaited the slip-up that would bring Hawkins into custody. Nothing happened. No one turned him in, no one betrayed him. No one reported to the authorities that Hawkins was seen playing Santa Claus to Jackie Cirian. Hawkins's whereabouts remained unknown.

After the holidays, Yocum and Candisky scanned their old note-books, address books, and messages, hoping to find an overlooked tip or lead. Nothing. They were dry. They had followed up everything in their notes at least once before. The reporters decided to go to the Franklin County Courthouse and visit Abraham on the morning of Tuesday, January 3, 1989. Perhaps he would throw them a bone.

Abraham was always friendly with the reporters, but reticent—a far cry from the chatty Bob Smith. The assistant county prosecutor considered his amassed information private until it had been made public in court. In his mind, premature disclosure constituted unprofessional behavior that could jeopardize his case. At one point, the reporters complained to Prosecutor Mike Miller about Abraham's reserve. The newspeople's reaction to the differences between Abraham's methods and Smith's amused Miller. As an elected official Miller was well aware of the benefits of keeping reporters happy. He conceded that Abraham had a responsibility to share some information and promised to talk to Abraham. "I'll ask him to loosen up a little," Miller promised.

The reporters found Abraham at his desk when they popped in on their surprise visit. "No," Abraham said, closing a brief he was reading and flipping it over on his desk. "Nothing new. You guys knew that Hawkins's parents were in town last week?" The reporters gaped. Abraham grinned. "You didn't know? I thought for sure you guys would have known."

"We hadn't heard," Candisky said. "Did you see them?"

"Oh yeah. They were here."

"What did they want?" Yocum asked.

Abraham shrugged. "I don't know what they wanted, really. I think it was a little fishing expedition to see what I would tell them."

John Hawkins, Sr., and Jackie Cirian had acted more like celebrities than parents concerned about the future of their son. They paraded into Abraham's office wearing sweat shirts emblazoned with the Just Sweats logo and name of the company their son had founded and then nearly ruined. Hawkins, Sr., sat down and announced his presence with a resonant belch.

His former wife didn't seem to notice the gaucherie. "There are no charges pending against my son," she proclaimed as if before a standing-room-only crowd. "I called the authorities in Los Angeles and they said they had no charges against Johnny."

"Maybe they don't," Abraham said. "But theft charges have been filed here."

Both of Hawkins's parents claimed that they hadn't seen their son recently, but Cirian admitted she had last seen him in August in Las Vegas. Both mother and father insisted that they had no idea of how even to contact their son; yet they asked Abraham what would happen to Hawkins if he turned himself in.

Abraham told them, "I can't make any promises. I'm taking this case to the grand jury to seek multiple indictments against both John and Hanson, but obviously the first one in the door would have the best chance to negotiate a plea bargain if he's willing to cooperate."

"And? Anything else?" Yocum asked.

"That was about it," Abraham said. "They still said they didn't know how to get a hold of him, and they kept saying he was innocent.

Then they left. I haven't heard from them since."

"That's all they came to town for?" Candisky asked.

"No, they were out at Just Sweats. They talked to Ed Laramee, and I think they talked to Erik DeSando, too."

The reporters instinctively knew their next two destinations.

Laramee was sitting behind a desk in an outer lobby of the small Just Sweats headquarters. The ashtray on his desk barely contained a heap of cigarette butts, but Laramee was busy lighting another. "Haven't seen you two in a while," he commented.

"We thought we ought to leave you alone for the Christmas rush so you could get some work done," Candisky said.

"Oh, if it's not you guys it's someone else. I had a guy in here last week who claimed he was from the *Wall Street Journal.* I think he was an undercover investigator working for Volpi."

Yocum and Candisky knew that Volpi used that ploy as one of his tactics. They had heard that Gus, the alleged reporter from *Rolling Stone,* who had paid DeSando $500 for information, actually worked for Volpi as a detective. But the reporters had also learned that someone from the *Journal* had really been in town working on the story.

"He might have been legit, Ed," Candisky said.

"Well, I humored him, answered his questions. But I thought he was a detective."

"We heard you had some other unexpected visitors last week," Yocum suggested.

Laramee laughed.

"What did they want?" Candisky asked.

"Good question," Laramee replied. "They didn't really say. I think, mostly, they wanted to know who owned the company. I explained the bankruptcy thing. It was pretty casual, more like a social call than a business meeting. They didn't seem overly concerned about their son."

The week before Christmas Jackie Cirian had called Melissa Mantz and told her, "I might be coming to Columbus real soon."

"Don't expect everyone to welcome you with open arms," Mantz retorted.

Cirian called Mantz again the next week. "John's dad and I are in town; we'll be over in fifteen minutes."

Hawkins, Sr., and Cirian conversed briefly with Laramee and Mantz at the Just Sweats headquarters, then went to the Just Sweats store next door and bought several sweat shirts. "You know, my son started this store," Cirian boasted to a clerk as her ex-husband tore a bill off of a wad of hundreds and paid for the sweat shirts.

At Laramee's suggestion, Hawkins, Sr., and Cirian went to visit Abraham. They then went to DeSando's northside condominium, equipped with a U-haul trailer for retrieving any and all of their son's belongings.

The reporters found DeSando at home in an almost empty apartment. DeSando's apartment was practically naked. "What happened to all your furniture?" Candisky asked.

DeSando looked around the apartment and shrugged. "This is all courtesy of John's parents."

"They took everything?" Yocum asked.

"Damn near."

DeSando said he didn't even know Cirian and Hawkins, Sr., had come to Columbus until he arrived home from work one afternoon and found them waiting in the parking lot. He was stunned when he saw John's parents step out of their car. "I wanted to get back in my car and leave," DeSando confided. "After telling the FBI about John's confession the night at the R 'n' R, I had hoped I would never have to face Jackie again. Wrong! I said, 'Jackie! Mr. Hawkins! What are you doing here?' Then Jackie comes running up to me and gives me a big hug. She said, 'It's so good to see you.' I'm thinking, 'What the hell is going on?' She said they were in town to take care of some business and wanted to stop in for a visit and maybe spend the night."

"She just came right out and asked to spend the night?" Candisky marveled.

DeSando nodded. "Yeah, and she really caught me off guard. I mean, what are you going to say? I told them they could. I really didn't want them around, but they were acting pretty friendly, and I felt obligated."

"So, what happened?" Yocum inquired. "You guys sit around and reminisce about the good old days, before her son became a fugitive from justice?"

"Hardly. Once Jackie got inside she turned off the charm. Man, she was in my face. She sticks her finger in my face and starts yelling, 'You'd better start keeping your mouth shut about Johnny. We talked to the district attorney in California and he said there are no charges against Johnny.' "

DeSando said their conversation was interrupted by a telephone call from Julie Gertz, an airline stewardess from Boston and one of

Hawkins's old girlfriends. Gertz had spoken with Hawkins after he left Columbus and wanted to know if DeSando had heard from him. When she realized that a friend of her son's was on the telephone, Cirian grabbed the receiver. "Don't talk to Erik," Cirian said. "Everything he says about Johnny is a lie."

"So what did you do all night?" Candisky asked.

"I didn't do anything with them. I left," DeSando said.

The reporters looked at DeSando in disbelief. "Left?" Yocum asked. "Erik, you've got to be kidding. Why would you leave them here alone?"

"I couldn't handle it," he said. "They show up with no warning and make themselves at home. I had to leave."

"Is that when they cleaned you out?" Candisky asked.

DeSando nodded. "Not too smart on my part, but I didn't know they were going to take everything." DeSando scanned the near-barren apartment. "I wish I'd never met John. There's just no getting away from this shit. I suppose you heard what happened up in New Hampshire."

Yocum and Candisky shook their heads.

"I went up last week to visit my mom and stepdad. I just wanted to take a week off where no one had ever heard of John Hawkins. So I'm driving through Keene and I get stopped for speeding. This cop asks to see my driver's license, and the next thing I know there are a dozen cops surrounding my car with their guns aimed at my head."

"They take their speeding pretty seriously, huh?" Yocum commented.

"No, the FBI had my name listed as an alias for John. They thought they had John. They hauled me out of the car, frisked me, put me in handcuffs, and took me to the police station. My mom had to come down and verify I was her son before they would let me go."

Candisky squinted at Erik. "How could John use your name, Erik?"

"I don't know. Maybe they just put my name down since we were friends."

Yocum knew what Candisky was implying and took it a little further. "But he'd need a piece of identification to become Erik DeSando," Yocum said.

"Like a birth certificate," Candisky contributed.

After months of denying that Hawkins had his birth certificate, DeSando finally admitted that he had given it to his former roommate. "Honest to God, I thought he wanted it to set up a bank account and hide some money," DeSando said. "I didn't know he was going to use it for an alias."

The reporters stood and started for the front door. "So what happened with Jackie and John, Sr.?" Yocum asked. "Were they here when you got back?"

"No. I came back the next day and they'd cleaned me out. They took the furniture, paintings, that goofy statue, and the cassette from the answering machine—for whatever the hell that was worth—and my hot tub."

"They took your hot tub?" Candisky repeated.

"Yeah, and it was mine, not John's. Never mind that it isn't even paid for. The company I bought it from wants me to file theft charges against them. So, I called Jackie to try and get it back, and she starts reciting Bible verses to me. Jackie Cirian reciting the Bible. It was like Psychos-R-Us. This whole thing is a nightmare."

48

Robin Yocum drifted in that haze between consciousness and sleep, sprawled out on the couch in his family room. The *Sporting News* he had been reading lay across his chest. The ringing telephone sounded like an air-raid siren. He bolted upright and sent the tabloid pages flying.

Yocum didn't know if he had been asleep for ten minutes or ten hours. He fumbled for the telephone receiver. "Yeah, hello."

"Guess what?"

Yocum took a deep breath and shook his head to get his bearings. Despite his grogginess, he recognized his partner's voice. "What?"

"Did I wake you up?"

"Yeah. No. I'm okay."

"Well, guess."

She laughed. Her call had to involve Just Sweats. Yocum wiped his eyes and squinted at his watch. It was 11:45 P.M., Sunday, January 29, 1989.

"Uh, they caught Boggs."

"No. Boggs hasn't been hiding, remember?"

"Right. Uh, Hawkins?"

"Nope."

"Hanson?"

"Yes," she shrieked.

"That's great. Hanson. Where? Who told you?"

"Volpi just called. He said customs called him and said Hanson was arrested tonight at the Dallas–Fort Worth Airport."

"The airport? What the hell was he doing in an airport?"

"Don't know. All Volpi knew was that he was coming in on a flight from Acapulco. They caught him in the airport with a bogus ID."

"Wolfgang von Snowden?"

"I don't know. I've told you about everything I know."

Yocum checked his watch again. "There probably isn't enough time to get this in the paper. Besides, I'd want to confirm it."

"Right. Plus, at this hour all we'd be able to get in the paper is two paragraphs in the final makeover. That's just enough to tip off radio and television. Besides, we need some kind of confirmation with fingerprints. This could be some poor guy who bought a hot ID, or the real Wolfgang von Snowden, if there is such an animal."

Yocum called the *Dispatch*'s metro editor at home and told him of Hanson's capture. He and Candisky weren't coming into the office in the morning. "We're going to bang on some doors and see what we can find out."

By the time Yocum picked up Candisky at her apartment at 8 A.M. on January 31, word of Hanson's arrest had already gone out on the morning radio news. The reporters drove Yocum's pickup truck to Volpi's, but he didn't have any more information than he had the previous night. He said he might be going to Fort Worth with Abraham later that day. The assistant prosecutor had only been on the case for a few months and was less familiar with it than Volpi.

The reporters went to the Columbus office of U.S. Customs, but no one there knew anything. Doug Ogden, agent in charge of the Columbus FBI office, said he too was awaiting information. At the Franklin County Prosecutor's office Abraham told them he was meeting with Prosecutor Mike Miller later that morning to discuss the possibility of flying to Texas that afternoon. The reporters sensed Abraham and Volpi both knew they were going to Fort Worth, but neither of them was going to admit it.

Yocum and Candisky then drove to Clintonville to update metro editor Gary Kiefer on their progress. "You've got to call the office," he said. "Everyone's trying to get a hold of you. They didn't think you knew Hanson had been arrested."

Dispatch editor Luke Feck wanted a reporter on a plane to Texas immediately, and he had decided it would be Yocum. He and Candisky went to pack at Yocum's house on the southwest side of town. They had forty minutes to get him on the airplane.

Candisky dropped Yocum off and drove back to the office to make calls and begin writing a story on Hanson's arrest. Yocum dashed into the airport ten minutes before the flight was scheduled to leave. A *Dispatch* secretary had ordered his tickets, so Yocum had only to pick them up at the counter. Volpi and Abraham stood ahead of him in the ticket line.

Yocum said nothing. He smirked when he finally caught Volpi's eye. "Howdy, boys," Yocum said. "You're takin' the one-twenty flight for Dallas–Fort Worth, too, huh? What a coincidence."

Abraham, briefcase in one hand and garment bag in the other, forced a smile. He did not look pleased to see the reporter. Yocum had figured that Volpi had been deliberately evasive about their travel plans. They didn't want a journalist poaching on what they considered their territory. Abraham, no doubt, would prefer to interview Hanson without the company of the press.

Yocum chose a seat in the middle of the uncrowded plane. He allowed Volpi and Abraham to huddle together in the back. The reporter felt confident of his ability to find out what the investigators were planning.

While Yocum and the Ohio authorities flew in from the east, another plane carrying Glendale Police Detective Jon Perkins and California Department of Insurance investigator Jerry Treadway flew in from the West Coast.

The reporters had been told that Perkins, a short man with an overgrown moustache that compensated for his balding head, possessed an especially overinflated ego. Although he had been with the police department since November 1973, at the time of his assignment to MacKenzie's Just Sweats task case, Perkins had served as the Glendale Police Department's race relations officer. His superiors had appointed him to that position, reporters in Los Angeles had told Yocum and Candisky, because Perkins couldn't get along with other detectives. He seemed to have some difficulty relating to others in general: when a reporter asked him for his business card, Perkins smirked and said, "I don't carry business cards. It's my trademark. I carry bullets."

Treadway, a ten-year veteran of the department of insurance fraud bureau, had been on the case for several months. A former investigator with the California Department of Alcohol and Beverage Control, he had also spent three years in army intelligence.

The California authorities considered the Just Sweats crime to be their case. After all, the murder had occurred in their state. But Ohio had issued the only charge holding Hanson in jail.

A nasty jurisdictional clash was about to take place in Fort Worth.

Candisky still had no details on Hanson's arrest. Her first call in search of further information went to Ogden at the FBI.

"Have you heard anything more?" Candisky asked.

"Not much," replied the always-cautious Ogden. "Did you hear how many different IDs he was carrying?"

"No. How many?"

"Fourteen is what they told us, including Ellis Greene's California driver's license."

"Ellis Greene! The dead guy Ellis Greene?"

"You know any others?" Ogden challenged.

Candisky knew Ogden never joked about such matters. Still, she thought, it seemed too ludicrous to be true. Why would Hanson keep the driver's license? A souvenir? "Doug, are you kidding me?"

"No kidding. I'm as anxious as you to hear him explain how he got that."

Joe Dealey, director of public relations for the Dallas–Fort Worth International Airport, provided Candisky with some additional details about the arrest. He also arranged a telephone conference call between the reporter and the two customs officers who had apprehended the fugitive.

Hanson, Dealey said, had been an easy target. He got off American Airlines Flight 150 from Acapulco at 7:30 P.M., and two customs officers immediately spotted him. He wore red gym shorts, a T-shirt, and sneakers. His nervousness and furtive glances around the terminal as he waited for his luggage to come off the carousel gave him the look of a drug runner.

"He was dressed the part, but he didn't look like a regular tourist," Customs Inspector Dave Berry told Candisky. "This guy had a narcotics-smuggler look. He stood out from everyone else and appeared to be in a hurry."

Berry and Inspector Jim Starnes pulled the man aside. Starnes asked the man if he was a U.S. citizen and where he had been. The man produced a Massachusetts driver's license in the name of George Soule and told authorities he was returning from Mexico. When asked what he had been doing in Acapulco, Soule became very nervous. At first he said he had been on vacation; then, that he had been living there in a condominium.

"Is your declaration correct?" Berry asked.

Soule nodded. "I have nothing to declare."

Berry searched Soule's leather knapsack and found a plastic bag stuffed with fifty-dollar bills. The bag appeared to contain more money than the $10,000 people entering the country can possess without declaring the sum to customs. Berry dangled the bag in front of George Soule's face. "If this is more than $10,000, you've got a problem."

It was. The agents counted out $14,000—280 fifty-dollar bills. George Soule—aka Wolfgang von Snowden, aka Melvin Eugene Hanson—had problems that were just beginning. Hanson first claimed that he was going to use the money to buy an antique car. He later changed his story: The money was for a condominium in Acapulco.

"He still was acting so nervous after we found the money that we knew there had to be something more," Starnes said. The customs officials placed Hanson in a holding room while the agents searched the rest of his luggage.

Starnes said he found an eyeglass case that contained a driver's license and birth certificate for a Wolfgang E. Von Snowden. "When I asked who Wolfgang was, he claimed it was his business partner," Starnes reported. "I asked him why he was carrying his business partner's ID, but he just sort of shrugged." Customs officers came upon identification for fourteen different aliases stashed in the side pocket of a suitcase. Agents also found a book, *How to Change Your Identity,* long-overdue from the Dade County Library.

"He kept asking for coffee because he was stressed out," Berry said. "We wanted him to calm down, too, but it was late and the coffee machines had been turned off, so we gave him a soda."

Berry and Starnes began entering the aliases into their computer. The computer was hooked into the U.S. Treasury Enforcement Communications System, a database that would flag any name with an outstanding warrant. When they checked the third name on their list, Wolfgang Von Snowden, the computer responded. Customs learned that the name was an alias for Melvin E. Hanson, who was wanted in Ohio on a federal warrant for unlawful flight to avoid prosecution. The inspectors informed Hanson that he was under arrest.

"Let's just say Hanson was not the least bit cooperative," Dealey said. "He wasn't too keen on getting fingerprinted and wouldn't answer any questions." Authorities held the erstwhile Mr. Soule in the two-cell airport holding facility Sunday night, January 29. About noon on Monday they transferred him to the Tarrant County Jail in Fort Worth.

After Candisky typed notes from the Texas interviews into her computer, she composed an obvious and appropriate lead.

"Nothing out of the ordinary led to Melvin E. Hanson's arrest—it was just sweat."

49

Yocum punched the buttons on the imaginary phone in the palm of his hand and talked out loud. "1-800 . . . 1-800-4 . . . 1-800-46 . . . 46 something, dammit."

He could never remember the paper's out-of-state WATS number. He ended up calling Candisky collect during his flight layover in Memphis.

"Did Dan or Vince tell you anything?" she asked.

"No. They were huddled in the back of the plane, speaking, shall we say, very discreetly. How are things on your end?"

"Pretty good. We've got a pretty good story in the bag for tomorrow," Candisky said. "I've got something you're not going to believe. When they arrested Hanson, one of the IDs he was carrying belonged to Ellis Greene."

Yocum thought he hadn't heard her right. "Whose ID?"

"Ellis Greene's."

"Get out!" Yocum exclaimed. "He's not that stupid."

"Well, apparently he is. Ogden said Hanson was carrying Greene's driver's license, some other papers, personal checks, and bills. He also said Hanson has scars around his eyes from the plastic surgery."

There had been a conspiracy, and Hanson had been right in the middle of it. And all the men's detailed planning and scheming the men had been undone by a piece of plastic—Ellis Greene's driver's license. Hanson's possession of that license left little doubt that he had been involved in the death of Ellis Greene. It was almost too simple.

Yocum called Hanson's mother in Jacksonville. Katherine Lawley expressed her feelings at news of her son's arrest. "I've been afraid he was dead. I've been praying for him every day. This is a relief to me, even with all the problems Gene faces."

Lawley, a devout Baptist, had difficulty grasping the reality of her son's situation. "We raise our children the best we can, but you never know what they will do," she said. "I really don't know how he could have done the things they say he did, but of course, I'm biased. I'm supposed to be."

As Yocum's plane had been taking off for Dallas–Fort Worth on Monday, January 30, Hanson was being arraigned before federal magistrate Gene Grant on Ohio's charge of theft by fraud. Because Hanson was a fugitive, Grant set his bond at $5 million, an amount almost impossible to raise.

Yocum rented a car at Dallas–Fort Worth and tried to make the fifteen-minute drive to downtown Fort Worth following the directions he had been given. An hour later, he was still on the outerbelt, trying to read a map by the dome light. He finally arrived at the Tarrant County Jail after 8:00 P.M.. The reporter wanted to interview Hanson that night, but a deputy said that would be impossible. "Come back tomorrow," the officer said.

"When tomorrow?"

"The sheriff comes in at seven in the morning. I'd be here then if I wanted to get an interview."

By the time Yocum left to find a hotel room, Hanson was already on a first-name basis with Volpi and Abraham, who were interrogating him in a small room at the jail. After being reminded of his constitutional rights as given to him by customs officials the previous day, Hanson said he didn't have an attorney, but was willing to listen to what the men had to say. He didn't want the conversation taped.

Volpi issued to Hanson the investigator's standard statement. Authorities now had extensive knowledge of the insurance scam; whether Hanson cooperated or not, his conviction was almost assured. Hanson could see the prosecutors had a strong case against the alleged conspirators. Careful not to make any promises, Volpi and Abraham told Hanson that he might receive more leniency during sentencing if he cooperated. The private investigator wanted to know the extent of Hanson's involvement in the scam and the location of the rest of the money.

Hanson acknowledged his true identity and signed a waiver that he understood his rights and agreed to make limited statements without an attorney present. First, he exonerated his Columbus attorneys, Austin Wildman and Richard Curtin, from any participation in the scheme. He then professed his unconditional love and concern for John Hawkins, who he said feared Boggs and had promised to kill himself before going to prison.

An hour into the interview, Hanson finally allowed investigators to turn on a tape recorder. Hanson rambled, but eventually told them he had $30,000 in a bank account in the Cayman Islands, a much smaller amount in a St. Petersburg bank, and the $14,000 he was carrying when he was arrested. He also had some property in St. Petersburg Beach, and some personal items he had left in Acapulco. When asked where he had gotten the money, Hanson said he had received $85,000 from someone, but refused to identify his benefactor.

Hanson stopped short of confessing to the insurance fraud. Volpi later told the reporters that Hanson had made some incriminating statements. However, the investigator refused to divulge the particulars of the two-hour interrogation, only to say that Hanson carefully avoided incriminating Hawkins. The interview ended about 9:30 P.M., and Hanson asked Abraham and Volpi to return the next day so he could talk to them before he waived extradition to Ohio. Only after returning to Ohio, Hanson said, would he make a full statement.

When Tarrant County Sheriff Don Carpenter arrived at the jail at seven the next morning, Yocum met him at the door. The reporter took an immediate liking to Carpenter, a gregarious country boy with a long Texas drawl, a head of silver hair, and a cheek full of chewing tobacco. Yocum told him the story of Hanson and the elaborate murder-for-insurance scheme. "Go on," Carpenter said in amazement, cramming his mouth with a fresh wad of chewing tobacco. "He was carrying the dead guy's driver's license? That wasn't too smart, was it?"

"Not really," Yocum said.

"You want a chaw?" Carpenter offered the reporter a foil packet of tobacco. Yocum declined. "I wonder what makes a man do something like that?" Carpenter continued. "Greed, I expect. I've never understood it." Carpenter spit into a Styrofoam cup. "One of the deputies said this Hanson's a homosexual. That right?"

"That's what I hear."

"Well, I never understood that, either." He spit again. "So, you want to interview this Hanson fella, huh?"

Yocum nodded. "That would be nice."

Carpenter winked. "Let's see what we can do." He called upstairs to one of the jail deputies. "Go talk to that boy from Ohio. Tell him there's a gentleman from the . . ." He looked back at Yocum.

"*Columbus Dispatch.*"

". . . *The Columbus Dispatch.* And he wants an interview. See if he won't come down here."

Yocum had hoped to speak to Hanson before Abraham or the

California authorities showed up and ruined the fun. Carpenter's phone rang a few minutes later. "He does, huh? Good," Carpenter said. "Bring him down to my office." The sheriff smiled. "He says he'll talk to you. I'm interested to hear this myself."

The telephone rang again a minute later. Hanson had changed his mind. Yocum felt as if he had been kicked in the crotch. The phone rang for a third time. Hanson had decided to talk with the reporter and was on his way down.

The prisoner looked like hell. The dark green jailhouse jumpsuit fit badly over his slumped shoulders. He shuffled along in an attempt to keep his prison-issue rubber sandals on his feet. Without his wig, he seemed to have aged twenty years. The shaking that resulted from more than thirty-six hours without a cigarette consolidated the image. Hanson had become an old and broken man.

Yocum extended his hand. "Robin Yocum. I'm a reporter with *The Columbus Dispatch.*

Hanson shook Yocum's hand, nodded, and then looked away. "Uh. I'm sorry, but, uh, I don't want to speak to you right now, not until I've talked to the prosecutor from Ohio. I hope I didn't waste your time," Hanson said, avoiding Yocum's eye.

Yocum turned to Carpenter, who could only shrug. "Okay," the sheriff said. "Take him back."

An hour later, authorities from Ohio and California were questioning Hanson in the office of Carpenter's chief deputy. Yocum sat across the hall in the lobby of Carpenter's office and stared at the closed door. "You don't have an intercom hooking up these two offices, do you, sheriff?" Yocum asked.

Carpenter laughed around his chaw. "Naw. It might make for some interesting listening, though, huh?"

Yocum moved to a bench in the outer hall and waited nearly two hours before the detectives took a break. Shortly before ten, Jon Perkins and Jerry Treadway walked into the lobby. "What's going on in there?" Yocum asked, tossing his newspaper to the bench as he jumped up. "Anything you can . . ."

Perkins and Treadway continued down the hall without giving the reporter even a glance. Abraham followed. "Danny . . ."

"Robin, not now. I'll talk to you later."

Volpi walked slowly into the hall, hands in his pockets, his jaw tight. He looked at Yocum and shook his head. "Making any progress?"

Yocum asked.

"Not much, thanks to those dicks from California."

"What's the problem?"

"They want to run the show. Perkins comes in like Dick Tracy, trying to throw his weight around. He told Danny it was their investigation because the homicide had occurred in California. They keep forgetting that they haven't filed any charges."

"Danny isn't letting them push him around, is he?"

"No, he told them the only thing keeping Hanson in custody was the charge from Ohio." Volpi chuckled. "They backed off, but I don't think they like it. If we drop our charge, he walks. This is the same stunt they pulled in Florida. They walk in and try to take over, and they don't know shit."

"Perkins knows it was you who was doing the investigation in Florida, right?"

"Oh, he knows. He hasn't spoken to me yet. He won't even look me in the eye," Volpi said, running his fingers back through his hair.

"I wouldn't let it bug me," Yocum said. "You know most cops don't like private detectives. You should expect it by now." Volpi nodded. "So, what's Hanson saying?"

Volpi shrugged. "I better not say. You'll have to get that from Danny. But I'll tell you this, he's making a lot more headway with Hanson than Perkins or Treadway. Danny's got a nice approach—slow, methodic, nothing sneaky. Perkins was like a fuckin' pit bull. He thinks he can pressure Hanson into a confession. But Hanson's not stupid and he's got an attorney."

The counsel for the defense, Danny D. Burns, was short and dark-haired, with a ruddy complexion that gave him the look of a street fighter. The Fort Worth lawyer and part-time boxing manager had stayed with Hanson during the questioning. Burns wasn't about to let his client confess to spitting on the sidewalk, let alone murder or insurance fraud.

Yocum cornered Burns as he finished using a pay phone at the end of the hall. "How's Gene holding up?" Yocum asked.

"Not real good. It's hard to tell if he's scared or the problem is not having a cigarette for a day and a half."

"I heard he's not too fond of the guys from California?"

"That's a bit of an understatement," Burns laughed. "He won't even look at Perkins. But, he's worried. I think he's going to waive extradition to Ohio. Perkins promised him they were going to file murder charges with death penalty specs. I think he'd rather try to straighten it out in Ohio."

After lunch, Hanson asked Burns to leave the room so he could talk to the investigators alone. "I told him it was a bad move, but if he doesn't want me in there while he is talking to them, that's his prerogative," Burns told Yocum when they later sat in the hall. "I could be making more money back at the office."

"So, what's going on in there? Hanson kicking in to anything?"

Burns shook his head and waved an open hand toward the closed door. "Hell no. It's just a bunch of chit-chatty and a waste of time."

"So he hasn't confessed to anything?"

"There's nothing to confess to," Burns said. "The man is innocent of all the charges."

"Oh," Yocum said, fighting off a grin. "So, ah, how does he explain everything that's happened, like, getting caught with the dead guy's ID?"

"He says it's simply a misunderstanding. He's anxious to get back to Ohio. He just wants to clear his name."

"Really?" Yocum could no longer stifle his amusement. "Which one?"

Burns smiled back at the reporter. "No comment."

Later in the afternoon, authorities shuttled Hanson—looking tanned and tired and still wearing his jail-issue jumpsuit, thongs, leg shackles, and handcuffs—from Carpenter's office through a throng of lawmen and cameramen to an upstairs courtroom for his extradition hearing. When District Court Judge George S. Kredell asked Hanson if he was "Wolfgang E. Von Snowden, also known as Melvin E. Hanson," Hanson replied, "Yes, I am." Hanson waived extradition to Ohio and said he would like to return "as expeditiously as possible." He joked nervously with Kredell, "If they don't want to come and get me and you want to let me go, that's fine with me."

Texas police then led Hanson away and, at his request, he was removed from the general population and placed in a one-man cell reserved for homosexuals. He also asked to use the telephone and called his mother for the first time in fifteen years. Katherine Lawley later told Yocum she felt relieved to hear her son's voice, even though the first words she heard him say were "Mom, you know I'm a homosexual."

The next morning, Wednesday, February 1, Yocum talked to Abraham at the sheriff's department. "Where's Vince?" Yocum asked.

"He flew back to Columbus."

Yocum didn't give it another thought, assuming Volpi had other obligations in Ohio. Abraham said that Hanson was probably flying back to Ohio later in the day. The assistant prosecutor planned to present the case to the grand jury and hoped to obtain a nineteen-count robbery and conspiracy indictment against Hanson.

Late that morning, Yocum was trying to learn when Hanson would be shipped back to Ohio. Authorities liked to sneak suspects out of back doors or under the cover of darkness, always claiming that the prisoner's protection required it. Mostly, however, the back-door maneuver is done to pimp the reporters. Yocum wanted to talk to someone who would play straight with him. The reporter called Volpi long distance to see if he had heard when Hanson was to return.

"I don't know if I'm ever talking to anyone about this case," Volpi said.

"And a pleasant good morning to you, too." Yocum replied. "What's wrong?"

Volpi said Abraham had unceremoniously told him to take his private investigator's badge and go back to Columbus. Apparently Perkins and Treadway didn't want him around any longer. Then, to make matters worse, Volpi's name wasn't even mentioned in Wednesday's *Dispatch* article on Hanson.

"Okay, okay, Vince, I'll take care of it. We'll make it up to you." Yocum called Candisky. "I need you to stroke Vince a little. He's all bent out of shape because he didn't get treated very well in Texas. He did a lot of work on this and we didn't give him a mention. Can you do a little piece on him?"

"I thought he didn't want his name in the paper," Candisky argued.

"I guess things have changed."

Candisky wasn't quite sure why Volpi was angry with them. He had always given them information on the sly, and the reporters assumed that he wanted his name kept out of the paper. He had never complained before, but since he was a valuable source they wanted to keep him happy. The sidebar in the next day's *Dispatch* featured Volpi in a story on the work he had done on the case, along with a photo of him and his girlfriend's German shepherd, Watson.

50

Candisky had kept Dr. Jeffrey Tardiff's name and telephone number on a stack of papers on her desk for weeks. Volpi had given it to the reporters after the California authorities had botched his Florida investigation. However, prior to the Hanson arrest, *Dispatch* editors had begun to lose interest in the story. Neither reporter had bothered to followed up with Tardiff.

The reporters had little hope of getting an interview with Tardiff, the micro–plastic surgeon from Miami who, in May 1988, had rid Hanson's face of wrinkles during eleven hours of surgery. Doctors are notoriously closed mouthed and protective of their patients. Jeffrey Tardiff, on the contrary, took great pride in the work he had done on Hanson—the man he knew as Wolfgang Von Snowden—and he was delighted to tell Candisky the details.

Hanson had heard of Tardiff through mutual friends in the Miami homosexual community. The doctor had amassed a small fortune conducting plastic surgery and "removing the scabs from AIDS patients." Tardiff said he was introduced to Wolfgang Von Snowden, then 47, by a mutual friend, Miami real estate agent Malcolm Briggs, who had helped Hanson find the penthouse apartment. "He said he wanted to look strikingly younger because he was dating men twenty to twenty-five years his junior." Tardiff told Von Snowden it would cost him $5,000.

"He didn't care about the expense and said he wanted no one to see any incision lines," Tardiff said. "He said he had seen other patients and wanted me to duplicate the work on him. He looked haggard and tired. He had an obvious smoking problem and a bad case of bronchitis. I told him I would not operate on him unless he promised to quit smoking and get rid of the bronchitis. He said okay. He had a four-pack-a-day habit, but he said he would quit if I'd perform the operation."

Despite the promise, three weeks later Tardiff found "nicotine in toxic levels" when he did blood work on Von Snowden.

"He said, 'Okay, you got me,' " Tardiff noted.

The next time Von Snowden came to the office, Tardiff found only traces of nicotine in his blood. The plastic surgeon went ahead with the surgery.

Von Snowden had severe, deep-set wrinkles and bags around his eyes. Tardiff said he performed two procedures: a complex bletharoplasty—a seven-and-a-half-hour procedure to remove wrinkles from around Von Snowden's eyes; and a meloplasty—a three-and-a-half-hour operation to reconstruct his cheeks. The surgeries entailed incisions on the patient's upper and lower eyelids. Tardiff extended the incisions on the lower eyelids onto Von Snowden's cheek to remove the wrinkles around his eyes, cheeks, and the sides of his mouth and nose. The surgeon also extended incisions to his jawline to remove additional wrinkles.

Tardiff planned to reconstruct Von Snowden's chin to give him an even more youthful appearance. But, after the eye surgery, Von Snowden began smoking again, and Tardiff refused to perform the second procedure. "He said he wanted the surgery done on his chin, but obviously he didn't want it bad enough to quit smoking. He said there was a lot in his life he had to worry about. I didn't understand what he meant then, but I understand it now. He never told me he wanted to change his looks. I had no clue he was into that stuff."

Tardiff first suspected that Von Snowden might be hiding something after the surgery was completed. Von Snowden asked for the photographs the doctor had taken. "I told him I needed them for my records. He said that I did such a fantastic job and he wanted to show them to his family. He sounded so sincere and I gave them to him." When Tardiff's secretary asked Von Snowden to sign a release for the photos, the patient misspelled his own name, signing "Von Schnowden."

"My secretary showed it to me. She said, 'Ah-ha, I told you there was something fishy about that guy.' But by then Von Snowden was gone. I haven't seen him or heard from him since.

"My secretary didn't like him. She kept saying, 'There's something about him that I just don't like.' I thought he was very pleasant and personable. But, I was concentrating more on the procedure than his personality."

51

Yocum sped down a lower hallway in the sheriff's department carrying a mug shot of Hanson taken when he was admitted to the jail. A photographer at the *Fort Worth Star-Telegram* had offered to transmit it back to the *Dispatch*. Yocum had intended to walk the few blocks to the newspaper until he spotted Abraham alone in an office using a telephone. Yocum stopped and leaned against the doorjamb to wait for Abraham to finish his call.

"Busy day?" Yocum asked.

Abraham sat down on the edge of a desk. "Very. Where've you been?"

"I just ran over to the jail to pick up a mug shot of our buddy." Yocum held up the photo. "How about you?"

"I'm getting ready to head back home."

"With your prisoner, I assume."

Abraham nodded. "I've done about all I can here."

Yocum smiled. "And what, may I ask, did that entail?"

Abraham shook his head. "Nothing you don't already know. I interviewed Hanson and arranged for his extradition. No big deal."

"Did he kick in to anything?"

"No. Nothing that exciting."

"Did he implicate Boggs or Hawkins?"

Abraham shrugged. "You know I can't talk about that."

"Come on Dan, what the hell went on in there? Did he tell you where he's been since he left Miami? He'd gotten out of the country. Why was he coming back?"

"He apparently needed the money," Abraham said as a matter of fact.

"What? Did he have money stashed somewhere?"

"He might, but he said he was going to St. Petersburg Beach to sell some property. He was coming in for the closing and planned on

257

going right back. He had a round-trip ticket from Acapulco to St. Petersburg."

"What was he selling? A condo? A house?"

"I don't know. I can't remember."

"Who was handling the closing for him? Did he have a real estate agent or a lawyer down there?"

"I think there was a real estate agent involved, but I couldn't tell you who."

"He was dealing with an agent named Briggs, last I heard."

Abraham shrugged. "I don't know. I haven't heard any names."

"So when he left Miami last August, he must have gone to St. Petersburg."

"Eventually. He said something about spending some time down in the Keys. Supposedly, he rented a place and opened a bank account using Ellis Greene's name."

"Pretty incriminating."

Abraham rolled his eyes. "Your words, not mine."

After dropping off the photo, Yocum returned to his hotel room and called Candisky. "Here's the quote of the day," Yocum said. "One of the deputies asked Hanson if he could post the $5 million bond and he told them, 'If they let me die a few more times I can.' "

"He did not!"

"I got it from one of the sheriff's chief deputies."

"Not too incriminating. What's going on down there?"

"I was just talking to Abraham and they're probably bringing Hanson back this afternoon. We ought to get some photogs at the airport. How about on your end? Any luck with Hanson's connections in St. Petersburg Beach?

"I've got one lead. Vince gave it to me," she said, flipping through her reporter's notebook. "Supposedly Hanson was staying someplace called the Island's End. It's in some ritzy area called Pass-A-Grill."

"In St. Pete Beach?"

"Yeah. But I haven't checked it out."

"That's enough for me to get started with. I'll buzz you back later."

Yocum contacted information for St. Petersburg Beach and got the number of the Island's End Resort. He called and asked to speak to the owner. Millard Gamble had no trouble remembering Wolfgang Von Snowden. Gamble said Von Snowden came to his resort on a secluded peninsula in St. Petersburg Beach in an old gray Volvo shortly before Labor Day, 1988. On August 31, using the Von Snowden alias, Hanson tried to rent a cottage at the Island's End. "If I was trying to hide, I'd stay here," Gamble stated.

"I didn't have any cottages available, so he left his name and checked into the Hilton in St. Petersburg. Once the Labor Day crowd left, I called him to see if he was still interested in a cottage. He said he was and came right out."

"So, did he rent a cottage?"

"Yeah. One of the little ones. Pretty modest actually, a bedroom, living room, bath, and a deck. But it backed right up to the water."

"How much?"

"Three-hundred-fifty dollars a week."

"Pretty reasonable."

"He said that was all he needed. We had one available for $770, with a private pool, but he took the cheaper one."

"How long did he stay?"

Gamble thought for a minute. "Quite a while, actually. About eight weeks. He said he didn't know how long he was going to stay. Most people stay for a week, but he just stayed on and on."

"Did you get to talk to him much? Did he say what he did or where he was getting his money?"

"He didn't talk much. Sort of kept to himself. He did say he was in the clothing business, and I got the impression he was carrying a lot of money because when he first checked in he asked if we had a safe. We don't, and I told him he'd be smart to rent a safe-deposit box. I guess he did appear a little suspicious, but he didn't strike me as a drug dealer. He certainly wasn't ostentatious with his money. He didn't flaunt it."

"How did he pay you? Cash?"

"At first. Then he got a checking account down at Florida Federal and started paying me with checks."

"Did he pay you on time?"

"Always."

"Well, did he say what he was doing? Did he say he was on vacation, or what?"

"At first he didn't say anything. He just hung out. Then, after a few weeks, I guess, he said he was interested in finding a place to buy in St. Petersburg Beach. In fact, he asked me several times if the Island's End was for sale. I said it wasn't, and I told my secretary to call Mike Seimetz. He's a local real estate agent and a friend of mine. A few days later he drove over and took Wolfgang around to see some places."

"Do you have a number for Mr. Seimetz?"

Mike Seimetz said he found Von Snowden "pleasant and very intelligent. He told me he wanted to find some property he could fix up for resale. He said, 'I've got $100,000 to invest—green—you know what I mean? Cash. I'd prefer not to deal with banks.' He didn't tell me much about his past though, only that he had been in business in Ohio. I asked what he was looking for and he said he wanted to live in a section of town that would accept him. He made it a point to tell me early in our conversation that he was a homosexual. I suggested the Pass-A-Grill section. It had old money, but it's fairly liberal thinking. It was also near the only gay bar in town."

When Seimetz began looking for a place suitable for a homosexual German businessman, Von Snowden became a regular visitor to the offices of Capalbo Realtors. "He knew where the coffee pot was," Seimetz said. "He was a flashy dresser, always running around in this little red kit car. He'd come in after he got done working out. Wolfgang worked out everyday—he was kind of a health nut—but he was a chain smoker and he was was always coughing."

"So he eventually bought something, didn't he?"

"Something, yeah, a shack. It was this little three-room frame about a block from the beach. It was tiny. Sat on a thirty-by-fifty-foot lot."

"What did he pay for it?"

"Fifty-eight thousand dollars. It wasn't much of a house, but the property in Pass-A-Grill is expensive," Seimetz said. "I negotiated a deal with the owner—this guy from New Jersey—to see if he might be willing to carry the mortgage. He really wanted to sell, so he said yes. Once I started working on the contract, Wolfgang began bringing cash to the office."

"What for?"

"A down payment. At first he brought in $1,000, then he made four or five payments of $4,000 or $5,000 each. They were all in fifty-dollar bills. The serial numbers followed in sequence on a lot of them. We make photocopies of cash payments as proof of payment, and that's how I noticed. Every four or five days he'd bring in a wad of bills. As soon as I had the $25,000 down payment, we went ahead with the contract. Wolfgang mortgaged the $33,000 balance through the owner."

"Do you recall the date he bought it?"

"Not right off hand, but I've got it around here somewhere. Hold on." Yocum could hear file drawers opening and closing. Seimetz returned to the phone a few minutes later. "October 14, with monthly payments of $354."

"October 14. That's ironic. That's the same day the insurance company filed charges against him. So, you stayed in contact with him after he bought the place?"

Seimetz laughed. "Yes. I was witness to the entire fiasco. Let's just say it was an absolute comedy of errors."

"How so?"

"Wolfgang bought the house and immediately got a remodeling permit. I warned him that because of housing regulations in St. Pete Beach, his remodeling could not exceed 50 percent of the value of the house. If you exceed 50 percent, which isn't much, you have to comply with new housing specifications, which include putting your house on stilts. 'No problem,' Wolfgang said. 'I'm not going to do that much.' Two days later I went down to see how Wolfgang was doing. I found him and this carpenter standing in the front yard looking at three walls. That's all that was left. One entire wall and the roof were gone. I told him, 'I think you've done more than 50 percent here, Wolfgang.' He said he would get it fixed, but the next Monday the building department came out and yanked his remodeling permit. He said, 'Mike, what am I going to do now?' I told him, 'Shit, I'm not a builder, but I'll sell the lot for you.'"

Seimetz sold the lot. A local developer, Paul Skipper, bought it contingent on Skipper's being able to obtain a building permit. "In the meantime, Wolfgang said he had to leave town to go to a clinic for treatments. He had this nagging cough the whole time I knew him. I asked him if he was going to get treated for his cough. He said, 'Actually, it's an AIDS clinic.' I thought to myself, 'Oh Christ, why me?' Then he says I'm not going to be able to call him at the clinic because they won't let calls come through because of privacy laws. He said he'd call periodically and see how the closing was going. When he called I asked him how the treatments were going and he said fine. He said he was feeling better and stronger."

The building department approved Skipper's permit, but it went into effect only after a thirty-day waiting period in which neighbors had a chance to appeal the decision, Seimetz said. The delay angered Von Snowden, who was anxious to consummate the deal. "By January, he was calling me day and night from Boston, Acapulco, the clinic in San Francisco. I thought, 'Christ, I've got a real dope dealer here.' He asked me to send him copies of the closing papers to an address in Boston, but they were never picked up. Finally, he called and said he would be in St. Pete on January 30 for the closing. To no one's surprise, he didn't show. The next afternoon I get a call from his lawyer in Fort Worth. He tells me Wolfgang had gotten arrested trying to come into the country with too much money. So I told him, 'Well, tell him to pay the fine and let's go with the closing.' "

"I would," Danny Burns told Seimetz. "But it seems that we have another problem. Mr. Von Snowden is wanted in two states for some kind of murder and insurance scam."

"When things go wrong I guess they really go wrong," Seimetz said. "He couldn't even remodel his house. They had to tear it down. If you want to talk to someone who got the short end of the stick, you should talk to George Cecilio, the guy who sold Wolfgang the house."

When Cecilio answered the phone at his home in Blackwood, New Jersey, he told Yocum that he rued the day he had ever heard of Wolfgang Eugene Von Snowden. "I was suspicious of this guy from the begining," Cecilio said. "I thought, what the hell kind of name is that? Wolfgang?"

But since Cecilio had been trying to sell the house for quite a while, he was happy to get rid of it. "That's why I agreed to carry the mortgage. I got paid in November, and I haven't heard from him since. I was told he had gotten in over his head. My understanding was he had permission to remodel, but he proceeded to demolish it to the ground. My sister-in-law lives down there and she called me one day and said, 'Your house is gone.' I said, 'Damn, I'm going to have to get an attorney.' "

52

"Office of the District Attorney, can you hold please?"

"Sure," Candisky said to a receptionist who had already left the line. It was midafternoon on Thursday, February 2, and the reporter was desperately trying to reach Albert MacKenzie. He had always returned her calls promptly, but not today.

"What's going on?" asked city editor Mark Ellis.

Candisky cupped the receiver and shook her head. "Something's going on. The DA won't return my calls. They're scrambling."

"Why? What's the hurry?"

"With Hanson in custody they've got to be afraid that Boggs is going to bolt."

"You think they're going to file charges against Boggs?"

"I'm sure they want to, but as far as I know they still don't have a cause of death. How do you charge someone with murder when you can't even prove the guy was murdered, let alone that Boggs did it?"

"Do you think Hanson will help them out?" Ellis asked. "Try to save his own tail?"

Candisky shrugged. "I don't know, but it's going to be a while before California gets a whack at him. Even if they file charges against him today, it'll be months before he's extradited."

"Sorry for the wait," the DA's receptionist said. "Who are you holding for?"

"Albert MacKenzie."

"Mr. MacKenzie is not available right now. Can I take a message?"

"Yes, this is Cathy Candisky. I've called a couple of times today and I really need to talk to Albert."

"Uh-huh. I have your messages, Ms. Candisky. I'll see that he gets them."

"Thanks," Candisky responded. She flung her pen across her desk. "Something's going on," she told Ellis.

"Let me know when you figure it out," Ellis said.

Candisky picked up the little blue address book the reporters had bought months earlier and began flipping through the pages. She and Yocum were no longer in control of the story. For months they had been the ones breaking new ground, setting the pace of the investigation. Now, they waited at the mercy of investigators who no longer needed what the reporters offered. Candisky called Abraham and was told he was gone for the day. Ogden's secretary said he was in a meeting. Weinstein was with a client. Candisky had just begun dialing Volpi's number when Ellis held up his phone. "For you," he said.

She picked up the phone.

"Cathy, it's Vince."

"Hey, I was just trying to call you."

"Your timing is good. I've got a little tip for you," Volpi said. "California is going to file charges against Hawkins, Hanson, and Boggs tomorrow."

"How solid is that?"

"Don't print it until you confirm it, but it's solid. It comes from a good source."

"But they still don't have a cause of death, do they?"

"Nope. Apparently they feel the circumstantial evidence is so strong they don't need it."

Candisky hung up and immediately called MacKenzie. This time he answered his phone. "Albert, I heard you are going to file charges against Boggs, Hawkins, and Hanson tomorrow."

"I can't comment on that, Cathy," MacKenzie said in his typical slow and deliberate tone. "I promise you will be the first to know."

"I appreciate that, Albert, but let me ask you this. If we flew out to L.A. tonight, would we be making a wasted trip?"

There was a moment of silence. "No."

Candisky gave the news to her editors and left to pick up Yocum at the airport.

When he got off the plane, Yocum had on the Tarrant County Sheriff's Department cowboy hat that Don Carpenter had given him. "Howdy, ma'am," he said, pushing up the brim of his hat with his index finger.

"Want to go to L.A.?" Candisky asked.

"Sure. What for?"

"The arrest of Dr. Boggs."

*   *   *

He was born Richard Pryde Boggs on May 15, 1933, the oldest of three sons born to Pryde and Beulah Boggs. The family lived in Hot Springs, South Dakota, where his father tried to scratch out a living with an oil-drilling company during the Depression. The father's job took the family to Casper, Wyoming, and then on to Los Angeles where the company had relocated. In 1943, the family settled in Glendale.

Boggs graduated from Glendale High School in 1951, then worked his way through college, including spending one summer canvassing Wyoming, South Dakota, and Colorado selling children's schoolbooks. He received his bachelor's degree in zoology from the University of California at Los Angeles in 1956. A family friend lent him the money to attend the College of Medical Evangelists in Loma Linda, California. (The school, supported by the Church of Seventh-Day Adventists, later changed its name to Loma Linda Medical School.)

Boggs adopted the strict ways of the Adventists, abstaining from tobacco, alcohol, and meat. In 1961, shortly before he graduated from medical school, he married Lola Cleveland, a sturdy Midwesterner with thick brown hair and strict morals whom he had met while working a summer job in Lincoln, Nebraska.

After their marriage, Boggs finished his medical training while Lola supported them by working as a math teacher. The young doctor did a two-year residency at Boston City Hospital under Dr. Derek Denny-Brown, the renowned Harvard neurologist.

Returning to Los Angeles, the couple adopted two boys, Dana and Kevin, born just a week apart, and raised them as twins. The doctor moved his young family into a Tudor mansion in the exclusive La Canada Flintridge section of Los Angeles, and soon after became the youngest chief of neurology at Rancho Los Amigos Hospital in Downey, California. He and his wife had two children of their own, a daughter, Heather, and a third son, Jonathan. Life was good for Dr. Richard Boggs, but he simply couldn't control his lust for success and money.

He established a private practice in Glendale, then left Rancho Los Amigos in 1972. His private practice was, by all appearances, very successful. Some patients thought Boggs a genius and swore by his compassion and caring. They considered him a neurologist with few equals.

Rita Pynoos, the wife of Beverly Hills developer Morris Pynoos, suffered from a degenerative thoracic nerve that had left her nearly paralyzed. She feels she owes her life to Boggs, who diagnosed and treated the problem. The grateful Mrs. Pynoos said, "He was absolutely brilliant. He's the best."

Others, such as Rose L. Simpson, had a different view of Boggs. The courts awarded Simpson $85,000 in damages after Boggs performed an unsuccessful operation to relieve her headaches. According to a lawsuit filed by Simpson, the surgery that was supposed to last ninety minutes stretched out instead to more than six hours. Not only did Simpson continue to suffer headaches, but she was also left partially paralyzed and with vision problems.

Hers was not the only legal filing. Since 1970, Boggs had been the target of more than forty civil lawsuits filed in Los Angeles County Superior Court and Glendale Municipal Court. He was sued by patients, landlords, bankers, professional partners, medical vendors, friends, and, ultimately, his family.

In 1970, Boggs founded one of the country's first health maintenance organizations. After finding investors for his "Satellite Health Systems," Boggs set up his corporation on Sunset Boulevard, recruited twenty-two doctors and dentists, and began seeing patients at offices in Glendale and Hollywood. Boggs envisioned that Satellite would handle the medical needs of 100,000 patients. At its peak, Satellite served 25,000 patients.

The venture, according to longtime friend John Pasek, earned Boggs a telephone call of encouragement from then-President Richard M. Nixon, who opposed socialized medicine and was eager for the private sector to get involved in preventive medicine.

But Satellite was resembling a comet reentering the earth's atmosphere. During each month of the four years it was in business, Satellite Health Systems lost money. By the time it closed in 1974, Boggs owed millions of dollars to the U.S. Small Business Administration, banks, leasing agencies, friends, and other physicians.

Then more legal problems hit.

Dr. Kathleen Revel accused Boggs of literally stealing her practice from her. In April 1973, Boggs recruited Revel for the group for a salary of $36,000 a year, insurance, and a company car. Revel turned over her own office, equipment, and list of patients to Boggs. She never saw the car, and the paychecks stopped coming by year's end. When Revel attempted to resurrect her practice, she found that her office locks had all been changed. Boggs then tried to steal her patients by telling them that Revel had moved her practice. Revel eventually won a $57,000 judgment against Boggs.

In March 1974, one of the Satellite clinic physicians sued Boggs, claiming he was owed $11,000 in back pay. A medical equipment firm sued Boggs in May 1975 over a $6,377 debt. Six months later, a medical leasing company filed suit, claiming Satellite owed it $115,899. In 1978 a dentist sued Boggs for defaulting on a $13,000 loan the dentist had co-signed.

"I find that sometimes professional people—doctors, lawyers, psychiatrists—have a feeling that they have achieved such a level that they are good in everything," said Boggs's brother, James, an insurance salesman in Spokane, Washington. "My brother is a very good doctor, but that doesn't make him a very good businessman."

Those who know Boggs said he never recovered from Satellite's failure. In 1976, Glendale Memorial Hospital and Verdugo Hills Hospital removed him from their staffs for disciplinary reasons that the hospitals refused to disclose.

Boggs and Lola divorced in 1978. Lola said her former husband was a caring father and dedicated physician who began to change in the mid-1970s, when he acknowledged he was a homosexual and was forced to declare bankruptcy. In 1981, Lola and the four children charged Boggs with contempt of court after he failed to make $33,000 in child support–payments over three years.

About the same time, Boggs had a falling out with his brothers. James Boggs said Richard wanted their mother to invest in a business deal. However, Beulah Boggs's two youngest sons, James and William, a Drug Enforcement Agency agent assigned to the United States embassy in Copenhagen, Denmark, advised her against it. "He had gotten involved with some business deals, individual investments, and he wanted my mother to get involved. My brother and I felt it wasn't in her best interests and we advised her to get out. Richard felt we were butting in," James Boggs recalled.

By the time his marriage finally ended, Dr. Richard Pryde Boggs, the once-devout Seventh-Day Adventist, had already begun to hang out in gay bars in West Hollywood and had bought a condominium in the area. The doctor who once had the respect of his community now chased young boys in seedy bars. The former crack diagnostician earned a reputation around West Hollywood for being "loose with the 'scripts,' " street talk for a doctor willing to write prescriptions in return for sex or money. At least one former colleague called him a sociopath. Boggs carried a gun to protect himself against patients he perceived were out to get him. During a hearing involving his family's lawsuit for back child support, Lola Boggs testified that he had threatened to kill her on several occasions. The *Los Angeles Times* reported that Lola recalled that he once said he "could get someone to do that."

By the mid-1980s, Boggs appeared consumed by his homosexuality. His office had become a playground for his boyfriends, such as his live-in boyfriend, Hans Jonasson, and other male "office assistants." A close associate said Boggs simply could not control his lust for young boys. Boggs had male prostitutes make regular appointments as patients at the office. While the waiting room filled with sick people, Boggs would take his "patients" into the examination rooms and have anal intercourse with them. The doctor would pay the men handsomely for their time. However, ever the clever businessman, Boggs would recover his money by billing their insurance companies for the "treatments."

"It makes you wonder what the hell happened to the guy," said a friend of Boggs for twenty years. "Here's a guy who had it all—brains, money, a great family—and he ends up chasing little boys in bars. It doesn't make sense. Something must have snapped somewhere."

53

Yocum's flight landed at the Burbank Airport at 10 P.M. He rented a car and drove to the Holiday Inn in Glendale. All the restaurants in the vicinity of the motel had already closed, so the reporter bought his dinner from vending machines: cheese crackers and an ice cream bar. Then, he crashed.

He awoke at 7 A.M. to a miserably cold and rainy Friday. He called MacKenzie's office, but the DA hadn't yet arrived. Famished after his junk-food meal of the night before, Yocum went downstairs for a breakfast of grapefruit and oatmeal. He called MacKenzie a half a dozen times and finally reached the DA about nine. "You're at the Glendale Holiday Inn?" MacKenzie asked. "Good. Stay there and I'll call you in a little while."

"Are you filing charges this morning?" Yocum asked.

"Robin, I just can't comment on anything right now. Just stay there and I'll get back in touch with you."

MacKenzie continued to play it by the book. He wasn't about to tell Yocum anything that might jeopardize the case.

Yocum knew that at any minute the police would arrest Boggs. The reporter also knew that he hadn't flown across the country to learn about the arrest through a press release handed to him by some officious bureaucrat. He called reporter Priscilla Lee at the Glendale office of the *Los Angeles Daily News*. Although she had a doctor's appointment at the moment, her editor promised she would meet Yocum at the Holiday Inn. They could tag-team Boggs's arrest. Lee arrived in a beat-up blue Pinto with the back window smashed out of it. A basketball-sized piece of concrete lay on the back seat and only a huge hole remained where the radio used to be.

"Someone broke into my car and ripped off my stereo last night. Sorry for the mess," Lee said. When she turned the key, sparks jumped from the loose radio wires.

Yocum edged a little closer to the door. "No problem."

The reporters first drove to Boggs's condominium on South Street, but found no sign of the police there. They sat in front of the building for fifteen minutes before driving to the medical building on Central Avenue.

A flotilla of police cruisers had crammed into the parking lot behind Boggs's office. A dozen faces pressed against the glass of the rear foyer. The upstairs windows resembled framed portraits as office workers intently watched detectives and uniformed officers scurry around the lot. "Cheesus, it's happening. Stop the car," Yocum said as he hopped out.

Yocum scanned the back seats of the police cruisers, searching for Dr. Boggs. They've already taken him away, the reporter thought. Just then, the crowd inside the back door parted. Two detectives—one on each arm—led a handcuffed Dr. Richard Pryde Boggs out of the building and into a light drizzle. Boggs, wearing a tan jacket and a look of bewilderment, walked with a slight limp and stared blankly around the lot. Dr. Boggs nodded as a detective opened the rear door of a cruiser. The plainclothesman shielded the top of the doctor's head, solicitously protecting his suspect from injury as he slid into the back seat.

Yocum ran up to one of the detectives as he was leaving the building. "What's Boggs been charged with? Murder?"

The detective shot back a who-the-hell-are-you look and kept walking. Yocum asked the same question of the next detective who came out. "I'm not the one you need to talk to. You'll need to talk to Captain Rutkoske or Sergeant Durand," he said, never breaking his stride.

"Which one's Rutkoske?" Yocum asked, turning to Lee who was behind him.

"Hey, Priscilla. Get out of there," yelled a thick-faced man driving an unmarked cruiser. "Get out of their way and let them do their work."

She nodded in the man's direction. "That's him. That's Rutkoske."

"Hey, captain," Yocum said as he started toward the car. "Can I ask you a few . . ."

Rutkoske rolled up his window and drove away.

Yocum and Lee tried another tack; they walked into the foyer of the medical building. "You know any of these people?" Yocum asked.

"No, but I assume they work here."

Lee pulled out a pen and notebook and approached the two women standing closest to the door. "Hi, I'm with the *Daily News*. Did you . . ."

"No. No, no, no. We're not talking," said a heavyset woman as she disappeared into a medical office. Three other women left abruptly.

"We've got to work on your approach," Yocum said, winking at Lee. "Come on, I've got to find a phone."

He ran across the street to a pay phone and called Candisky. "Where have you been?" Candisky asked. "You know they arrested Boggs."

"Yeah, they . . . How did you know that?"

"Albert called. I've got the charges—a ten-count indictment against all three."

"Murder?"

"Yep. Where are you now?"

"Standing in the rain, right across from Boggs's office. They just hauled him out of here."

"Did you see it?"

"Yeah."

"Great. Give me some color."

Yocum described the arrest, and Candisky wrapped it into the story they had been waiting five months to write.

Boggs, Hawkins, and Hanson had been charged with murder for financial gain, which carried a possible death sentence; conspiracy to commit murder, insurance fraud, and grand theft; insurance fraud for claiming $1 million from Farmers New World Life Insurance Company; grand theft for accepting the money from Farmers; insurance fraud for making a claim on the $500,000 policy from the Golden Rule Insurance Company; grand theft for accepting a $15,000 advance from Golden Rule for funeral expenses; insurance fraud for making a claim on the $50,000 policy with Globe Life Insurance Company; insurance fraud for making a claim to Farmers for $15,000 on a group life-insurance policy held by Just Sweats employees; insurance fraud for making bogus claims to Farmers for medical treatment of Hanson the night of his alleged death; and assault with a stun gun, stemming from the April 1, 1988, attack on Barry Pomeroy.

Candisky made a round of calls to Wildman, Weinstein, Mantz, and Laramee for their reactions to the arrest, then she polished the story. Meanwhile, Yocum and Lee drove to the Glendale police headquarters. The reporters climbed up to the second-floor looking for Sgt. Dean Durand. "Wait here a minute," Lee told Yocum. "I think I know where he might be."

A few minutes later, Durand came storming down the hall, muttering through clenched teeth as he blew past Yocum. "What's wrong with him?" Yocum asked Lee.

"No one told him anything about the arrest and he's mad. He's supposed to be the one who deals with the press and they didn't tell him anything."

A calmer Durand appeared a few moments later.

"We have most of the details of the arrest and charges," Yocum said. "But Boggs had to know something was coming. Did he try to skip town after Hanson was arrested?"

"No. He might have wanted to, but we didn't give him the chance. We've been conducting an around-the-clock surveillance for a considerable amount of time," Durand said.

"Did he know that?"

"Oh yes. He saw our cars tailing him and he made a few feeble attempts to elude us. He drove over to his office early this morning and was arrested as he left about 1 P.M."

"Where is he now?"

"Right here, in the city jail."

"Good. Listen, since you filed charges, do you know how Greene was killed?"

A faint smile pursed Durand's lips. "We've got some ideas."

"Care to share them?"

"No."

"Think you can prove it in court?"

Durand shrugged. "We'll see."

When Yocum and Lee got back to the *Daily News* office they found a copy of the complaint against Boggs, Hawkins, and Hanson, which the paper's court reporter had picked up in Los Angeles County Municipal Court. Yocum returned to his motel room with a copy of the complaint and holed up most of Saturday cranking out stories for Sunday and Monday. The complaint listed the ten charges along with 114 alleged acts that linked the men in a conspiracy. The list revealed the elaborate planning that had gone into the scam and fascinating details of Boggs, Hanson, and Hawkins's movements before Hanson's reported death. They had been in almost daily long-distance phone contact with each other in the weeks before and after they allegedly killed Ellis Greene. The trio called each other at least twenty-eight times from April 1 to April 16, 1988, the morning Greene was found dead in Boggs's office. They made an additional fifteen calls over the next ten days. MacKenzie said investigators had reviewed records of more than ten thousand telephone calls in the months before and after Hanson's reported death. Boggs made at least twenty-six calls from California, Hanson made thirteen calls while living in the Miami penthouse, and

Hawkins made four calls from his Columbus condominium.

MacKenzie said Boggs and Hanson killed Greene in the physician's office in the early morning hours of Saturday, April 16, 1988. Although Hawkins was in Columbus at the time, he was aware of the slaying and had plotted in the conspiracy.

The actual plotting of the scheme had taken more than two years. The conspiracy began to unfold on April 15, MacKenzie said, when Hanson, using his own name, flew from Miami to Los Angeles. At 1:22 A.M., April 16, someone used Boggs's telephone credit card to call the doctor's office from a pay phone at the Rawhide, one of the bars Ellis Greene had visited the night before his death. The call lasted six minutes.

About 6:30 A.M., Hanson checked into the Glendale Holiday Inn under the name of Wolfgang E. Von Snowden. He telephoned Hawkins from the room. Later that day, while police interviewed Boggs in his office, Hanson, under the Von Snowden alias, flew back to Miami. Meanwhile, Hawkins, who had been informed of Hanson's death, flew to Los Angeles to make arrangements for Hanson's funeral. Hawkins checked into the Los Angeles Hyatt.

On April 17, Hanson in Miami called Hawkins at the Los Angeles hotel.

Using warrants and tidbits of information they had collected on Hawkins's whereabouts, Yocum and Candisky put together a story that charted Hawkins's travels since he had left Columbus in July 1988.

On August 5, 1988, Hawkins got a Colorado driver's license—and later a passport—in the name of Jerry Anthony Greene. The real Jerry Anthony Greene was the brother of Tim Greene, Hawkins's boyhood friend from St. Louis. The photographs on the identification showed that Hawkins had cut his hair and dyed it black, and had started wearing glasses. In mid-August 1988, Hawkins visited Michelle Ford, an old friend in Denver, Colorado, who saw Hawkins using a Colorado driver's license in the name of Greene. In addition to Colorado, Hawkins traveled to St. Louis and Washington, D.C., before going to Las Vegas to visit his mother.

From Vegas, Hawkins went to Los Angeles, where he met Amy Blizzard in late August for their trip along the Pacific coast. On August 28, Hawkins checked into an Inglewood, California, motel using the Greene alias.

Jill Birdwell of Seattle, whom Hawkins had met in Hawaii, said she received a call from him in mid-September. In a telephone interview with Yocum, Birdwell said she hadn't heard from Hawkins since turning down an offer of world travel. "He called me one day, out of the blue, and told me he was in Arizona and that he had sold Just Sweats and made a business deal that would make him a millionaire. He told me he was going to take a trip around the world and he wanted me to go with him. I told him no way and I haven't heard from him since," Birdwell said. "He was cute, but weird."

Days later, Hawkins called Blizzard from a pay phone in Camden, New Jersey. He was en route to visit Julie Gertz, his stewardess friend in Boston. By early November he had made it to Hawaii. From there he telephoned Michelle Ford and asked her to meet him after Christmas in St. Thomas, Virgin Islands. Ford declined the offer.

During the Thanksgiving weekend, a Xenia, Ohio, woman thought she saw Hawkins aboard a plane from Boston to Dayton, Ohio. She described the man's coat and knapsack, and her descriptions matched those of what Hawkins was wearing that friends had given investigators. Subsequently, Hawkins told a few friends that he was soon going to Canada and then flying to Australia.

54

Yocum scanned the crowded Los Angeles County municipal courtroom. On this typically busy Monday morning lawyers and teary relatives jammed the courtroom. After observing the action for a few minutes, Yocum threaded his way through the throng of television cameras and tapped an official-looking man on the shoulder. "Excuse me. Are you the bailiff?" the reporter asked.

"More or less."

"My name's Rob Yocum. I'm covering the Boggs hearing for *The Columbus Dispatch* and . . ."

"My condolences," the bailiff smirked. The snide remark had been made for the benefit of the television cameramen, and the comment fetched a few laughs.

"Boggs's attorney, Samuel Weiss. Do you know him?" Yocum asked. The bailiff chuckled. "Everyone knows Sammy Weiss."

"Well, I don't. Is he here?"

The officer made a cursory check of the courtroom. "Nope."

"What does he look like?"

"Let me say this. Missing Sammy Weiss in a court of law would be like missing the Statue of Liberty in New York Harbor." The bailiff turned his attention to other business and left before Yocum could ask for something a little more specific.

However, Yocum soon saw the truth in the bailiff's analogy. Five minutes later a short man with wavy red hair and a wiry beard strolled into the courtroom. On the lapel of his tailored suit he wore a rhinestone-jeweled brooch of what appeared to be a Scottish terrier.

Sammy Weiss informed the sea of reporters that he had represented Boggs on a few other matters, all considerably less serious than this murder charge with its death penalty specifications. However, Weiss said, he felt his client had actually been victimized in the masterfully crafted scam in which he was implicated. "I feel Dr. Boggs was tricked and bamboozled by Mr. Hanson and Mr. Hawkins," Weiss said. "If Dr. Boggs was truly guilty, he would have absconded a long time ago."

"But, how could your client have been duped when he was the one who identified the corpse as Melvin Hanson?" Yocum piped up.

"Well, in fact, Dr. Boggs had not seen Mr. Hanson for several months. He genuinely believed that the man who came to his office was Mr. Hanson. When you're treating a hundred patients a month, you don't look at everyone's face."

"Maybe not, but Dr. Boggs said Hanson had been a patient for seven years," Yocum persisted

Weiss turned to address a television reporter's query. The attorney tried his best to answer the questions fired at him by the dozen reporters massed around him. Yocum could see that Weiss hadn't had the time to prepare for the newspeople's assault.

When someone asked why Boggs hadn't stayed with his patient throughout the medical crisis, the attorney answered that Boggs had left Hanson alone in the examination room so the doctor could call the hospital. However, when speaking to police investigators, Boggs only said that he left his patient to tend to other business. The doctor never mentioned calling a hospital. Weiss also contended that Boggs had shown his innocence by refusing to sign Hanson's death certificate. "He could have signed the death certificate immediately, but he didn't; he asked for an autopsy," Weiss said.

"That's not what the police say," Yocum interjected. "They said Boggs wanted to sign the death certificate, but they wouldn't let him because they were suspicious and ordered an autopsy. Any comment on that, Mr. Weiss?"

Weiss glanced at Yocum, then moved across the courtroom without responding.

Half the reporters on the scene had come for the Boggs hearing; the other half was covering the arraignment of actor Todd Bridges on attempted murder charges. The former star of the hit television sitcom "Different Strokes" later won acquittal of stabbing a man over a drug deal.

Yocum leaned against a wall in the back of the courtroom and scanned some notes he had taken from a conversation with Candisky an hour earlier. With murder charges on file against Hanson in California, Franklin County Prosecutor Michael Miller had dropped Farmers' theft charge against Hanson, allowing MacKenzie to pursue the death penalty. During an arraignment that morning in Columbus, Hanson began his fight to prevent being extradited to California by claiming he wasn't Melvin Eugene Hanson. He had repeatedly invoked his fifth amendment right against self-incrimination and denied any involvement in the scam.

It seemed like an absurd defense to Yocum. But, he reasoned, why should the case start making sense now?

After Bridges's brief appearance, marshalls led Boggs into a courtroom holding cell. The doctor, unshaven and dissheveled, still wore the clothes he had on when arrested three days earlier. He looked tired and yawned several times during his arraignment. Judge David Milton asked Boggs if he understood that he faced the death penalty or life in prison with no chance of parole if convicted. Boggs nodded and softly answered, "Yes." The doctor pleaded not guilty, and Milton ordered him held without bond in the Los Angeles County Jail. The entire hearing took only a few minutes, then authorities returned the doctor to the lockup. Like Hanson, Boggs had requested a private cell; the guards placed him in the jail's "Queen Tank," a separate area for the confinement of homosexuals and informants.

After the hearing, MacKenzie surprised Yocum by telling him that Ellis Greene may not have been Boggs's only murder victim. "There is another matter under investigation, a homicide. I can't comment on it, but Dr. Boggs is the primary suspect in the investigation," MacKenzie said. "It's separate from the insurance scam."

55

The events that led to the arrest of John Hawkins on July 14, 1991, began when his photograph flashed on TV screens throughout the Netherlands during a rerun of the "Oprah Winfrey Show." The talk show that day featured another popular television program, "America's Most Wanted," which enlists viewers in helping to capture fugitives. A 24-year-old Amsterdam woman nearly jumped off her living room couch at the sight of Hawkins's photograph: she had met the man the previous summer on the Spanish island of Ibiza. The woman was shocked to learn of Hawkins's alleged crimes and stunned to hear of his bisexuality.

She immediately called FBI agents in both Brussels and Washington, D.C. The Feds then contacted Dave Hanna, agent in charge of the Columbus office. Hanna had learned not to get too excited over reported Hawkins sightings. Agents had received hundreds of calls since "America's Most Wanted" and "Unsolved Mysteries" had featured the fugitive's profile. Most of the tips had come from well-meaning citizens who had just spotted a lookalike.

The woman from Amsterdam told Hanna that she had dated Hawkins. She also gave a complete description of him, including the unpublicized fact that Hawkins lacked skin pigmentation on a part of his penis. Federal authorities knew about the skin flaw, and the woman got Hanna's attention. Hawkins had traveled to Amsterdam to visit her several times, but the woman hadn't heard from him in three months and she didn't know his exact whereabouts. Last she knew, Hawkins was sailing the Mediterranean in a red, forty-foot catamaran named *Carpe Diem,* Latin for "seize the day."

Another Dutch viewer also recognized Hawkins from the photograph. The man's son had sailed the Mediterranean with Hawkins for several months. The father gave the FBI office in Brussels much of the same information that the woman had. He told agents that his son and Hawkins were sailing between Spain, France, and the islands of Corsica and Sardinia.

From earlier tips that had proved solid, agents knew Hawkins's lifestyle hadn't changed. Unlike Hanson, he hadn't permanently altered his appearance through plastic surgery, and he still enjoyed the good life of a charismatic jet-setter. Informants had spotted him skiing in Colorado and later sailing in the West Indies. He kept out of the authorities' reach by constantly staying on the move and disguising himself with facial hair, glasses, and hair coloring.

Hanna knew he had John Hawkins in his sights. The woman's description was so detailed that the agent felt it had to be accurate. The father's information supported the lead. Hanna sent photographs of Hawkins to agents in Brussels, who showed them to the woman. When she positively identified them as pictures of Hawkins, agents contacted the U.S. Naval Investigative Services in La Maddalena.

Military investigators, acting on the woman's tips, learned the *Carpe Diem* flew under the Dutch flag, and Hawkins had purchased the boat seven months earlier in the south of France for 150 million lire—about $113,000. Within a week, the investigators learned the sailboat was bound for Sardinia and a man meeting Hawkins's description was aboard.

Hanna sent Sardinian police a packet of photographs of Hawkins, a list of his known aliases, his fingerprints, and a description of the birthmark. With the Naval Investigative Services monitoring the ship's route to Sardinia, authorities now had all they needed to land their catch.

The red catamaran glided into the dock on the Costa Smeralda on the northern coast of Sardinia. The *Carpe Diem*'s captain, a tanned and muscular man in an orange muscle shirt, stepped from the sailboat and tied it to the dock.

Beyond the rows of wooden docks that harbored an array of sail- and powerboats, a uniformed officer inched forward. "Patience," Police Captain Aldo Iacobelli whispered. "Wait until he has moved away from the boat."

The captain of the ship, hands on his hips, stretched his back before starting up the dock. Shortly after midnight on a steamy August 2, 1991, Iacobelli nodded and his men, assisted by U.S. military police from the nearby nuclear submarine base in La Maddalena, swarmed onto the docks. The sailor stepped back slightly, his eyes wide as he scanned his reception committee. A wall of uniformed officers had surrounded him in a semicircle, hemming him against the water.

Captain Iacobelli stepped forward. "Good evening, sir. I am Captain

Aldo Iacobelli of the Olbia Police Department. Do you have any identification?"

The sailboat captain reached into the hip pocket of his shorts, pulled out a British passport, and handed it to Iacobelli. "There's no problem, is there?" the man asked.

Iacobelli ignored the question as he thumbed through the book. "Glenn Donald Haweon. Northern Ireland," Iacobelli said, squinting at the passport photo in the dim light. "Is this your boat?"

"Yes sir."

"You are Mr. Haweon."

The man smiled. "Yes I am."

"Are you sure you are not the American John Hawkins?"

"John who?" he asked, shaking his head. "No. I'm Glenn Haweon, just like the passport says."

Iacobelli pursed his lips as he slid the passport into his breast pocket and brandished an Interpol warrant. "Sir, we are placing you under arrest. We have reason to believe you are the John Hawkins wanted by the United States government for murder."

For perhaps the first time in his life, he did not have a chance to talk his way out. John Hawkins looked back toward his boat and the Mediterranean. As an officer confronted him with a pair of handcuffs, Hawkins inhaled and made one desperate dash. The police were ready. Hawkins drove a forearm into the face of an Italian officer, knocking him back, but the man grabbed Hawkins's shirt and dragged him down to the ground. Three officers quickly set upon him. They pressed the fugitive to the dock, handcuffed him, then led him to a waiting police van.

Iacobelli ordered his men to search the sailboat for weapons, drugs, pieces of identification, money, credit cards—anything that might confirm his identity or implicate him in a murder. "Thoroughly," Iacobelli commanded.

Hawkins sat in the police van while officers searched the sailboat. Within an hour, the police had located nineteen pieces of identification, each bearing a different name. Iacobelli thumbed through the documents. "It's his picture, but all with different looks," he said to a nearby military officer. "Different hair color and length, glasses, beard. But all him."

"Is it our man though?" asked a U.S. officer.

Iacobelli nodded. "He looks like the man in the FBI photos. Let's take him back to the station for fingerprints and to check for the birthmark." The captain leered. "He won't be fond of that."

The authorities drove Hawkins fifteen miles to the police station in the seaside town of Olbia. There they fingerprinted the erstwhile sailor, then led him to a holding cell in the rear of the building.

"We need to check for a birthmark," Iacobelli informed his prisoner. "Could you remove your shorts?"

"What?" Hawkins screeched. "No."

"We can assist you if you prefer."

Hawkins paced the cell twice, then bent over to pull down his shorts. "I can't believe this. You're making a big mistake."

Iacobelli tried to keep a professional attitude, but his glee overwhelmed him. He smiled broadly as he examined the birthmark John Hawkins couldn't hide. The FBI had told Italian authorities to look for a lack of skin pigmentation that had left white spots on Hawkins's penis. The man in custody had such marks. Iacobelli walked away. Hawkins jerked his shorts back up and slouched onto a cot, as embarrassed and angry as he used to be when his friends teased him about the spots. Now his friends had ratted on him and told authorities about the birthmark.

Hawkins lay back, tears trickling from the corners of his eyes. After three years, the running was over.

Hours after his arrest, Italian authorities transported Hawkins 150 miles south to the jail, Di Buon Cammino, in the Sardinian capital of Cagliari. As four uniformed officers led Hawkins to his initial court appearance, a reporter for the independent Italian daily *La Repubblica* asked him if he was guilty of the murder. Hawkins sneered. "I don't have anything to do with any murder," he said. "The doctor is responsible. I didn't kill anyone. He is the architect of the whole thing. I had to flee because they suspected I was involved. It would be a crime if you sent me back."

Epilog

Unlike its co-founders, Just Sweats still thrives, though now under the name of J. S. Attitudes. In early 1989, Dennis Tishkoff, owner of a Columbus-based shoe and warehouse business, followed his wife into the Just Sweats store on East Broad Street. Mrs. Tishkoff wanted to buy a sweat shirt and Mr. Tishkoff didn't want to wait in the car. A shrewd businessman, he saw the potential for Just Sweats and purchased the then-bankrupt company for a paltry $145,000.

Tishkoff immediately began remodeling the stores, upgrading the merchandise, and hired former Ohio State University All-American and two-time Heisman Trophy winner Archie Griffin as the company spokesman. Mantz was retained by Tishkoff and moved into a merchandising position. Laramee was fired. Although he had worked tirelessly to keep the company operating throughout the turmoil, Tishkoff said there wasn't any need for him in the new company. Within eighteen months, Tishkoff had opened more than twenty new stores in Ohio, Indiana, and Kentucky, and the company was again making a profit.

A jury of six men and six women deliberated just three hours the afternoon of July 12, 1990, before returning verdicts of guilty to all nine counts. Boggs was convicted on charges of murder for financial gain, conspiracy, insurance fraud, theft, and assault with a stun gun.

Opening statements in Boggs's trial were heard on May 29, 1990, before Los Angeles County Superior Court Commissioner Florence-Marie Cooper. During the ensuing six weeks, Assistant Los Angeles County District Attorney Albert MacKenzie presented overwhelming circumstantial evidence against Boggs. Despite Boggs's claim that the man who had died in his office was the only Gene Hanson he had ever known, Jean Walker, the doctor's longtime receptionist, failed to recognize photographs of the corpse and testified that she had never seen the man. She did, however, identify a photograph of Hanson as

Boggs's patient of seven years.

Boggs's former lover, Hans Jonasson, testified that Boggs had received a $6,500 wire transfer from Hawkins six weeks after Hanson's reported death. Jonasson, who worked as a physical therapist in Boggs's office, also testified that on several occasions the doctor asked questions about drugs that would kill without leaving any trace in the system.

When pathologists could not find traces of any poison in the blood and tissue samples saved from the autopsy, MacKenzie presented jurors with a theory that Greene had been suffocated. An expert witness, Dr. Michael Baden, the chief forensic pathologist for the New York State Police, testified that Greene had met his death through "burking," a method of suffocation perfected by eighteenth-century Scottish grave robbers William Burke and William Hare.

An attentive jury listened to Baden describe how Burke and Hare began their careers by robbing graves for dissection at the medical schools in Edinburgh. When guards were posted at cemeteries to prevent the grave-robbing, the duo began suffocating derelicts, drunks, the retarded, and prostitutes. To ensure no traces of violence on their cadavers, Burke and Hare would ply their victim with alcohol until he or she had fallen asleep. Then one of the murderers would sit on the victim's chest while the other held a pillow over the victim's face.

Defense attorneys Dale Rubin and Charles Lindner countered Mac-Kenzie's theory by calling their own expert medical witness to testify that Greene died not from suffocation, but rather from an overdose of "poppers." The drug was popular in the homosexual community and was used as an aphrodisiac. Dr. Griffin Thomas, a retired pathologist who had conducted autopsies on Japanese victims of the atomic bomb, testified that poppers—amyl nitrite inhalants—are often available in adult book stores under the brand names of "Locker Room," "Thrust," and "Rush." They are muscle relaxers and are used by homosexuals to ease the pain of anal intercourse. The effect of the drug is instantaneous: it causes light-headedness, rapid heartbeat, flushing of the face, and dizziness. Thomas said Greene died of acute cardiovascular failure, prompted by an accidental overdose of poppers, alcoholism, and a diseased liver. The poppers caused the oxygen-carrying molecules in the blood to dysfunction, which resulted in a chemically induced suffocation, the pathologist told jurors.

The jury quickly decided on Boggs's guilt. However, the panel remained deadlocked 10-2 in favor of the death sentence while deliberating during the penalty phase of the trial. After two-and-a-half days, Cooper declared a hung jury and dismissed the members on August 8, 1990. As allowed under California law, MacKenzie opted to seat a new jury for another penalty hearing, rather than settle for the lesser penalty of life in prison.

Boggs came to the witness stand for the first time during his second penalty hearing. He pled for his life, telling jurors his world began to unravel when he had separated from his wife a decade earlier. Boggs said when he left Lola and their four children, he resigned from his church and moved in with a man. The doctor had known for some time he was a homosexual.

Boggs said his fear of being exposed as a homosexual led him to help Hanson and Hawkins in their scam. The doctor insisted he had nothing to do with Greene's death. He had only agreed to sign a phony death certificate after Hanson threatened to ruin Boggs's practice by telling his patients he was gay. "He indicated that if I would cooperate and sign the death certificate, he'd make it worth my while. If I did not, then I'd have some problems," Boggs told jurors. "They would ruin my practice by publicizing the fact that I lived with another man."

The second jury, seven women and five men, deliberated just under two days before returning with a recommendation of life in prison without parole. On August 30, 1991, Commissioner Cooper imposed the recommended sentence. Dr. Richard Pryde Boggs remains in Pelican Bay, a maximum-security prison in northern California.

After admitting his identity in a Fort Worth courtroom and returning to Columbus on February 3, 1989, five days after his arrest, Melvin E. Hanson launched a fourteen-month battle to block his extradition to California. Shortly after he arrived in Columbus, Hanson again began denying his identity. Before giving him a chance to plead guilty to a single theft charge, Franklin County prosecutors dropped their case against him. With no charges pending in Ohio, Hanson faced immediate extradition to Los Angeles and prosecution on the more serious charges with a possible sentence of death.

His last-minute appeal to the Ohio Supreme Court failed. On April 19, 1990, Hanson, sans toupee and again showing the twenty years he had lost with surgery, was hurried to the Columbus airport and flown to Los Angeles. MacKenzie offered Hanson life in prison without parole in exchange for his guilty pleas and testimony against Boggs and Hawkins. Hanson immediately declined and pleaded not guilty to the charges.

Melvin Eugene Hanson remains in the Los Angeles County Jail without bond awaiting trial.

Although U.S. military police had positively identified John Hawkins through fingerprints, he continued to deny his identity while in the Italian jail, holding fast to his claim that he was Glenn Donald Haweon, a ship's captain from Northern Ireland.

On January 2, 1992, Hawkins attempted to escape his Italian captors by slipping through the second-story window of his cell and using sheets to lower himself into a courtyard. He was spotted coming out of the window and captured as he hit the ground.

Italian officials agreed to extradite Hawkins, but not until prosecutors in California dropped the death penalty specifications against him. Italy does not have capital punishment.

On January 24, 1992, John Barrett Hawkins was placed aboard a jet for the United States. Like Hanson, he is being held without bond in the Los Angeles County Jail awaiting trial.